Human Rights
and Participatory Politics
in Southeast Asia

PENNSYLVANIA STUDIES IN HUMAN RIGHTS

Bert B. Lockwood, Series Editor

A complete list of books in the series is available from the publisher.

HUMAN RIGHTS
AND PARTICIPATORY POLITICS
IN SOUTHEAST ASIA

CATHERINE RENSHAW

PENN

UNIVERSITY OF PENNSYLVANIA PRESS

PHILADELPHIA

Published by
University of Pennsylvania Press
Philadelphia, Pennsylvania 19104-4112
www.upenn.edu/pennpress

Printed in the United States of America on acid-free paper
10 9 8 7 6 5 4 3 2 1

Library of Congress Cataloging-in-Publication Data
ISBN 978-0-8122-5103-6

CONTENTS

List of Abbreviations   vii

Introduction   1

PART I. FOUNDATIONS:
LEGITIMACY OF A REGIONAL HUMAN RIGHTS REGIME
IN THE ABSENCE OF LIBERAL DEMOCRACY

1. Democracy and Human Rights in Southeast Asia   19
2. ASEAN's Turn to Democracy and Human Rights   39
3. The ASEAN Human Rights Declaration   57

PART II. APPLICATIONS:
ASSESSING THE REGIONAL DYNAMICS
OF HUMAN RIGHTS COMMITMENT AND COMPLIANCE

4. The Rights of Women at the Global, Regional, and Local Levels   99
5. Trafficking in Persons   123
6. ASEAN as a Purveyor of Human Rights in Myanmar   148

Conclusion   167

Notes   173
Index   231
Acknowledgments   245

ABBREVIATIONS

ACTIP	ASEAN Convention Against Trafficking in Persons
ACW	ASEAN Committee on Women
ACWC	ASEAN Commission on the Promotion and Protection of the Rights of Women and Children
AEC	ASEAN Economic Community
AFAS	ASEAN Framework Agreement on Services
AFTA	ASEAN Free Trade Area
AHRD	ASEAN Human Rights Declaration
AIA	ASEAN Investment Area
AICHR	ASEAN Intergovernmental Commission on Human Rights
AMM	ASEAN Ministerial Meeting
APF	Asia Pacific Forum of National Human Rights Institutions
ARF	ASEAN Regional Forum
ASC	ASEAN Security Community
ASCPA	ASEAN Security Community Plan of Action
ASEAN	Association of Southeast Asian Nations
ASEAN-PMC	ASEAN Post-Ministerial Conference
Banjul Charter	African Charter on Human and Peoples' Rights
CEDAW	Convention on the Elimination of All Forms of Discrimination Against Women
CLMV	Cambodia, Laos PDR, Myanmar, and Vietnam
CPP	Cambodian People's Party
CRC	Convention on the Rights of the Child
CSO	civil society organization
DEVW	Declaration on the Elimination of Violence Against Women in the ASEAN Region
DEVWC	Declaration on the Elimination of Violence Against Women and Elimination of Violence Against Children in ASEAN

EAS	East Asian Summit
ECHR	European Convention on Human Rights
EPG	Eminent Persons Group
HLTF	High Level Task Force
HRWG	Working Group for an ASEAN Human Rights Mechanism
IAI	Initiative for ASEAN Integration
ICCPR	International Covenant on Civil and Political Rights
ICESCR	International Covenant on Economic, Social and Cultural Rights
NGO	nongovernmental organization
NHRI	national human rights institution
NLD	National League for Democracy
NPA	National Plan of Action
RIA	Roadmap for the Integration of ASEAN
SAPA	Solidarity for Asian People's Advocacy
SEANF	Southeast Asian NHRI Forum
SLORC	State Law and Order Restoration Council
SOGI	sexual orientation and gender identity
SOM	Senior Officials Meeting
SPDC	State Peace and Development Council
SUHAKAM	Malaysian Human Rights Commission
TIP	trafficking in persons
TOR	terms of reference
Trafficking Protocol	United Nations Protocol to Prevent, Suppress and Punish Trafficking in Persons, Especially Women and Children
TVPA	United States Trafficking Victims Protection Act (2000)
UDHR	Universal Declaration of Human Rights
UN Women	United Nations Entity for Gender Equality and the Empowerment of Women
UNESCO	United Nations Educational, Social and Cultural Organization
UNGA	United Nations General Assembly
Women's Caucus	Southeast Asia Women's Caucus on ASEAN
ZOPFAN	Zone of Peace, Freedom and Neutrality

Introduction

Southeast Asia, home to the world's newest regional human rights system, has been in tumult in recent years. In Myanmar (Burma), Aung San Suu Kyi's National League for Democracy won a landslide victory in the 2015 general elections, presaging what seemed to be a new democratic dawn for the former pariah state. Two years later, however, the Burmese military carried out a "clearance operation" in the northern part of the country, aimed at driving out the minority Muslim population, the Rohingya. The military torched Rohingya villages, raped women and girls, and used grenades and helicopters to fire on civilians. The United Nations High Commissioner for Human Rights called it a textbook example of ethnic cleansing. Aung San Suu Kyi, Nobel laureate and human rights icon, refused to criticize the actions of the military.

In neighboring Thailand, the military coup d'état of May 2014 was followed in 2016 by a constitutional referendum in which a majority of Thai people endorsed a continuing role for the military in politics. Under its interim constitution, Thailand is ruled by the National Council for Peace and Order, a military junta, which governs under a regime of surveillance and censorship, restricting media freedom and prohibiting criticism of its actions.

In the Philippines, the presidential elections of May 2016 brought to power Rodrigo Duterte, who began a campaign of state-sanctioned extrajudicial violence against drug addicts and people involved in the drug trade. By 2017, more than thirteen thousand people had been killed in Duterte's war on drugs—more than the number who died during the twenty-year dictatorship of President Ferdinand Marcos. In the communist states of Vietnam and Laos, human rights organizations continue to protest the arrest and imprisonment of political dissidents and activists. In Cambodia, in 2017, authoritarian prime minister Hun Sen consolidated power by arresting the leader of the main opposition party on grounds of treason. Even Indonesia, a moderate Islamic state with a flourishing, multiparty democracy, suddenly seems susceptible to intolerance and political extremism. In December 2016 hundreds of thousands of protestors took to the streets of Jakarta, demanding the arrest of the city's Chinese Christian governor on charges of blasphemy.

Meanwhile, at the regional level, the ten-member Association of Southeast Asian Nations (ASEAN) was engaged in an extraordinary flurry of institution building.[1] Long derided as a "club for dictators," ASEAN seemed determined to change its image, and its 2007 charter explicitly links ASEAN's purpose with the strengthening of democracy and the protection of human rights within the region.[2] The charter also provides for the establishment of an ASEAN human rights body, which was inaugurated on October 23, 2009, as the ASEAN Intergovernmental Commission on Human Rights (AICHR).[3] On November 18, 2012, in Phnom Penh, ASEAN adopted its Human Rights Declaration, which states that ASEAN's members affirm all the civil and political rights, and all of the economic, social, and cultural rights, in the Universal Declaration of Human Rights,[4] as well as other rights specifically relevant to the region, such as the right to a safe, clean, and sustainable environment;[5] the right to development;[6] and the right to peace.[7]

For many reasons, these are remarkable developments. First, Southeast Asia is characterized by a significant degree of political diversity. ASEAN includes two communist states (Vietnam and Laos); an Islamic sultanate (Brunei Darussalam); a democracy in transition from military dictatorship (Myanmar); two established multiparty democracies (the Philippines and Indonesia); and a group of other countries of less easily defined political hue. Among these are Cambodia, which Hun Sen rules under a system described as electoral authoritarianism;[8] Singapore, where only one political party has held power since the countries gained independence; and Thailand, a constitutional monarchy that has experienced multiple coup d'états. ASEAN's members cannot describe themselves in the same way the leaders of Western Europe did at the end of World War II, as "like-minded countries with a common heritage of political traditions, ideals, freedom, and the rule of law."[9]

Second, ASEAN states have traditionally been reluctant to engage with the international human rights treaty monitoring system. Only three of the eight major international human rights treaties have been ratified by all ten ASEAN member states.[10] Even in relation to these treaties, several ASEAN states have entered substantial reservations.[11] Only six ASEAN members have ratified the

International Covenant on Civil and Political Rights (ICCPR) and the International Covenant on Economic, Social and Cultural Rights (ICESCR).[12] Historically, most ASEAN states have been reluctant to subject their human rights policies and practices to external scrutiny.

Third, during the "Asian values" debates of the 1990s, several Southeast Asian leaders openly questioned liberal democracy's emphasis on liberty and autonomy, arguing that these values displace equally important values of familial and communitarian obligation, social order, and harmony. Singapore's prime minister Lee Kuan Yew, Malaysian prime minister Mahathir Mohamad, and Indonesia's president Suharto all argued that Asian cultural particularity justified the rejection of liberal democracy and the civil and political rights associated with it. These leaders argued that the welfare of the people depended on economic growth and political stability and that political opposition and the exercise of civil freedoms were detrimental to these. The Asian Values debate drew much of its force from the success in the early 1990s of the "tiger economies" of East and Southeast Asia. When these economies faltered in the aftermath of the 1997 Asian financial crisis, the Asian Values debate lost much of its strength. Nonetheless, arguments persist about the particularity of Asian political culture and the unsuitability of some Western political ideals to the circumstances of Southeast Asia.[13]

Against this backdrop, the emergence of a regional human rights system in Southeast Asia has puzzled onlookers, and it has been unclear to what extent these regional developments would affect the domestic behavior of ASEAN states. Optimists hoped that ASEAN would eventually mirror the work of regional organizations such as the Conference on Security and Cooperation in Europe, the Council of Europe, the Organization of American States, and the Economic Community of West African States in supporting and deepening democracy among their member states. Others, however, observing Southeast Asia's political diversity and noting that democracies "with adjectives" still predominated in ASEAN's membership, viewed the turn to human rights and democracy as at best futile and at worst a danger to regional stability.

Why did these disparate states agree to institutionalize human rights at the regional level? Was it merely a strategy to deflect criticism from the poor human rights records of some ASEAN members, or was it the beginning of a serious regional-level effort to protect and realize the rights set out in the Universal Declaration of Human Rights?[14] It was unclear how ASEAN's new regional human rights institutions would set about implementing rights in states that are not liberal democracies and addressing fears that ASEAN's new institutions would endorse a different, perhaps lower standard of human rights for Southeast Asia. The overarching question was whether and to what extent ASEAN's new institutions could shape the human rights behavior of member states and improve the lives of the peoples of Southeast Asia. That is the question this book takes up.

Global and Regional Rights Regimes

The creation of a regional human rights body in Southeast Asia follows the establishment of regional human rights institutions in Europe,[15] the Americas,[16] Africa,[17] and the Middle East.[18] Regional systems are, in general, characterized by small numbers of members, deep levels of integration, a degree of consensus around certain societal values, similar geographic characteristics, and shared economic and security interests.[19] There are notable exceptions in the Middle East and South Asia, where intraregional rivalries and conflict undercut possibilities of cohesion. Nonetheless, the features of regionalism seem to provide a more effective foundation for the governance of human rights, compared to the more heterogeneous and unwieldy global level.[20] States seem more willing to subscribe to binding human rights norms when they are promoted by regional organs rather than by worldwide institutions.[21] Some scholars have observed that there seems to be a "directness of association" between members of regional organizations, which positively influences the processes by which states internalize human rights norms ("socialization").[22] In 1980, the United Nations Commission to Study the Organization of Peace reported that the comparative success of regional human rights systems could be attributed to:

(1) the existence of geographic, historical, and cultural bonds among States of a particular region;

(2) the fact that recommendations of a regional organization may meet with less resistance than those of a global body;

(3) the likelihood that publicity about human rights will be wider and more effective; and

(4) the fact that there is less possibility of general, compromise formulae which in global bodies are more likely to be based on considerations of a political nature.[23]

Regional human rights systems emerged after World War II partly as a consequence of the failure to establish an effective worldwide institution for the protection of human rights.[24] In the brief period of hope and optimism following the end of World War II, before the Cold War took root, the construction of a legalized global human rights order seemed at least a possibility.[25] Some world leaders talked of the creation of an international court of human rights, which would guarantee the rights of the individual, change the way states behave, provide individual remedies, and deter would-be perpetrators of abuse.[26] In the end, however, the practical impediments to the establishment of an international human rights court were insurmountable. There was little confidence that a court with such breadth of jurisdiction could cope with the vast amount of litigation that it would attract or accommodate the various domestic laws and policies in diverse contexts.[27] Few states were ultimately willing to entrust judicial review of matters as fundamental as rights to an international tribunal.[28]

The leaders of Western Europe, however, reeling from the horror and barbarism of the Holocaust, were determined to find a concrete means for preserving the core liberal rights they regarded as essential to democracy. The European Convention on Human Rights was drafted primarily to serve as an "early warning system" that would alert the newly formed Council of Europe should one of its members slip into undemocratic practices that might pave the way to totalitarianism.[29] The convention was drafted to include the basic civil and political rights that were assumed to already exist as a common denominator in the domestic legal systems of Western European nations.[30] By the end of the 1970s, the European experiment was widely viewed as a success.[31]

But it was not clear, in the decades following the establishment of the European Court of Human Rights, whether the European experience could be replicated in other regions. The most promising region was the Americas, which had a long history of regional solidarity.[32] The 1948 American Declaration on the Rights and Duties of Man preceded the Universal Declaration of Human Rights by a matter of months. But three decades were to pass before the adoption of the Inter-American Convention on Human Rights and the establishment of the Inter-American Court of Human Rights. Responsibility for stagnation lay with the region's hegemon, the United States of America, which showed no willingness to participate in a legally binding regional human rights system on the grounds that its constitution and the federal structure of its government made participation in such a convention impossible.[33]

In Africa, there were for many years problems more urgent than the creation of a regional human rights system. The continent's postwar upheaval, as it shed slavery and colonialism and struggled to address conflict and poverty, left little space for collective efforts toward the creation of regional human rights institutions.[34] Moreover, the egregious human rights violations committed by leaders of African states led to deep skepticism about their commitment to human rights.[35] The African Court on Human and Peoples' Rights did not commence operations until 2006.

In the Middle East, there was even less grounds for optimism. The League of Arab States (LAS) established the Permanent Arab Commission on Human Rights in 1968. Although the commission's mandate was to promote human rights and to prepare an Arab Charter on Human Rights, its activities were mainly concerned with the situation in the occupied territories.[36] In 1994, the LAS adopted the Arab Charter of Human Rights, which failed to secure ratification by any member states. A revised Arab Charter, which established the Arab Human Rights Committee, was adopted in 2004 and took effect in March 2008.[37] In September 2014, the LAS Ministerial Council adopted a statute for the creation of an "Arab Court for Human Rights," which at the time of writing has not been established.[38]

In Asia and the Pacific, at various times, subregional conventions were proposed, often at human rights conferences sponsored by the United Nations or the International Commission of Jurists.[39] But for many Asian and Pacific states, sovereignty was too newly won, there was too little feeling of solidarity with neighboring countries, and there were other priorities, such as peace and development. No regional or subregional human rights institution was to emerge from any part of Asia or the Pacific until ASEAN established its Intergovernmental Commission on Human Rights in 2009.

At first, regional human rights organizations were viewed merely as institutions for a transitional period during which the foundations of a genuinely global human rights order could be built—as a temporary detour until the time was ripe for the creation of universal institutions.[40] But as prospects for establishing a centralized human rights body with global jurisdiction receded, the building and strengthening of regional human rights institutions came to be seen as the most practical and achievable way to promote and protect human rights. The 1993 Vienna Declaration and Programme of Action states that "regional arrangements play a fundamental role in promoting and protecting human rights," and it reiterates "the need to consider the possibility of establishing regional and subregional arrangements for the promotion and protection of human rights where they do not already exist."[41]

However, deep concerns remain about the regional human rights project. One of these is that the effectiveness of regional institutions seems to depend on whether most states in the region are liberal democracies and already subscribe to fundamental human rights principles. Another concern is that in nondemocratic regions, weak human rights institutions may in fact impede progress toward the realization of human rights by enabling states to deflect criticism for violations of such rights.

Then, too, there are fears that regionalism may challenge the universal nature of human rights. In theory, regional institutions implement and apply universal standards in varying, context-sensitive circumstances.[42] In reality, however, the different interpretations of rights in different contexts have the potential to dramatically change the way a particular right is understood. The problem in this regard is that the existence of many regional variations may undermine the principle of universality, which holds that all people, everywhere, possess the same rights. The history of ASEAN's attempt to establish a regional system for the protection of human rights sheds light on all these matters.

Southeast Asia as a Region

ASEAN was formed in 1967 by Indonesia, Malaysia, the Philippines, Singapore, and Thailand. Burma was offered membership in ASEAN at the time of its creation but declined. From Burma's perspective, ASEAN was an anti-communist organization, comprised wholly of anti-communist regimes.[43] China had declared that ASEAN was a tool of U.S. imperialists aimed at containing China and other communist powers. Burma, committed to a precarious policy of Cold War nonalignment, had no wish to antagonize its powerful neighbor to the north by joining ASEAN.[44]

The primary purpose of ASEAN at the time of its birth was to increase the security of member states. The perceived threats were many and various: communist insurgencies; unsettled ethnic populations; unresolved territorial disputes left behind by departing colonial powers; a rising China; and an economically voracious Japan. The perception of vulnerability, coupled with a fierce desire to remain independent from Great Power spheres of influence, provided the impetus for the creation of ASEAN.[45] These circumstances led to what Indonesian foreign minister Adam Malik called a "convergence in the political outlook of the five prospective member nations."[46] ASEAN's founding document, the 1967 Bangkok Declaration, refers to "mutual interests and common problems among countries of South-East Asia" and asserts that "in an increasingly interdependent world, the cherished ideals of peace, freedom, social justice and economic well-being are best attained by fostering good understanding, good neighbourliness and meaningful cooperation among the countries of the region already bound together by ties of history and culture."[47]

ASEAN was not the first attempt at regional institution building. The Association of Southeast Asia (ASA) had been launched in 1961, promoted primarily by Malaya and joined by Thailand and the Philippines. But Indonesia, under the presidency of Sukarno, refused to join ASA, perceiving it to be little more than a front for the Western-oriented South East Asian Treaty Organisation (SEATO). Burma and Cambodia, reluctant to offend China, were similarly put off by ASA's anti-communist stance.[48] Sukarno favored a different organization, Maphilindo, a confederation of the three Malay-speaking nations (Malaysia, the Philippines, and Indonesia). However, Indonesia's aggression against Malaysia during the period of Konfrontasi, which only ended with Suharto's overthrow of Sukarno in 1966, doomed Maphilindo to failure.

At the time of ASEAN's formation, few were optimistic about its prospects for survival.[49] It was far from clear, in 1967, that ASEAN would succeed in allaying Malaysian suspicions about Indonesia's declared peaceful intentions; or defuse the serious dispute between Malaysia and the Philippines over the latter's claims on the territory of Sabah; or reassure the tiny city-state of Singapore, which had been violently ejected from the new state of Malaysia in 1965. For the first nine years of its existence, as relations between the superpowers and a rising (and later nuclear) China made the geopolitical environment increasingly uncertain, ASEAN did little.[50]

The Second Indochina War (1954–73) between the forces of the Republic of South Vietnam, supported by the United States, and the North Vietnamese Army, supported by the Soviet Union and the People's Republic of China, convinced ASEAN that it needed to be proactive in preserving the independence of its members from Great Power intervention.[51] In 1971, ASEAN states signed the Declaration on an ASEAN Zone of Peace, Freedom and Neutrality, which notes the "right of every country to lead its national existence free from outside interference in its internal affairs as this interference will adversely affect its freedom, independence and integrity."[52] In 1976, ASEAN member states produced the Declaration of ASEAN Concord, which notes that "the stability of each member state and that of the ASEAN region is an essential contribution to international peace and security" and that "the elimination of poverty, hunger, disease and illiteracy is a primary concern of member states. They shall therefore intensify cooperation in economic and social development."[53] In 1976 the Treaty of Amity and Cooperation was signed, establishing a code of conduct to govern interstate relations in Southeast Asia. The treaty underscores commitment to sovereignty and noninterference as the hallmarks of peaceful relations.[54] These principles became the cornerstones of what is known as the "ASEAN Way" of "consensualism, informality, confidentiality, gradualism, and the "front state principle" (i.e., accepting the lead of the member most exposed to specific external developments)."[55] The ASEAN Way for creating and maintaining peace was a steadfast policy of noninterference in the internal affairs of other member states. Former Thai deputy foreign minister M. R. Sukhumbhand Paribatra described the nonintervention principle as "the glue keeping ASEAN together."[56]

ASEAN's original five members had long held the view that all geographically proximate members of the region should belong to the regional association.[57] Only then, it was thought, could the association truly represent "one Southeast Asia" on the international stage.[58] Brunei became a member of ASEAN in January 1984, after gaining independence from Britain. The original plan was for the remaining Southeast Asian states (Myanmar, Laos, Cambodia, and Vietnam) to become members of ASEAN by the time of the association's thirtieth birthday in 1997. Vietnam and Laos joined ASEAN in 1995 and 1997, respectively. The end of the Cold War had mitigated regional tensions, and the communist political systems of these countries were no barrier to their admission into ASEAN. Myanmar was also admitted in 1997, while under the rule of a military junta that had ignored the results of democratic elections in 1990. Myanmar's admission to ASEAN, which I discuss in Chapter 6, caused ASEAN significant problems diplomatically in its relationships with Western states. Cambodia's admission to ASEAN was delayed until 1999 because of the domestic turmoil that followed Hun Sen's coup d'état.

Since 1976, ASEAN has managed not only to survive but to flourish, spawning an array of affiliated regional organizations, associations, groupings, and forums, of which ASEAN remains at the center: the ASEAN Regional Forum (ARF); the ASEAN Free Trade Area (AFTA); ASEAN +3 (with Japan, South Korea, and China); ASEAN +6 (with Japan, South Korea, China, India, Australia, and New Zealand); ASEAN-Europe Meeting (ASEM); the East Asian Summit (EAS); and Asia Pacific Economic Cooperation (APEC). In a period that witnessed the end of the Cold War, the Asian financial crisis, 9/11 and the War on Terror, environmental crises and natural disasters, coup d'états and revolutions among its member states, and serious conflict in the South China Sea, ASEAN has maintained peace in a politically, religiously, and ethnically diverse region and remained a forum for engagement and the formulation of regional policy. The ASEAN Way has prevailed as the modus operandi of relations between member states.

Human Rights in Southeast Asia

ASEAN's early history was marked by the reign of authoritarian leaders, who carried out gross violations of civil and political liberties in order to maintain power. At the time of ASEAN's birth, Indonesia was under the rule of President Suharto. The Philippines was controlled by President Marcos, who placed the country under martial law from 1972 until 1981. Thailand's monarchs shared power with predominantly military or military-backed governments until 1973. Malaysia, facing first a challenge from communism and then persistent religious and ethnic tension, was dominated by one party that placed the country under successive states of emergency. Singapore had one prime minister and one ruling party between 1959 and 1990. For the first thirty years of its existence, ASEAN could not criticize policies such as detention without trial, curbs on press freedom, and draconian laws because these practices were commonplace among all members of the association. ASEAN did not respond to President Marcos's declaration of martial law in the Philippines in 1972 or to Indonesia's invasion of East Timor in 1975 and the annexation that followed a year after.[59] ASEAN did not issue a response to the massacre of East Timorese civilians by Indonesian soldiers in Dili in November 1991[60] or to the Thai military's lethal crackdown on pro-democracy demonstrators in May 1992.[61]

ASEAN's expansion to include Vietnam, Laos, Myanmar, and Cambodia reinforced the image of ASEAN as a champion of authoritarianism.[62] Vietnam and Laos were (and remain) single-party communist states. Political party pluralism is not permitted and political dissent is commonly suppressed.[63] Cambodia suffered the genocidal rule of Pol Pot and the Khmer Rouge, the war with Vietnam, and the famine that followed. Myanmar, at the time of its admission to ASEAN, was ruled by the State Law and Order Restoration Council (SLORC). The SLORC maintained power by intimidation, the sup-

pression of all dissent, the persecution of political dissidents, torture, and repression of civil and political liberties. The litany of human rights abuses
committed by the SLORC and its successor, the State Peace and Development
Council (SPDC), are manifold.[64] The Burmese army, the Tatmadaw, was also
engaged in a brutal war with ethnic armies. The reports of UN Special Rapporteurs detail the targeting, torture, rape, and abuse of civilians.[65]

In September 2007, when the Burmese military opened fire on protestors
in the streets of Yangon, ASEAN broke its long tradition of not criticizing the
human rights behavior of its member states. ASEAN's foreign ministers,
meeting in New York on the sidelines of the UN General Assembly, expressed
revulsion at the Burmese government's use of violent force. But any hope that
ASEAN's response to the "Saffron Revolution" presaged a new era of regional
responsiveness to human rights abuses was short-lived. In March 2010, thousands of protestors occupied central Bangkok, demanding the resignation of
military-backed Prime Minister Abhisit Vejjajiva. The Thai military ended the
street campaign by storming the protestors' encampment, killing and injuring
scores of protestors.[66] On May 22, 2014, Thailand's military chief, General
Prayuth Chan-ocha, took power in a coup d'état, suspended the constitution,
arrested protestors, and placed severe restrictions on freedom of speech and
association. Using sedition laws and *lèse-majesté* laws that prohibit insults to
the monarchy, the military-backed government persecuted its critics.[67]

ASEAN did not respond to the 2014 coup d'état in Thailand or to the
human rights violations that followed.[68] Individually, some ASEAN members
expressed concern. Indonesia's president Susilo Bambang Yudhyono, for example, urged ASEAN to act.[69] But for other ASEAN members, the coup in
Thailand and the military's treatment of opponents were matters for Thailand's internal governance, not matters that could or should be the subject of
public comment or action by ASEAN. ASEAN adopted the same attitude of
noninterference in December 2016, when the prime minister of Malaysia accused the Burmese military of genocide in its persecution of Myanmar's minority Muslim population, the Rohingya.[70]

The human rights history of Southeast Asia appears to provide strong
evidence for the argument that democracy is a necessary condition for the
realization of human rights. Yet democracy, when it did arrive in some
ASEAN states, did not always immediately improve the human rights situation. In the Philippines between 1965 and 1986, Ferdinand Marcos tortured
and killed thousands of political opponents and jailed tens of thousands.[71]
After Marcos was deposed by the "People Power" revolution of 1986, the new

leader, Corazon Aquino, moved quickly to establish a national human rights commission, sign most major international human rights treaties, and promulgate a new constitution guaranteeing most major civil and political rights. Yet under Aquino, the war in rural regions intensified and the number of political detainees who were imprisoned actually increased.[72] In Cambodia, the UN-backed elections of 1993 installed an unstable government between Hun Sen's Cambodian People's Party and Prince Sihanouk's Funcinpec faction.[73] In the period after the election, politically motivated killings, committed by both sides, increased. Meanwhile, leaders in other parts of Southeast Asia referred to the chaos that followed democratic transitions in Cambodia and the Philippines as a justification for continuing their authoritarian rule.[74]

In 1993 the Vienna World Conference on Human Rights called on all states to consider establishing a regional human rights system if they had not already done so. Most Southeast Asian states responded with caution. While some ASEAN governments rejected the notion of supra-state oversight of human rights altogether, others viewed a regional human rights system as an opportunity to create a human rights system on their own terms, with an emphasis on priorities relevant to the region. For their part, the region's nongovernmental organizations (NGOs) responded very warily to the notion of Southeast Asia's authoritarian states establishing a regional system on terms congenial to the rulers. Civil society organizations questioned whether a human rights system constructed in a region where a majority of states were not democracies would have any effect.

Global and Regional Human Rights Dynamics

This book has two main purposes. The first is to record and explain the human rights developments that have taken place in Southeast Asia since the signing of the ASEAN Charter in 2007. The reasons why ASEAN's human rights institutions were created and the negotiations that took place between different ASEAN states in the lead-up to the establishment of the new human rights institutions, and between states and civil society organizations, reveal much about the way human rights are understood in Southeast Asia and the potential and limitations of the region's new human rights institutions in effecting change.

At the time of writing, the ostensible achievements of ASEAN's human rights institutions are meager. The ASEAN Intergovernmental Commission on Human Rights (AICHR) has held meetings, carried out research, conducted human rights training, and consulted stakeholders. AICHR has produced one thematic report, on corporate social responsibility in the region.[75] Other thematic reports promised in AICHR's first five-year plan—on migration, peace, and the death penalty—have not yet been produced.[76] AICHR, working on the basis of consensus in decision making and according to principles of noninterference, has not commented on or condemned the human rights practices of any ASEAN government. The ASEAN Human Rights Declaration has not been invoked in any jurisdiction in Southeast Asia. ASEAN's human rights commissioners argue that they are still in the stage of "institution building," and they point to the fact that the European Court of Human Rights did very little in the first ten years of its existence. Civil society actors, NGOs, and human rights defenders argue that they need "a champion for their cause, a body that will investigate violations, seek the truth and then talk truth to power, and insist that governments cannot get away with violations, and see to it that all human rights are enjoyed by all."[77] ASEAN's human rights institutions are navigating between the high expectations of civil society and the ongoing reluctance of most ASEAN states to submit their policies and practices to external scrutiny. The core problem is Southeast Asia's democratic deficit, which undercuts the legitimacy of the region's nascent human rights institutions and stymies their potential as instruments of change.

The second aim of this book is to consider whether regional human rights institutions have the potential to influence human rights practices in ways that global institutions cannot. In order to answer this question, we need to know something about the theory of why states change their human rights practices.

One of the most influential and convincing explanations to emerge in recent decades is "the spiral theory of human rights" put forward by Thomas Risse, Stephen Ropp, and Kathryn Sikkink.[78] In *The Power of Human Rights: International Norms and Domestic Change* the authors show how states became socialized to human rights through a process that begins with tactical concessions, such as signing human rights treaties. The tactical concession provides domestic and international actors with the leverage to pressure states to make further changes, such as bringing domestic laws into conformity with international norms and setting up national human rights institutions.[79] In this process, domestic civil society supplements pressure that comes "from above" (the international community) with pressure "from below."[80]

The final stage of the spiral process occurs when norms about appropriate behavior are internalized and become part of how states define themselves (their identity). At this point human rights norms are regarded as right and appropriate, requiring no further justification in order to secure compliance. States automatically behave in ways that they regard as appropriate within a community of rights-respecting states to which they now belong.[81] An important part of the final stage is socialization: communication, interaction, argumentation, and advocacy around human rights issues.[82]

Theories of human rights socialization explain how domestic and international NGOs, members of civil society, political opposition groups, and the international community use normative standard setting to persuade, shame, or coerce states into compliance.[83] But change is often very slow. Many states (both predatory and decent) are resistant to influence. In circumstances of exception (civil conflict, war, political crisis) when human rights are most vulnerable to abuse, the processes are least effective.[84] Some states remain frozen at the stage of tactical concessions and do not progress to rule-consistent behavior. External sources of pressure, such as shaming and sanctions, do not always move states from tactical concessions to human rights conformity. Indeed, external processes are in some circumstances counterproductive to internal forces for change.

In this book I argue that regional and global influences operate differently to effect change in the human rights behavior of states. For example, civil society's efforts to persuade states to translate norms into domestic legislation are sometimes enhanced if other states within the region also endorse the norm. This is because a "community of states" or a "group of peers" situated at the regional level has more influence than the amorphous "global society" to which all states belong. In relation to interaction and learning between states, again, proximity within regions enhances these processes. On the other hand, there are cases where regions are marked by intractable political or religious differences between states, or where the presence of a hegemonic power distorts socialization processes, or where states belong to a region where the predominant norms are not "good," liberal, democratic, human rights–oriented ones.[85] In these latter cases, regional influences work to socialize states *away* from human rights norms. Those agitating for human rights change within the state might find that an appeal to global norms and mechanisms is more effective. As I explore how states in Southeast Asia respond in different ways to the global and regional dynamics of human rights, I consider how much this difference has to do with the relative legitimacy of global and regional norms and the legitimacy of the institutions that promote them.[86]

PART I

FOUNDATIONS:

LEGITIMACY OF A REGIONAL
HUMAN RIGHTS REGIME
IN THE ABSENCE
OF LIBERAL DEMOCRACY

THE FIRST THREE chapters of this book show how the political character of a majority of ASEAN states limited the possibility that a robust regional system for the protection of human rights would emerge in Southeast Asia. The first chapter explains the relationship between democracy and human rights and why there is resistance, at the regional level, to principles of liberal democracy. The second chapter shows how ASEAN's reservations about democracy played out in the drafting processes for the ASEAN Charter, the ASEAN Intergovernmental Commission on Human Rights, and the ASEAN Human Rights Declaration (AHRD). The third chapter pulls apart the text of the AHRD, revealing the way different conceptions of religion, politics, and culture manifested themselves in the form of the text. The chapter demonstrates how the legitimacy and potential of the region's primary human rights instrument were weakened by the absence of democratic processes for deliberating about conflicting views on rights.

The democratic deficit in Southeast Asia is the reason why many people were deeply skeptical about ASEAN's potential to change the human rights behavior of member states through the institutionalization of human rights. Since the fall of the Berlin Wall and the end of communism, Western states have generally assumed that "internationally recognized human rights require a liberal regime,"[1] that liberal democracy and human rights are "two sides of the same coin,"[2] that "human rights, equal rights and government under law are important attributes of democracy,"[3] and that liberal democracy is a necessary precondition for realizing human rights.[4] Much of the literature on both democracy and human rights—and many of the statements emanating from the United Nations—considers liberal democracy and human rights codependent.[5]

In 2002 and 2005, for example, the UN Commission on Human Rights requested that the High Commissioner for Human Rights convene an "expert seminar on democracy and the rule of law."[6] The first seminar noted the inseparable and interdependent character of democracy and human rights as concepts that had spread around the globe but emphasized that there was no single universal model of democracy. The second seminar stated that free, fair, and periodic multiparty elections were a key component of democracy, the rule of law, and the protection of human rights and that "elections also had an autonomous value as a means of self-realization and recognition of human dignity."[7]

In the following chapters, we see how the absence of democracy affected the form and structure of ASEAN's nascent human rights system. First, at the regional level, ASEAN was not a community of democratic nations that identified as liberal, rights-respecting states belonging to a community of similar nations. For this reason, more progressive states, such as Indonesia and the Philippines, possessed very limited ability to shame, encourage, or coerce ASEAN's nondemocratic members into forging a more robust human rights system based on principles that conform to international human rights standards.[8] Most ASEAN members cared, to an extent, about the reputational costs that would follow from establishing an ineffectual regional human rights body. But among a group of nondemocratic peers, they did not care enough to relinquish long-standing and important ASEAN norms like sovereignty and noninterference.

Second, because ASEAN did not possess a homogeneous, liberal, rule-of-law culture, the character of transnational relations between governmental elites and bureaucrats within ASEAN did not support or reinforce liberal norms. Government negotiators involved in drafting and deliberations were broadly divided into two camps. The first was the "CLMV" group (Cambodia, Laos, Myanmar, and Vietnam), whose representatives were firmly opposed to the adoption of a European-style system of human rights oversight. The second was composed of Thailand, the Philippines, and Indonesia, whose representatives pressed for a stronger human rights mechanism and whose internal political systems provided space for engagement with local stakeholders, civil society actors, and human rights activists. A third group, from Brunei and Malaysia, raised persistent concerns about conflict between fundamental human rights principles such as freedom of religion and principles of Sharia law. In sum, decisions were not based on a shared set of assumptions about the importance and value of human rights and liberal democracy. ASEAN was not a "transnational society" capable of socializing members to liberal norms. The drafting processes for the ASEAN Charter, the Terms of Reference of the ASEAN Intergovernmental Commission on Human Rights, and the AHRD lacked transparency and inclusiveness, and the final texts reflect the interests of states, not the interests of rights-holders. The result of this is that at the outset, the legitimacy and potential of ASEAN's nascent human rights system were severely constrained.

CHAPTER 1

Democracy and Human Rights in Southeast Asia

The 1967 Bangkok Declaration, which ASEAN's five original members drafted and signed, makes no connection between peace, democracy, and human rights. In contrast, other regional and international instruments make the connection between these principles explicit. The Preamble to the 1945 constitution of the United Nations Educational, Scientific and Cultural Organization (UNESCO), drafted in the aftermath of World War II, states: "The great and terrible war which has now ended was a war made possible by the denial of democratic principle."[1] The Preamble to the European Convention on Human Rights (ECHR), which came into force in 1953, affirms a "profound belief in those Fundamental Freedoms which are the foundation of justice and peace in the world and are best maintained on the one hand by an effective political democracy and on the other by a common understanding and observance of the Human Rights upon which they depend."[2] The Charter of the Organization of American States (1948) declares that "democracy is an indispensable condition for the stability, peace and development of the region."[3]

If we adopt a very broad definition of democracy—for example, that democracy is political representation that functions with a maximum level of inclusiveness in the systems of power[4]—we can readily see how basic civil rights (for example, the rights of freedom of expression, peaceful assembly, and freedom to form and join associations) are necessary preconditions for democracy. But is democracy necessary for the realization of human rights? Three lines of argument suggest that it is.

First, a long line of liberal thinkers have argued that developed democratic states rarely if ever make war upon each other.[5] As conditions of war inevitably lead to human rights violations, it follows that democracy is necessary to preserve peace and protect human rights.[6]

At the end of World War II, the situation in Southeast Asia was significantly different from that in the West. Departing colonial powers left behind unresolved territorial disputes, civil conflict, and communist insurgencies.[7] But it was not clear that democracy was the remedy for these problems. At the time of ASEAN's birth, Southeast Asia had no consolidated democracy that could take the lead in promoting a "democratic peace" at the regional level, and democratization did not begin there until some twenty years later.[8] In these circumstances, other means for peaceful coexistence needed to be found. Noninterference and mutual respect for sovereignty emerged as Southeast Asia's pragmatic response to the problem of creating and maintaining regional peace. The Philippines president, Ferdinand Marcos, exhorted Asians to "work together as brothers, not at cross-purposes but for each other's prosperity and happiness."[9] "Working together" meant suspending suspicion and hostility, respecting the internal governance of other states, and subordinating "dogmatic theories to practical issues."[10] Respect, not political like-mindedness, became the key to peace. In the first two decades of its existence, ASEAN contributed to ending Indonesia's period of *konfrontasi* and Vietnam's invasion of Cambodia, and it defused other latent conflicts among member states.[11]

Thus, instead of references to "democracy" as the essential ingredient of peace and prosperity, ASEAN's founding declaration refers to the importance of economic and social cooperation in "an increasingly interdependent world."[12] "Democracy" is not mentioned in the 1971 Zone of Peace, Freedom and Neutrality (ZOPFAN) Declaration, which notes the "right of every country to lead its national existence free from outside interference in its internal affairs as this interference will adversely affect its freedom, independence and integrity,"[13] or in the 1976 Declaration of ASEAN Concord, which notes, "The stability of each member state and that of the ASEAN region is an essential contribution to international peace and security" and that "the elimination of poverty, hunger, disease and illiteracy is a primary concern of member states. They shall therefore intensify cooperation in economic and social development."[14] The 1976 Treaty of Amity and Cooperation underscores commitment to sovereignty and noninterference as the hallmarks of peaceful relations.[15] ASEAN's modus operandi for creating and maintaining peace was not encouraging (let alone forcing) members of the regional association to adopt democratic political systems. It was, above all else, a policy of noninterference between states, few of which could be called "democratic."

Part of the argument underpinning the liberal peace thesis is the notion that economic interdependence among democratic nations leads to a preference against wars with fellow democracies by creating transnational ties that encourage accommodation rather than conflict. This idea has become a central tenet of liberal thinking.[16]

The first article of the 1967 Bangkok Declaration appears to reference this idea, when it proclaims ASEAN's purpose to be "to accelerate the economic growth, social progress and cultural development in the region through joint endeavours in the spirit of equality and partnership in order to strengthen the foundation for a prosperous and peaceful community of South-East Asian Nations." The 1976 Declaration of ASEAN Concord also provides that "the stability of each member state and of the ASEAN region is an essential contribution to international peace and security. Each member state resolves to eliminate threats posed by subversion to its stability, thus strengthening national and ASEAN resilience." The ASEAN Vision 2020, the Hanoi Plan of Action (1999–2004) and succeeding Plans of Action, the Initiative for ASEAN Integration (IAI), and the Roadmap for the Integration of ASEAN (RIA), as well as ASEAN's many other statements and declarations, all pronounce an imperative for ASEAN to deepen and broaden economic integration in order to promote regional peace and stability, security, development, and prosperity.[17] For example, part of the ASEAN Vision 2020 is the creation of an "ASEAN Economic Community" in which there is a "free flow of goods, services, investment and a freer flow of capital, equitable economic development and reduced poverty and socio-economic disparities."[18] The "ASEAN Economic Community" envisions a single market and production base, created through initiatives such as the ASEAN Free Trade Area (AFTA), ASEAN Framework Agreement on Services (AFAS), and ASEAN Investment Area (AIA). Central to the idea of an "ASEAN Economic Community" is addressing the "development divide" between ASEAN's original members and Cambodia, Laos, Myanmar, and Vietnam.

But respect for economic sovereignty and the lack of regional institutions to implement and enforce compliance with AFTA, AFAS, and AIA have proven to be major impediments to achieving an integrated market in Southeast Asia. ASEAN states remain in competition with one another for access to outside markets, and Southeast Asia continues to lack a strong regional economy to act as a foundation for regional trade. Consequently, the region's medium- to small-sized nations continue to value trade and investment links with the outside world (recently with China, Japan, and South Korea) more than intraregional economic integration.[19] Thus ASEAN's economic interdependence has not significantly grown, despite the association's many declarations of increasing common interests.[20] In 1967, the year of ASEAN's birth, 23 percent of ASEAN exports were directed to other ASEAN countries.[21] In 2010, ASEAN chair Surin Pitsuwan noted that trading among ASEAN member states still accounted for only 25 percent of their total trade.[22] The intraregional cooperation that does exist is connected to Singapore, which is the richest non-oil-producing country in the world. But Singapore has a small economy, limited market, and weak democratic credentials.[23] The 1997 Asian financial crisis demonstrated the limits of such theories of pacific interdependency in Southeast Asia by showing how economic disparities among states reduce the potential political gains of interdependence and how interdependence can even "serve as a transmission belt for spreading security problems through the region."[24]

A second line of argument supporting the link between democracy and human rights is based on the work of Nobel Laureate Amartya Sen. Sen argues that democratically elected governments, which are susceptible to criticism from the media and the informed public, promote the political incentive for governments to be responsive, caring, and prompt in addressing deprivation and right violations. For example, in relation to the right to food (Article 11 of the International Covenant on Economic, Social and Cultural Rights [ICESCR]), Sen shows that substantial famines do not occur in independent and democratic countries that possess a relatively free press. This is because democratic governments, which face elections and criticism from opposition parties and independent newspapers, are forced to undertake the efforts required to prevent famines.[25]

The 1979 Cambodian famine, which caused 1.5 to 2 million deaths, resulted from the civil war that lasted from 1970 to 1975, followed by the rule of the Khmer Rouge from 1975 to late 1978, and then Vietnam's invasion of Cambodia in 1979.[26] From this famine, Southeast Asia drew stark lessons about the connection between civil conflict, state insecurity, and starvation. But Southeast Asian leaders did not necessarily draw from the Cambodian experience the lesson that democracy improves state security and, consequently, economic security. Instead, leaders concluded that order and stability were preconditions for economic growth and that any political order that claimed to advance human dignity must be founded upon that growth.[27]

Southeast Asia experienced rapid economic development after World War II, but democratization—where it occurred—played a marginal role in generating development or in distributing the benefits of development among the region's peoples. The oldest democracy in the region, the Philippines, has been far less successful than the electorally authoritarian states of Malaysia and Singapore in providing access to adequate housing, medical care, and economic security.[28] Indeed, the post-Marcos Philippines stands for many within the region as an example of the pitfalls of Western-style democratization. With arguably the most democratic constitution in Southeast Asia and one of the region's first independent national human rights institutions, the Philippines has one of the worst economic records in ASEAN and is marked by the poverty, insecurity, and human rights abuses that result from economic instability.[29] In 1996, Singapore's prime minister, Lee Kuan Yew, asserted that "the liberal democracy practiced in the Philippines was an obstacle to economic progress, which required collective discipline and firm central control."[30] More recently, former ASEAN secretary-general Rudolf Severino has written:

> In ASEAN, for example, some members of the Filipino elite may denigrate the restrictions on the rights of assembly and free speech imposed on the people of Singapore. On the other hand, many Singaporeans are appalled by the inability of the Philippines political system to deliver a better standard of life and social justice for the Filipino people. Under the stringent rule of the Vietnamese Communist party, the average Vietnamese is increasingly regarded—whether accurately remains to be seen—as having better prospects of a higher standard of living than the average Filipino or the average Indonesian, who, unlike the Vietnamese, enjoys the right to demonstrate on the streets and write freely in the newspapers.[31]

The 1997 Asian financial crisis, which devastated the "tiger" economies of the East (and toppled the Suharto regime),[32] impressed upon the region that their economies were interrelated and that crises would need to be addressed in concerted fashion. But the financial crisis did little to unseat the belief that the strong state was a driver of economic progress. Within Southeast Asia, many did not blame "Asian values" (among them authoritarian-style government) for the Asian financial crisis.[33] In fact, authoritarian states such as Singapore and Malaysia emerged stronger after the crisis, while the region's new democracies, such as Indonesia, the Philippines, and Thailand, were slower to recover economically.[34]

In Malaysia, elections following the Asian financial crisis were held under the banner of *reformasi*. The opposition focused predominantly on issues of "governance" in the sense of addressing corruption, cronyism, and nepotism rather than on human rights and social justice.[35] Acharya points out that in the wake of the 1997 crisis, demonstrators in Indonesia were not demanding "greater democracy" but an end to the corruption they saw as intrinsic to Suharto's rule.[36] From this perspective, the solution to Asia's economic problems did not lie in greater democracy but in "sound banking laws, rigorous supervision in the financial sector, and proper corporate governance."[37]

In short, the argument that democracy is necessary for economic development has not accorded with Southeast Asia's historical experience.[38] Indeed, the contrary proposition seems to have empirical substance: authoritarianism supports economic development, while democracy hinders it. Good governance, constituted by principles of accountability and transparency, long-term orientation by government in deciding policy options, and social justice (meaning equality of work opportunity irrespective of race or religion) are valued ideals. But these values do not necessarily entail democratic principles of inclusiveness and participation in politics.

Consequentialist arguments for democracy as a condition for the fulfillment of human rights are unconvincing in the context of Southeast Asia. But there is a third argument for emphasizing the interrelatedness of human rights and democracy. This is the argument that democracy *is* an autonomous human right itself, not just a means for securing the realization of other rights.[39] Proponents argue that democracy is one of the values that define our intrinsic humanness and as such should be protected and promoted.

Western political philosophers as well as human rights lawyers have taken up the idea that democracy is in itself an individual right, premising the principle on the first Article of the Universal Declaration of Human Rights, which states that human beings are born "free and equal." Once one accepts that idea, it is, in the words of Joshua Cohen, "natural to conclude that there ought to be widespread suffrage and elected government under conditions of political contestation, with protections of the relevant liberties (of participation, expression and association)." This is because the extension of individual equality and freedom to political arrangements "expresses the respect owed to persons as equals, with political capacity." A political democracy is a natural concomitant to the idea of equality and equal respect because its design reflects the equality principle in its methods for collective decision making by endorsing (1) equal rights of political participation, association, and office-holding, including equal rights of voting and equally weighted votes; (2) equal rights of political expression; and (3) equal opportunities for effective political influence.[40]

International human rights instruments that set out the basis for rights of political participation—such as Article 21 of the Universal Declaration of Human Rights (UDHR)[41] and Article 25 of the ICCPR—extend the idea of equality to participatory political arrangements. Article 25 provides that every citizen shall have the right and the opportunity, without unreasonable restrictions:

(a) To take part in the conduct of public affairs, directly or through freely chosen representatives;

(b) To vote and to be elected at genuine periodic elections which shall be by universal and equal suffrage and shall be held by secret ballot, guaranteeing the free expression of the will of the electors;

(c) To have access, on general terms of equality, to public service in his country.[42]

Six of the ten ASEAN states have signed the ICCPR.[43] However, Article 25 is unclear on whether rights of political participation require political pluralism or can be satisfied in a one-party state. It also does not clarify whether the absence of opposition political parties is inimical to "genuine periodic elections" or what obligations rest on states to foster their development and freedom to operate. There is no guidance on what "direct" participation in the conduct of public affairs means.[44]

The collapse of the Soviet Union in 1989 sparked a new enthusiasm on the part of the UN General Assembly, the Human Rights Committee, and the Human Rights Commission to develop the meaning of Article 21 of the UDHR and Article 25 of the ICCPR. In 1991, the General Assembly adopted a resolution titled "Enhancing the Effectiveness of the Principle of Periodic and Genuine Elections," which reaffirmed and detailed the electoral entitlement outlined in the UDHR. The resolution stressed that determining the will of the people requires an electoral process that provides an equal opportunity for all citizens to become candidates and put forward their political views, individually and in cooperation with others.[45] At its next session, the assembly, with only four dissents, passed Resolution 46/137 of December 17, 1991, which again reaffirmed that periodic and genuine elections are a "necessary and indispensable element" and a "crucial factor in the effective enjoyment . . . of a wide range of other human rights."[46]

In 1996, the United Nations Human Rights Committee adopted General Comment 25, which explicates the rights set out in Article 25 of the ICCPR. According to this general comment, the conduct of public affairs is a broad concept, which covers all aspects of public administration, as well as the formulation and implementation of policy at the international, national, regional, and local levels. The comment provides that allocation of powers and the means by which individual citizens exercise the right to participate in the conduct of public affairs should be established by the constitution and other laws. The general comment maintains that democracy requires freedom of expression, assembly, and association (paragraph 12); enshrines nondiscrimination with respect to the citizen's right to vote (paragraph 3); rejects any condition of eligibility to vote or stand for office based on political affiliation (paragraph 15); calls for voters to be free to support or oppose the government without undue influence or coercion of any kind (paragraph 19); and requires states reporting under the covenant to explain how the different political views in the community are represented in elected bodies (paragraph 22).[47]

In 1999, the Commission on Human Rights adopted a resolution, sponsored by the United States, titled "A Right to Democracy," which stressed the connection between democracy and human rights, maintaining that "democracy fosters the full realisation of all human rights, and vice versa." The resolution was adopted with 51 votes in favor and none against. There were two abstentions: China and Cuba.[48] The following year, the Commission on Human Rights again addressed the issue of democracy in Resolution 2000/47, "Promoting and Consolidating Democracy." Resolution 2000/47 expanded on the 1999 document and for the first time added the notion of multiple parties as an essential element of democratic elections.[49]

The reality of Southeast Asia stands in contrast to the model of electoral democracy that the human rights bodies of the United Nations have progressively articulated. For some states, such as Vietnam and Laos, such a model is not even an aspiration. It is arguable that Indonesia and the Philippines aspire to political systems and processes for voting that meet international norms of democracy. Indeed, in the eyes of many observers, Indonesia has already successfully established a modern liberal democracy.[50] Yet even in Indonesia, democracy is constrained by serious impediments to inclusiveness and participation, such as high levels of poverty, which militate against political participation, particularly in rural areas, and the continuing influence of the military and business elites in shaping government policy. In some parts of the country corruption and the absence of the rule of law undermine representative government.

Democratic gains in Southeast Asia are often fragile. In Thailand, for example, Thaksin Shinawatra was elected to power in 2001 on a platform that included a raft of policy reforms that challenged, among other things, the continuing influence and power of three of Thailand's key (unelected) institutions: the military, the king, and the senior bureaucracy.[51] In 2006, Shinawatra was unseated by a military coup. In the wake of the chaos, street protests, and deaths that followed the coup, calls came for a return to "Thai-style democracy," based on moral and king-centered politics,[52] a form of governance different from the Western-style, electoral-based democracy that was perceived (by many) to have failed Thailand. These calls were heard again in 2014, when the "bloodless coup" of General Prayuth Chan-ocha unseated the democratically elected Yingluck Shinawatra. In August 2016, Thai voters approved the nation's twentieth constitution, which authorizes the military to remove an elected government without resorting to a coup and creates an unelected senate.[53]

In Malaysia and Singapore, competitive multiparty politics is constrained by press censorship and by laws that restrict the rights of opposition political parties to associate, assemble, and communicate. The use of these laws—in certain cases, to arrest and charge opposition leaders—has entrenched single-party dominance in both states since independence from Britain in 1957. Ruling party tactics to consolidate power are subtle, including practices such as the exclusion from business enterprises and civil service opportunities of those known not to support the ruling party and the perpetuation of a climate of fear through the use of informants.[54] Singapore and Malaysia have been characterized as "semi-authoritarian" states where free and fair elections do not occur.[55] Yet in elections in Malaysia in May 2018, the Barisan Nasional coalition, which had been in power in Malaysia since the country's birth in 1957, was defeated by an opposition party led by former prime minister Mahathir Mohamad.

Of the other ASEAN states, Brunei is an absolute monarchy and does not hold elections. In Cambodia, Hun Sen's Cambodian People's Party (CPP) has ruled since 1993. From the time of the 1998 elections, the CPP has used "coercion, patronage, media control and other means to deny formally legal opposition parties any real chance of competing for power."[56] Vietnam and Laos have since 1975 held elections every five years for their respective national assemblies. In both countries, political parties other than the Communist

Party are not permitted to stand for election, although independent candidates and self-nominees (either belonging to the party or not) have been permitted to stand. In both countries, the Communist Party maintains a supermajority in the National Assembly and its members hold all central decision-making roles. The press is government controlled, and rights of assembly and association are limited.[57] Myanmar, transitioning to democracy after twenty-two years of direct military rule, has a constitution that reserves 25 percent of parliamentary seats for unelected members of the military.[58]

Southeast Asia's Skepticism About Democracy

Since the end of World War II and decolonization, resistance to liberal democracy in Southeast Asia has developed around three central themes. The first has its origins in the region's colonial past. For many there, liberal democracy remains associated with the West, and the West was responsible for the oppression and atrocities of colonialism.[59] In Sienho Yee's words, the effect of Asia's colonial history "is often unelaborated in writing but can hardly be underestimated."[60] The second theme derives from what are thought to be significant cultural differences between the West and Asia. This is a debate that takes form in arguments about "Asian values." Some Asian political leaders projected "Asian values" as a rejoinder to the idea that individual liberty and autonomy, as conceived by the West, are "universal" standards. At the same time, they linked "Asian values" to ideas about the overriding imperative of security for developing nations with unstable economies and social unrest. The third theme is the Marxist character of Vietnam and Laos. Both countries, despite embracing an economic perestroika since the mid-1990s, still formally uphold principles of communism.

Authoritarian leaders within Southeast Asia, attempting to deflect Western criticism of their nondemocratic practices, have often referred to previous human rights violations committed by Southeast Asia's former colonial oppressors.[61] They have charged the West with hypocrisy in its exhortations that Southeast Asian nations adopt democratic principles of "liberty" and "equality," because the powers now commending liberty and equality are the same powers that once conquered and ruled most of Southeast Asia.[62] The charge of neo-imperialism meets many exogenous attempts at political reform. In 1953, Indonesia's vice president Mohammad Hatta wrote that "the memory of the colonial status that bound them for centuries made them resist anything they consider an attempt to colonise them again, whether by economic or ideological domination."[63] In 2004, Myanmar's deputy minister for foreign affairs, U. Khin Maung Win, stated:

> Myanmar has existed as an independent kingdom for thousands of years. It has always been proud of its culture, traditions and values. Therefore, colonisation by Great Britain was a great shock to the psyche of the Myanmar people. After the regaining of independence in 1948, the Myanmar people are deeply jealous of their independence and sovereignty and are determined that they will never be subjugated by an alien power. Sense of patriotism and nationalism still runs very deep in Myanmar. A case in point, Myanmar became the first nation that refused to join the Commonwealth following the regaining of independence due to nationalism that refused to accept the British sovereign as head of state.[64]

Many Southeast Asian nations fought wars of independence against their imperial rulers, which had enduring consequences for the new nations. The Marxist-Leninist ideology that penetrated much of Southeast Asia (successfully taking hold in Laos, Vietnam, Myanmar, and Cambodia) was explicitly anticolonialist, drawing on notions of revolutionary liberation as well as economic redistribution.[65] The Communist Party of Vietnam, for example, continues to derive legitimacy from its thirty-year struggle against its French colonial rulers, and then from its struggle against the United States following World War II: "The Vietnam-American war was the mother's milk, the school and the testing ground of Vietnamese communism. It provides historical justification for the indispensable leadership of the Communist Party, endowing it with the 'mandate of heaven.' "[66]

The practices of colonial powers provided fertile ground for Marxism. In his classic *Philippine Society and Revolution*, Amado Guerrero describes what happened to the Philippines under the colonial rule of the United States, which had aided the Philippines in gaining independence from the Spanish in 1898: "The U.S. imperialist aggressors practised genocide of monstrous proportions. They committed various forms of atrocities such as the massacres of captured troops and innocent civilians; pillage on women, homes and property; and ruthless employment of torture, such as dismemberment, the water cure and the rope torture. Zoning and concentration camps were resorted to in order to put civilians and combatants at their mercy."[67]

Such readings of history have the rhetorical power to shape opposition to the values and ideals of the former imperialists, a significance those outside the region may too easily overlook. But the era of colonialism had other consequences as well. Wars of liberation fought in order to gain independence cemented the central role of the military in nation building and generated extreme forms of nationalism. The role of the military in the politics of ASEAN states—in some cases, a role preserved in state constitutions[68]—has deeply influenced their evolution. The Philippines, Thailand, Indonesia, and Myanmar provide particularly strong examples of this, as well as of the deleterious effect of military dominance on democratic development.

Colonial rule also exacerbated religious and ethnic divides, and leaders of some of Southeast Asia's authoritarian states have continued to connect the region's colonial legacy to problems of national unity and state building. In the Philippines, for example, the geographically oriented north-south divide between the Muslim population (the Moros) and the Christians was reinforced by a U.S. imperial policy that implemented a practice of civilian justice for the Christians and military justice for the Muslims, as well as policies of unequal land distribution that benefited Christians. Colonial policies alienated and radicalized Muslim populations, who resisted postcolonial efforts directed toward assimilation.[69] In Malaysia, the race riots of 1969 led to the strengthening of security laws such as the Internal Security Act, the Official Secrets Act, and the Sedition Act, which had originally been introduced by the British in the wake of the 1948 "State of Emergency." In Myanmar, the British divided "Burma proper" from the frontier areas, which were populated by non-Bamar ethnic groups.[70] As U. Khin Maung Win writes: "Myanmar is a Union composed of more than one hundred different national races, each with its own culture and traditions. Politically, there cannot be lasting peace and stability in the country without national unity. Unfortunately, the divide and rule policy practiced by the British colonialists resulted in suspicion and discord among the national races. This subsequently led to armed insurgency that spread to various parts of the country for decades."[71]

For many within the region, colonialism is the most important reason why a human rights system like that in Europe will not be established in Asia. The experience of being under colonial rule is the foundation of the principle of noninterference in the domestic affairs of another state and is "ingrained in the Asian psyche."[72]

From outside the region, the charge of neocolonialism is often perceived as a strategic invocation by authoritarian rulers to impede democratic reform.

But its effects are more complex. The shared experience of colonialism has translated into respect for the territorial integrity of state borders and for different political systems that exist within states, as well as into a deep suspicion of claims about the moral superiority of Western ethical traditions. Colonialism has also had real and enduring effects on the creation of national self-identities and has disrupted autochthonous movements toward democracy. Antipathy toward colonialism bred an attitude of general suspicion about the principles of democracy and spurred ideas about sovereignty and the inappropriateness of external intervention in the domestic affairs of states. As Rudolf Severino has explained: "All except Thailand fell under Western colonialism, that extreme form of interference in a society's internal affairs. . . . In the light of Southeast Asian countries' colonial and post-colonial experience, the immense diversity amongst them, the make-up of their populations, the still-delicate state of their relations, and their conceptions of their respective interests, it is difficult to see why ASEAN's policy and practice of non-interference in member's internal affairs should be the object of wonder or derision."[73]

The second theme of resistance to democracy forms part of the broad school of thought that has become known as the "Asian Values" debate. It is the idea some Asian leaders put forward that economic development is a necessary precursor to the realization of civil and political rights. The apogee of the debate was the 1993 Bangkok Declaration, drafted by the leaders of forty Asian governments in preparation for the Vienna World Conference on Human Rights. The declaration emphasized the right to development,[74] identified the main obstacles to the realization of the right to development as lying at the international macroeconomic level, reflected in the widening gap between the North and the South,[75] and affirmed that poverty is one of the major obstacles hindering the full enjoyment of human rights.[76] The Chinese representative to the Vienna Conference argued that "for the vast number of developing countries, to respect and protect human rights is first and foremost the full realization of the right to subsistence and development" and that it was permissible for governments to focus on fulfilling economic and social rights before addressing issues of civil and political rights. Many Southeast Asian leaders agreed with his statement that "human rights is a product of historical development, closely associated with specific social, political and economic conditions," and that "different historical development stages have different human rights requirements."[77] Indonesia's foreign minister called for "greater recognition of the immense complexity of the issue of human rights due to the wide diversity in history, culture, values system, geography and phases of development among the nations of the world."[78]

The claim in the Bangkok Declaration that caused the most consternation in the West—that "while human rights are universal in nature, they must be considered in the context of a dynamic and evolving process of international norm-setting, bearing in mind the significance of national and regional particularities and various historical, cultural and religious backgrounds"—seems less remarkable in historical perspective. After all, the Bangkok Declaration does not challenge the universality of human rights, and the idea of national specificity in the implementation of rights is well recognized by the West in doctrines such as the "margin of appreciation."[79] Furthermore, the notion that the human rights articulated in the UDHR and the two conventions have a historical specificity—for example, that the right to "a fair trial" presupposes the establishment of modern institutions and legal processes—is difficult to dispute.[80]

What lent such venom to the debate between Asian leaders and "the West" at the time of the Vienna World Conference was the charge by Asian governments of Western hypocrisy. The leaders of Asian states blamed "colonialism, foreign domination and poverty"[81] for the economic conditions that made it difficult for them to realize full-blown civil and political rights, and they resented the West compounding past injustices by insisting that Asian states respect rights the West had ignored during previous periods of imperialism, exploitation, and slavery. In 1993, examples of the West's "double standards and politicization" (in the language of the Preamble to the Bangkok Declaration) were readily at hand: the United States and the European Union hesitating in coming to the aid of the Serbs in Yugoslavia, remaining silent over events in Algeria, and linking economic aid and trade privileges to workers' rights in Malaysia and Indonesia in circumstances where it benefited American industry demands for protectionism.[82]

The West, for its part, read the claim that it was *poverty* that "makes a mockery of all civil liberties"[83] against a backdrop of events in Asia that included the Malaysian government's arrest of opposition political party leaders in 1987; the 1989 massacre of protestors in Tiananmen Square; the refusal of Myanmar's military junta to accept the results of the 1990 elections; and the shooting of civilian mourners in an East Timorese cemetery by the Indonesian army in November 1991.[84] Western observers (and many within Asia) viewed the idea of an "alternative Asian standard" of human rights as a dangerous capitulation to relativism. The West was willing to respect pluralism, a degree of "situational uniqueness,"[85] and what the Thai prime minister called "greater recognition of the immense complexity of the issue of human rights due to the wide diversity in history, culture, value system, geography and phases of development among the nations of the world."[86] But the argument that economic development might necessitate restrictions on human rights in order to provide a secure political framework in which rights can be pursued appeared to be a thinly disguised apology for authoritarianism and oppression.[87]

In several respects, the Asian Values debate challenged the importance of the civil and political rights that democracy supports and presupposes. For example, a white paper produced by the Singapore government in 1991, *Shared Values*, drew on Confucian ideas of political order. In *Confucian Traditions in East Asian Modernity*, Tu Wei-Ming writes, "In its political philosophy the Confucian tradition lacks concepts of liberty, human rights, privacy, and due process of law."[88] Drawing on such ideas, the white paper questioned the philosophical emphasis of Western liberal democracy on "the individual" and the political emphasis on competition and majority rule, which it argued were destructive to harmony and cooperation. Instead, the paper emphasized the individual's linkages to family, community, and nation through notions of obligation and duty. The Singapore paper questioned not only the Western means of ordering society but also its goal (individual freedom and the pursuit of individual interests). The white paper held up an ideal of social cohesion and fulfillment of the individual through a chain and hierarchy of duties. It drew on a family of philosophical ideas about the nature of man and society, which are linked by the notion that the individual is not atomistic and self-interested but is defined in terms of his or her connection with others. Ties of kinship and community should be the basis of political and social life, the aim of which is stability and the elevation of communitarian interests through consensus. Singapore's ambassador-at-large Tommy Koh (Singapore's member of the High Level Task Force [HLTF] who drafted the ASEAN Charter and the task force's chairman from August to November 2007) has stated: "East Asians do not believe in the extreme form of individualism practiced in the West. We agree that every individual is important. However, he or she is not an isolated being, but a member of a nuclear and extended family, clan, neighbourhood, community, nation and state. East Asians believe that whatever they do or say, they must keep in mind the interests of others. Unlike Western society, where an individual puts his interest above all others, in Asian society the individual tries to balance his interests with those of family and society."[89]

On such a view, elections are (somewhat) important because they select leaders, but once elected, it is the task of a governing elite to exercise independent judgment on what is in the long-term interest of the people and act on that basis. With the mandate of the people, leaders are able to adopt a long-term orientation to policy rather than follow what will please the people in the short term, free from the vicissitudes of popular opinion.[90]

Leaders from other parts of Southeast Asia have also drawn on religious teachings that support the idea of benevolent leaders who act in the best interests of the people. In predominantly Muslim Indonesia, President Sukarno referred to the spirit of *gotong rojong* (mutual aid), which was intended to ensure that everyone's views were considered in a spirit of tolerance and generosity, with one's own views put aside in the interests of all.[91] According to Sukarno, "true democracy" was "guided democracy" based on traditional village procedures of reaching unanimous decisions (*mufakat*) through deliberation and consultation (*musjawarah*). In Thailand, Buddhism is practiced by 95 percent of the population and has underpinned both pro-democratic and authoritarian movements within Southeast Asia. Within Myanmar, Buddhism is practiced by over 90 percent of the people. As U. Khin Maung Win writes, "Wealth in Myanmar not only means material affluence but also spiritual advancement, especially peace of mind and contentment. The Myanmar people are by nature kind, gentle, and tolerant. Moreover, good society to Myanmar is the equilibrium of *atta* (individual desire) and *para* (working for the good of the community). Thus, democracy is not just conferring basic rights but also obligations and duties to the state."[92]

Approaching the issue from various perspectives, critics of "Asian values" have attacked the idea that there is or should be a separate Asian standard of democracy. At the simplest level, critics have pointed to the contradiction between "claims of a consensus and harmonious society and the extensive arming of the state apparatus" in Southeast Asia.[93] In relation to the "communitarian" arguments of Asian leaders, Yash Ghai (among others) has argued that they overstate the individualism of the West's tradition of democracy (Rousseau, for example, strongly asserts the claims of the community) and that Asian governments wrongly conflate themselves (or "the state") with "the community."[94] In relation to the use of religious values to support political authority, Judge of the International Court of Justice Christopher Weeramantry points out that ideals such as equality, justice, and peace are present in all religions of the world,[95] and Amartya Sen notes that there is conscious theorizing about ideals such as tolerance and freedom in substantial parts of most

Asian traditions.[96] From the discipline of political philosophy, Cohen has demonstrated that proponents of Islam and Confucianism can occupy the "terrain of deliberation" about the nature and content of human rights (and their basic democratic premises).[97]

Most destructive to the credibility of an "Asian values" approach to democracy have been the deep contradictions that have resulted from the economic policies of many Asian governments (which uphold the market, capitalism, and individual property rights) and simultaneous claims that social and economic rights should take precedence over liberal ideas of democratic governance. Instead of upholding economic and social rights as a way of "mediating between the market and the community, to soften the impact of market forces, to act as a safety net," many Asian governments have in fact restricted social and economic rights in order to enhance economic competitiveness.[98] When the people are left without a democratic voice to oppose these restrictions, violations of economic, social, and cultural rights continue. Consciousness of rights remains low because of poverty, lack of education, and social division, and the capacity to challenge systems of oppression remains diminished.[99]

Finally, in two ASEAN countries, Vietnam and Laos, political ideology diverges radically from liberal democracy. The Socialist Republic of Vietnam and Lao PDR have both, since the mid-1980s, pursued policies of economic liberalization, permitting privatization of commerce and agriculture and opening their markets to foreign trade, aid, and investment. Accompanying these moves toward a capitalist market system have been attempts to implement the practices of "good governance": to end corruption, increase transparency, separate government from party organs, and promote respect for the rule of law.

But Laos and Vietnam remain single-party communist states. The constitution of the Socialist Republic of Vietnam provides that the nation "adheres to Marxism-Leninism and Ho Chi Minh's thought" and that the Communist Party "is the force assuming leadership of the State and society."[100] Article 5 of the Laos constitution notes that the National Assembly and all other state organizations "function in accordance with the principle of democratic centralism."[101] These strictures refer to the Marxist-Leninist principles that call for open discussion within a unit but demand that the minority accede to the will of the majority and that lower echelons obey the decisions of higher ones. The political systems of Laos and Vietnam derive from an understanding of democracy that is based on mass participation through local grassroots organizations, which are responsible for selection of parliamentary candidates and for policy implementation at the local level. During meetings held to discuss the ASEAN Charter's contents, a Vietnamese delegate noted that although his country was not a multiparty democracy in the Western sense, it still deserved the title because it practiced democracy *within* its one-party system.[102] Within this system, "democracy" operates within a single party, not via multiple political parties.[103] But tolerance of dissent is limited and democratic activism is curtailed.

If we accept for the purposes of argument that the political systems of Vietnam and Laos satisfy the broad definition of democracy I noted earlier, as any political system that provides for the ultimate authority of the people in determining their own political, economic, social, and cultural systems, what purchase does "human rights" have in these countries?

The starting point is Marx's theory of class struggle and capitalism, in which liberal ideas about human nature and abstract rights are "bourgeois hypocritical moral absolutism."[104] For Marx, the "human right of liberty" in capitalist systems is based not on human relations between individuals but rather on their separation in the marketplace where they are free to compete. This (apparent) disrespect for liberty prompted a succinct reaction from scholar Bertrand Russell: "Communism is not democratic. What it calls 'the dictatorship of the proletariat' is in fact the dictatorship of a small minority, who become an oligarchic governing class."[105]

More recently, Rhoda Howard and Jack Donnelly have argued that communist regimes are entirely inconsistent with international human rights norms:

> Communist society thus rests on a social utilitarianism fundamentally incompatible with human rights. The good of the society, as determined by the state/party, always takes precedence over all else. Because individual "rights" must always yield to social purposes, as enunciated by the state, such "rights" are worthless; no matter what the state does, it cannot be guilty of violating them. Whatever the opportunities and benefits citizens may (contingently) receive—and they are undeniably substantial in some communist regimes—communism represents a thorough denial of human rights.[106]

Communism is seen as subjugating the liberty and autonomy of the individual to a greater socialist purpose, so that the individual is not the respected, rights-bearing citizen imagined by liberal thinking. Under communist regimes, enjoyment of rights is held to be contingent on the discharge of social duties rather than on recognition of the equal and inalienable entitlements of all individuals.[107]

Marx and Engels provide no guidance on the question of multiple political parties in socialist societies. They assume that when the transition to socialist society takes place, the proletariat will constitute an overwhelming majority of the population, and the ideas and ideals of the workers will guide the functions of the state. In their view, different political parties are only necessary to represent the different interests of conflicting economic classes within a society. On Marx and Engels's view, if economic classes are done away with, politics and political classes would also be done away with (and of course ultimately the state as well). What is envisaged is a condition of social harmony, where "in place of the old bourgeoisie society, with its classes and class antagonisms, we shall have an association in which the free development of each is the condition for the free development of all."[108]

The importance of opposition political parties is that they liberate discourse about social values, their priorities and implementation, by providing political alternatives that challenge the policies and values of the ruling party. They provide autonomy in the sense of meaningful choice for citizens about the shape of society and their role within it. The Communist governments of Vietnam and Laos have not eliminated social conflict (evident in ongoing challenges from civil rights organizations, when they are permitted to establish themselves)[109] or economic conflict (resulting from the growing disparities in wealth as a consequence of policies of economic liberalization and market capitalism). In these circumstances, it is implausible to prohibit the establishment of political alternatives to Communist Party rule on the grounds that genuine democracy is practiced "within a single party structure." The political systems of Laos and Vietnam present a serious challenge to the legitimacy of ASEAN's nascent human rights regime.

The State of Democracy in Southeast Asia

As a region, ASEAN remains ambivalent about democracy. It might be argued that the divergent practices of governance and the democratic deficits that exist within most ASEAN states sufficiently explain the region's reluctance to endorse the substantive principles of democracy that now form part of the corpus of international human rights law. To different extents all ASEAN states—with the possible exception of Indonesia and the Philippines—regard their fellow ASEAN members in the way described by Aung Bwa, Myanmar's representative to the HLTF charged with drafting the ASEAN Charter: "Those who live in glass houses should not throw stones!"[110] But beyond this sentiment lie deep currents of resistance to the idea of liberal democracy as promoted by Western states and by the United Nations. Thus, while the post–World War II international legal order, by upholding the right of self-determination of former colonial peoples, has been effective at promoting democracy in Southeast Asia in its broad sense—as the right of a people to govern themselves—attempts at the regional level to specify what democratic governance means have been unsuccessful. The following chapter explains the ambiguous place of democracy in key ASEAN documents and entities and the effect this ambiguity has on the legitimacy of Southeast Asia's nascent human rights regime.

CHAPTER 2

ASEAN's Turn to Democracy and Human Rights

Democracy and the ASEAN Charter

Given the political character of most ASEAN states and their resistance to ideas of liberal democracy, it is somewhat puzzling that ASEAN included "democracy" in the 2007 charter.[1] Yet the document states that one of the association's purposes is to "strengthen democracy, enhance good governance and the rule of law, and to promote and protect human rights and fundamental freedoms, with due regard to the rights and responsibilities of the Member States of ASEAN."[2] The charter also provides that ASEAN and its members shall act in accordance with certain principles, one of which is "adherence to the rule of law, good governance, the principles of democracy and constitutional government."[3] Tracing how the association came to encode these particular statements reveals much about the precise meaning and place of democracy and human rights in Southeast Asia.

One plausible explanation is that ASEAN hoped the charter would enhance its credibility in the eyes of outside observers, particularly the European Union and the United States.[4] The regional human rights institutions and instruments of Europe, Africa, and the Americas all make a formal commitment to democracy. The European Court of Human Rights has consistently stated that "democracy appears to be the only political model contemplated by the Convention and accordingly, the only one compatible with it"[5] and has upheld the democratic principles expounded in Article 3 of Protocol 1 to the European Convention on Human Rights.[6] The Inter-American Democratic Charter, adopted by the Organization of American States in 2001, declares in

Article 1 that "the peoples of the Americas have a right to democracy and their governments have an obligation to promote and defend it,"[7] and the Santiago Declaration expresses an explicit commitment to democracy as a key principle of regionalism.[8] The Constitutive Act of African Union declares its objective as being "to promote democratic principles and institutions."[9] Article 13 of the African Charter on Human and Peoples' Rights provides for rights of participation in the government of the country, either directly or through chosen representatives.[10] The Organization of African Unity has endorsed democratic governance as a way of dealing with Africa's political conflicts and economic ills.[11] It is likely that ASEAN's leaders believed that the ASEAN Charter would be regarded as deficient in the eyes of outside observers unless it referenced democratic norms. Concerns about reputation outweighed reservations leaders may have had about the association's turn to democracy.[12]

This explanation, however, does not adequately capture the extent to which individual ASEAN states—in particular Indonesia—were genuinely committed to the inclusion of democracy as a norm in the charter.[13] Rizal Sukma, one of the most influential voices within Indonesia's civil society sector, stated at the time of the charter negotiations that "the inclusion of human rights and democratic principles in the charter is non-negotiable. Indonesia must fight for it because we will have no basis for protecting people's rights if the principles are not included in the charter."[14] Indonesian Foreign Ministry Director General for ASEAN Affairs, Dian Triansyah Djani, confirmed this position, stressing that Indonesia would continue to insist on the inclusion of articles on human rights and democratic values in the ASEAN Charter.[15] Ikrar Nusa Bakti, of the Indonesian Institute of Sciences, added that it was time Indonesia, the biggest country in the region, took the lead in fighting for values in which it believes and practices: "I think Indonesia now is the most democratic country in ASEAN. We should not let ourselves be bogged down by other ASEAN members."[16] This sentiment seems to be widely shared among both state and nonstate actors in Indonesia.

Indonesia had been advancing the idea of democracy as a regional norm at least since June 2003. At the ASEAN Senior Officials Meeting held that year, Indonesia proposed the creation of an ASEAN Security Community (ASC) with five key duties: setting norms, preventing conflict, resolving conflict, building peace after conflict, and political development. It was this last duty that caused consternation among other ASEAN states. Indonesia (the world's third largest democracy) defined "political development" as "people's participation, particularly through the conduct of general elections"; "good governance"; strengthening "judicial institutions and legal reforms"; and promoting "human rights and obligations through the establishment of the ASEAN Commission on Human Rights."[17] According to Indonesia, the ideological basis of the ASC was to be a commitment to democracy and human rights.[18] This was the first time that an ASEAN state had proposed "democracy" as a principle of the regional association.

Indonesia's proposal regarding "political development" was unsuccessful. The ASC, announced as part of its Concord II at the 9th ASEAN Summit in October 2003, contained only four aims: setting norms, preventing conflict, resolving conflict, and building peace after conflict. The controversial aim of promoting "political development" was deleted. Some months later, however, Indonesia achieved a partial victory in managing to secure reference to "political development" in order to achieve "peace, stability, democracy and prosperity in the region" as part of the ASEAN Security Community Plan of Action (ASCPA). The ASCPA stated that "human rights and obligations" were part of the strategy for political development and recognized that "political and social stability, economic prosperity, narrowed development gap, poverty alleviation and reduction of social disparity would constitute [a] strong foundation for a sustained ASC" rather than one limited to "a defence pact, military alliance or a joint foreign policy." ASCPA stated, "ASEAN Member Countries shall not condone unconstitutional and undemocratic changes of government."[19]

The precise wording of the ASEAN charter principle quoted at the start of this chapter had its roots in a series of consultations and meetings that began in 2005. That year, an Eminent Persons Group (EPG) began meeting to develop advice on the content of the ASEAN Charter.[20] The group engaged with the public and with civil society representatives in deliberations that influenced the recommendations it made in its final report.[21] That report stated that one of the fundamental principles of ASEAN was "the promotion of ASEAN's peace and stability through the active strengthening of democratic values, good governance, rejection of the unconstitutional and undemocratic changes of government, the rule of law, including international humanitarian law, and respect for human rights and fundamental freedoms."[22]

The EPG was not, however, responsible for ultimately drafting the charter. This task was allotted to a High Level Task Force (HLTF) composed of representatives of ASEAN states. In contrast to the consultative and collaborative process the EPG engaged in, the drafting process of the HLTF was "rather obscure, leading to the belief that it lacked legitimacy" and "did not reflect public opinion."[23] The language the task force came up with differed in one crucial respect from the language the EPG had recommended. The HLTF did not include a provision in the charter regarding ASEAN's obligation to reject unconstitutional and undemocratic changes of government but instead included a reference to "the rule of law, good government, the principles of democracy and constitutional government."[24] This principle was set alongside principles such as sovereignty, noninterference, territorial integrity, and national identity;[25] noninterference in the internal affairs of ASEAN member states;[26] the right of every member state to lead its national existence free from external interference, subversion, and coercion;[27] and the abstention from participation in any policy or activity, including the use of its territory, pursued by any ASEAN member state or non-ASEAN state or any nonstate actor that threatens the sovereignty, territorial integrity, or political and economic stability of ASEAN member states.[28] The provision relating to rejection of unconstitutional changes of government provoked sharp disagreement within the group because of the sensitive position of Thailand, which was at the time under military rule. A reference simply to "principles of constitutional government" was seen as a compromise.[29]

Within Indonesia, public disappointment with the watered-down commitment to democratic norms triggered a serious debate about whether the country would ratify the charter. In Indonesia, the People's House of Representatives, the Dewan Perwakilan Rakyat (DPR), ratifies an international treaty by passing a bill but only after the Commission on Foreign Affairs considers and votes on the bill. On the ASEAN Charter, members of the commission were divided. When the bill finally went to parliament, some prominent members of the ruling party wanted to delay ratification until provisions for the protection of human rights could be strengthened. Some members of parliament wanted to reject the charter outright because it wasn't clear on the human rights body's mandate and powers and because they were concerned about how it treated "budgeting, the decision-making processes and mechanism, the brutality of the Myanmar junta, ASEAN integration, and the idea of ASEAN as a people-centric movement."[30] They argued against the charter on other grounds, too: it did not provide for sanctioning noncomplying members; decision making was still through consensus; and enshrining the principle of noninterference in the charter might make it harder for ASEAN states to criticize members for violating democratic rights, human rights, and fundamental freedoms.[31]

The Indonesian media covered the parliamentary contest between pro-ratification and antiratification forces closely. This attention, combined with the March 2008 series of public hearings on the ASEAN Charter, contributed to widespread awareness of the charter within the country and to public discussions of its merits and shortcomings. Commentators reported on the divisions between parliamentary members and on claims from members of parliament that Foreign Ministry officials were not tough enough in negotiations with their ASEAN counterparts. Djoko Susilo, Indonesian member of parliament, recounted the view that Indonesian negotiators had "surrendered" to Myanmar, Laos, and Vietnam and had not taken public opinion, or the principles in the Bali Concord II, or the EPG Reports seriously enough. Instead, they had taken an "overtly Pajambon" (Foreign Ministry) position.[32] An editorial in the *Jakarta Post* in June 2008 described the charter as a "betrayal" of the EPG Report and argued that to ratify would be to "sell out on the values Indonesia stands for, including democracy, freedom and human rights."[33] The head of the House Commission on Defence, Security and International Affairs, Theo Sambuaga, countered that the difference in views "was normal in a democratic process."[34] Processes in Indonesia were "unlike in some of the other member states of ASEAN where governments can rush the ratification process."[35]

On May 5, 2011, a coalition of Indonesian NGOs, the Alliance on Global Justice, filed for a judicial review of the bill that would ratify the charter, arguing that it contradicted Indonesia's 1945 constitution.[36] The plaintiffs argued that Articles 1(5) and 2(2) of the charter, which are directed toward economic integration and creating a single market and production base within the Southeast Asian region, contradict Articles 33(1)(2) and (3) of the Indonesian constitution, which provide that "the economy shall be organized as a common endeavour based on the principle of the family system; that the branches of production which are important for the state and which affect the lives of most people shall be controlled by the state; and that land and water, and the natural resources found therein, shall be controlled by the state and shall be exploited for the maximum benefit of the people."

A *Jakarta Post* opinion piece characterized the lawsuit as a "dilemma arising from the interplay between international law and domestic law," where "the sovereignty to legislate by a country may be encroached by international agreements . . . the public will question who the government is working for: another government or its own constituency?"[37]

Most ASEAN states did not encounter the parliamentary processes, media scrutiny, public consultations, and judicial challenges that characterized Indonesia's domestic negotiation of the charter. In most of these states, treaty making is not within the prerogative of parliament. In Singapore, for example, the constitution does not require the involvement or consent of parliament before an international convention is ratified.[38] Brunei has no parliament with which to consult.[39] In Laos, legislative approval is simply a formality.[40] Unlike in Indonesia, where there was a range of differing opinions and these opinions were published and discussed without restriction by a free media, in Brunei, Laos, Myanmar, and Vietnam, public debate and deliberation about the charter were limited, and there was no involvement in the drafting or ratification process by representative parliamentarians who might have been responsive to the wishes of the people. The final result is a charter that reflects and protects the interests of ASEAN states, not the interests of the people of Southeast Asia.

The ASEAN Intergovernmental Commission on Human Rights

Article 14 of the charter provides for the establishment of an ASEAN human rights body. According to members of the HLTF charged with drafting the ASEAN Charter, discussion about the proposed human rights body was "the most explosive and tense" of all the debates[41] and the "most sensitive, controversial and difficult subject."[42] Aung Bwa, Myanmar's representative on the HLTF, describes how "the discussions on the issue were most heated and at times we almost came to blows—literally speaking."[43] There appears to have been a "common understanding that ASEAN needs to establish its own standards for human rights protection and promotion, and that human rights should not be left as an excuse for outsiders to interfere into ASEAN's own affairs."[44] Beyond this common understanding, there was clearly a division of opinion on the issue of the human rights body between the members from Cambodia, Laos PDR, Myanmar, and Vietnam (the CLMV states), who "got along very well most of the time,"[45] and Indonesia, Malaysia, the Philippines, and Thailand, states that had already established their own national human rights commissions and were pressing for a more robust regional human rights body.

The EPG had advised that ASEAN members should ultimately form an ASEAN union in which human rights and fundamental freedoms were protected by the rule of law.[46] The EPG did not go so far as to explicitly recommend the establishment of an ASEAN human rights court with powers of enforcement, merely noting that "the EPG discussed the possibility of setting up of an ASEAN human rights mechanism, and noted that this worthy idea should be pursued further."[47] When the question of a human rights body came before the HLTF responsible for drafting the charter, representatives were forced to tread "a fine line, particularly in striking an acceptable balance of competing pressures such as the need to conform to the Leaders' declarations, Ministerial decisions, the EPG Report and instructions from capitals."[48] Aung Bwa described the process of negotiations in relation to a human rights body as "give and take" but "never compromising on the vital issues that could be detrimental to the national interests."[49] Termsak Chalermpalanupap, special assistant to the secretary-general of ASEAN, writes that "the drafters had to follow official instruction from their respective superior" in a "government-to-government negotiation exercise" in which "public participation in the drafting was not possible."[50]

In the end, the HLTF did not decide the issue of a human rights body—whether it should exist and what form it should take. Members were unable to reach agreement. Brunei Darassalam's representative to the HLTF on the drafting of the ASEAN Charter, Pengiran Dato Paduka Osman Patra, states that "by the time of the Manila AMM in July 2007, consensus did not seem possible. They [sic] was no way forward. The Foreign Ministers, however, had other views. They grasped the political nettle and they reached a consensus that ASEAN should establish such a body."[51] Article 14 of the charter states: "In conformity with the purposes and principles of the ASEAN Charter relating to the promotion and protection of human rights and fundamental freedoms, ASEAN shall establish an ASEAN Human Rights Body. . . . The ASEAN Human Rights Body shall operate in accordance with the terms of reference to be determined by the ASEAN Foreign Ministers Meeting."[52]

The ASEAN human rights body referred to in the charter was established in 2009 as the ASEAN Intergovernmental Commission on Human Rights (AICHR). The Terms of Reference (TOR) of AICHR were drafted by a high-level panel comprised of representatives of each ASEAN state. After eight rounds of drafting, ASEAN's foreign ministers approved the TOR AICHR in July 2009, and AICHR was officially launched at the 15th ASEAN Summit in Phuket, Thailand, in October 2009.

The TOR AICHR provide that AICHR is an intergovernmental body and is consultative only.[53] The purposes of AICHR, as set out in the TOR, are to uphold, promote, and protect the human rights and fundamental freedoms of the peoples of ASEAN[54] and to pursue a broad range of goals that include promoting stability and harmony in the region, and friendship and cooperation among ASEAN member states.[55] The TOR specifically reference "national and regional particularities and mutual respect for different historical, cultural and religious backgrounds" and "the balance between rights and responsibilities."[56] The principles that are to guide AICHR, also set out in the TOR, reinforce the norm of noninterference in the internal affairs of ASEAN member states[57] and recognize that the primary responsibility to promote and protect human rights and fundamental freedoms rests with each member state.[58] In terms of the operation of AICHR, the TOR specify that decisions must be by consensus[59] and that AICHR should employ an evolutionary, constructive, and nonconfrontational approach to pursuing cooperation on the promotion and protection of human rights.[60] AICHR's commissioners, representing each of the ten member states, are appointed by member states (who may consult with stakeholders) and are also "accountable to" appointing states, who may decide, at their discretion, to replace them.[61] Commissioners are appointed for three-year terms, renewable once. AICHR's TOR were scheduled for mandatory review in 2014.[62] This review did not take place.

On August 1, 2016, for the first time, AICHR made its annual report available to the public.[63] The reason AICHR had for so long resisted doing this, despite exhortations from human rights activists, was because commissioners could not reach consensus on the issue of whether or not to publicize. Some commissioners believed that the reports contained sensitive information critical of their governments and should only be provided in confidence to the ASEAN foreign ministers.[64] Yet the report of commission activities for the period July 2015–June 2016 is very benign. The commission held meetings, ran workshops on issues such as trafficking in persons, engaged in policy dialogues with representatives from the European Union, and operationalized its guidelines on AICHR's relations with civil society organizations (CSOs) by granting "consultative relationship" status to eleven organizations.[65] AICHR discussed progress on its thematic studies, the first of which, on corporate social responsibility and human rights, was published in 2014.[66] These activities are representative of AICHR's work since its inception.

It is unsurprising that in the early years of its existence AICHR was unable to fulfill the strong protective role that civil society actors demanded of it. The inaugural appointments made to the commission by different ASEAN states were on the whole extremely conservative, with the notable exceptions of Indonesia and Thailand, who appointed, respectively, a human rights activist (Rafendi Djamin) and an academic and former national human rights commissioner (Sriphapa Petcharameesri). Most states appointed career diplomats or former bureaucrats, who were accustomed to acting in the interests of their governments. These appointments added to the perception that AICHR did not have the will or capacity to challenge states, particularly on issues that concern the means by which governments of the region attain power and the methods by which they hold onto it. Rafendi Djamin spoke of the "flaws" in AICHR, of his concern to make AICHR "more effective and credible," and of the difficulties he had encountered: "Until now, AICHR has never [held a] conference. Why? I cannot impose on AICHR members to meet the media [and will] leave it for others to judge."[67]

Yet even if AICHR produced reports and studies that were highly critical of ASEAN governments, it is unclear what effect this would have. The absence of democratic systems within most ASEAN states significantly reduces the likelihood they will be successfully pressured via domestic politics to comply with recommendations. Indeed, in several ASEAN states, the democratic avenues for civil society to raise political demands about compliance with international norms in order to secure domestic policy change do not exist.[68] Consequently, civil society's ability to leverage compliance through publicity is very limited. In many states, there are no domestic political repercussions for noncompliance.

In sum, by specifying the intergovernmental nature of the body, ASEAN's foreign ministers delimited aspirations toward strong regional oversight of human rights. By decreeing that AICHR is "consultative," the foreign ministers made clear that human rights of individuals and groups within the region would *not* be guaranteed by operation of the rule of law, overseen by an impartial third party (a court or commission), but would remain at the discretion of state parties. Yet despite AICHR's inauspicious beginnings, it seemed possible in the institution's early years that it might yet garner legitimacy through a gradual strengthening of its role. A pattern of principled decisions, complied with by a majority of ASEAN member states, would have gone some way toward rectifying the legitimacy deficit that existed at the time of AICHR's birth. Institutions can sometimes have unanticipated effects.[69] The litmus test of ASEAN's new human rights commission was to be its first and most significant task: the drafting of the ASEAN Human Rights Declaration.[70]

The Drafting of the ASEAN Human Rights Declaration

In 2009, when ASEAN's newly appointed human rights commissioners announced their mandate to prepare an ASEAN Human Rights Declaration for the region,[71] few people were optimistic that the product would be a muscular statement of rights that met international standards. There were sound reasons for skepticism.

First, the political diversity of the region, described in Chapter 1, led many to doubt that agreement could be reached on the content of core human rights principles.[72] Many regional human rights systems, at their inception, have included politically diverse systems of government.[73] Nonetheless, the fear was that ASEAN's political diversity would make it impossible for states to agree on anything other than a vacuous declaration that described rights at a level of generality that permitted multiple and conflicting interpretations or, worse, that explicitly constrained the rights of individuals and groups in favor of a broad discretion permitting states to limit freedoms on grounds such as public security, public health, or public morality. Responsibility for drafting the declaration lay in the hands of the commissioners of AICHR, who are accountable to their appointing states[74] and who must make decisions through consensus.[75]

Second, some were concerned that the declaration would revive old debates about the philosophical foundation and political utility of "international human rights" as an idea. During the 1993 Vienna World Conference on Human Rights, some Asian leaders, several of whom were from Southeast Asia, raised questions about the central premise of human rights: the principle of universality. These representatives asked how it could be the case, as the UDHR asserted, that human rights were applicable to *all* people, at *all* times, regardless of a state's economic development and social context. At the Vienna World Conference, Asian leaders echoed an observation that philosophers and scientists had made forty-five years earlier, when delegates were drafting the UDHR. They said that rights have a cultural and historical specificity: rights and duties cannot be absolute but are always relative to milieu.[76] Representatives of UN human rights bodies, and many civil society activists in Southeast Asia, were dismayed at the prospect of reopening the question of universality. In their view, the rhetorical power of "the universal" was an essential bulwark against slippage in state commitment to human rights protection.[77]

An antidote to all of these fears might have been a drafting process for the

ASEAN Human Rights Declaration that was transparent, fair, broad, participatory, inclusive, and wide-ranging and in which the marginalized and vulnerable people of the region, who were after all the primary intended beneficiaries of the declaration, participated. In such a scheme, drafts of the declaration would have been translated into the languages of the region and disseminated widely, including in rural areas. The opinions of religious leaders and philosophers would have been sought, as well as the views of legal experts and politicians, and these figures would have engaged with one another—and with ordinary people—in public forums about the scope and content of the declaration. In short, the ideal of deliberative democracy, which is in modern times understood as a central element of the legitimacy of law created within the political confines of the state, would have been employed throughout the process of the creation of the ASEAN Human Rights Declaration (AHRD).[78] In May 2012, when the United Nations High Commissioner for Human Rights, Nava Pillay, warned those responsible for drafting the AHRD that "the process through which this crucial Declaration is adopted is almost as important as the content of the Declaration itself" and asked AICHR to recognize the value of holding "meaningful consultations with people from all walks of life, in every country across the South-East Asia region," she was referring to precisely this sort of engagement. Pillay observed, "No discussion of human rights can be complete or credible without significant input from civil society and national human rights institutions."[79]

To CSOs and to UN actors such as Nava Pillay, it was self-evident that CSOs should play an important role in drafting the declaration. Yet the central role accorded to civil society in international lawmaking is a relatively modern phenomenon. In 1949, for example, at the time of the drafting of the European Convention on Human Rights (ECHR), a very different ethic of public involvement prevailed. The ECHR was largely the work of a handful of bureaucrats; it was certainly not drafted with the considered input of civil society organizations; nor was there any expectation that it should be.[80] The different expectations about the necessity of CSO involvement is, largely, one of the by-products of globalization. Discussion, debate, resolving conflicting positions, drafting submissions, creating consensus, and identifying positions of opposition no longer require physical contact between interested parties. Advances in technology mean that communication between CSOs, governments, representatives of international organizations, and others in different parts of the world is possible on a scale and at a level of intensity that were unimaginable when Europe and the Americas were producing the first regional human rights agreements. It was extraordinary, therefore, when the Cambodian AICHR representative, Om Yintieng, stated in June 2012 that there would be no public circulation of the AHRD prior to its adoption by ASEAN heads of state: "NGOs want to write it instead of us, but they don't know their duties. The declaration is for all 800 million ASEAN people, so if those 800 million people want to help, in 800 million years we will not be able to finish it."[81]

For several specific reasons, CSOs in Southeast Asia considered it imperative that the AHRD drafting process include their submissions and views. First, CSOs hoped that the declaration would eventually evolve into a legally binding convention, in the same way that the UDHR had eventually evolved into the ICCPR and the International Covenant on Economic, Social and Cultural Rights (ICESCR).[82] CSOs hoped to see the transformation of AICHR into a judicial body with powers of enforcement as a parallel development. The Cha-am Hua Hin Declaration on the Intergovernmental Commission on Human Rights, pronounced in 2009 at the time of the announcement of the commission's TOR, provided that AICHR would be reviewed every five years after its enactment "to strengthen the mandate and functions of AICHR in order to further develop mechanisms on both the protection and promotion of human rights."[83] The commission's first five-year work plan, which was not publicly released, also provided that AICHR would "work towards the ASEAN Convention on Human Rights upon the adoption of the ASEAN Human Rights Declaration."[84] Optimists hoped that by the time of AICHR's first five-year review, in 2014, there might be sufficient momentum among ASEAN states to support the transformation of the declaration into a formal convention. CSOs feared that a weak declaration, which failed to meet international standards for human rights protection, would be a precursor to a weak convention.

Second, CSOs hoped that the declaration would provide AICHR with a clearer mandate. Under the TOR of AICHR, one of the purposes of the commission is to "uphold international human rights standards as prescribed by the Universal Declaration of Human Rights, the Vienna Declaration and Programme of Action, and international human rights instruments to which ASEAN Member States are parties."[85] The TOR also states that AICHR is to be guided by the principle of "upholding the Charter of the United Nations and international law, including international humanitarian law, subscribed to by ASEAN Member States."[86] Because of the references to "human rights instruments *to which ASEAN Member States are parties*" and international law "*sub-*

scribed to by ASEAN Member States [emphasis added]," it was unclear whether or not the commission's mandate was limited to upholding only those human rights to which all ASEAN states had formally subscribed, either in international conventions or regional instruments. It confounded CSOs that AICHR had made no statements of condemnation on serious human rights issues that arose throughout the region during its first term in office. CSOs believed that the declaration needed to provide a clear statement of the rights that AICHR was mandated to take action on (even if action only amounted to oral condemnation).

Third, the organizations saw the declaration as a gauge of the extent to which the institutional limitations of AICHR would prevent it from operating to protect and promote human rights within the region. Observers were keen to assess the declaration, which was the commission's first task, given that the commission was required to meet only twice a year; decisions were to be made by consensus;[87] and commissioners were appointed by their government and were "accountable to the appointing government."[88] Some CSOs hoped that despite these limitations, independent-minded and courageous commissioners might yet be able to speak out on human rights violations within the region and, by a combination of awareness raising and "shaming," change the way governments in the region addressed human rights issues. The declaration came to be seen as the crucible for this hope.[89]

For these reasons, CSOs attached significant importance to the declaration and were determined to ensure that its fate would be different than the hundreds of hortatory declarations, statements, and "visions" that each year emanated from ASEAN, few of which ever came to fruition, or altered the way states behaved, or penetrated the consciousness of the people of the region. CSOs recognized that the declaration would be more effective as a tool for lobbying if it was perceived as legitimate, and they also recognized that the legitimacy of the declaration would be enhanced by the involvement of civil society in its creation and, to the greatest degree possible, by the involvement of the broader public as well.

The means for broad public engagement were available. In Southeast Asia, of the thousands of CSOs, many possess sophisticated, transparent, and highly democratic processes for engaging with one another and with governments and international organizations. Many CSOs had been active in lobbying for the creation of a regional human rights mechanism when the ASEAN Charter was drafted and possessed well-organized national and regional networks. Using the Internet to promote discussion and debate and to include the many grassroots NGOs whose views would otherwise have been overlooked, CSOs were well prepared to play an active and constructive part in drafting the declaration. Several joint CSO recommendations were prepared through participative processes at the national level, engaging diverse groups of national and regional NGOs.[90] Two of the most prominent networks of CSOs, which functioned as umbrella organizations, bringing together small and grassroots NGOs, were the Solidarity for Asian People's Advocacy (SAPA), which represents around eighty CSOs from across Southeast Asia, and the Working Group for an ASEAN Human Rights Mechanism (HRWG). As well as holding workshops on the declaration and disseminating information about it, these networks drafted several joint submissions on the content of the declaration to AICHR and later to the ASEAN foreign ministers. Several CSOs dedicated to specific issues, such as the Southeast Asia Women's Caucus on ASEAN and Earthrights International, also made submissions on AHRD.

Despite repeated calls from these groups for consultation and dialogue about the declaration[91] and the exhortations of the High Commissioner for Human Rights, AICHR held only two, daylong regional consultations with civil society groups. Both of these occurred in the latter half of 2012, when the declaration was already largely completed. The first regional consultation took place on June 22, 2012, in Kuala Lumpur, one day before AICHR held its final meeting on the draft declaration.[92] The second meeting took place on September 12, 2012, in Manila, at a time when the declaration had already been submitted to the ASEAN foreign ministers for review. Only four CSOs from each country were permitted to attend each of these consultations. How these four were selected was the subject of controversy. Each commissioner selected the representatives from his or her country, and in the case of Laos and Vietnam, the CSOs selected were affiliated with the government.[93] For these reasons alone, from the perspective of civil society organizations, the consultations were manifestly inadequate.

The June consultation in Kuala Lumpur involved little dialogue and debate between CSOs and commissioners. CSO representatives read out prepared statements; the commissioners listened without responding. After the first consultation, CSOs released a joint statement saying that they "are appalled that AICHR hopes to finalize such an important regional document, that is supposed to enshrine the rights of the peoples in the region, by holding merely one consultation with civil society at this late hour." They described the June 22 consultation as a symbolic "box-ticking" exercise so that AICHR could claim to have consulted civil society, not a meaningful engagement with civil society.[94] The Malaysian Bar Association labeled the drafting process "secretive and opaque" and demanded that the submission of the draft declaration to the ASEAN foreign ministers be delayed in order for comprehensive consultations to be carried out: "Since the intention is for the AHRD to be a foundational document that captures the hopes and aspirations of the peoples of ASEAN, then their voices must be heard."[95] On the other hand, AICHR's press release described the June 22 consultation as "engaging, constructive and productive as it brought many fresh ideas and different perspectives for AICHR's consideration for the further enrichment of the draft AHRD."[96]

The second consultation was, in the words of Indonesian CSO delegate Yuyun Wahyuningrum, "a step forward for ASEAN in engaging with the civil society."[97] CSOs had learned from the June experience and were determined that the September consultation would be more interactive: "No more listening mode, but rather to answer our questions."[98] Indonesian NGOs collaborated to prepare a joint approach on eight "priority issues" for the AHRD, which had apparently still not been agreed upon by AICHR commissioners: limitation of rights (including public morality); principles of self-determination; nonderogable rights; indigenous peoples' rights; right to an impartial and independent judiciary; migrant workers; and sexual and reproductive rights.[99]

In Manila, CSOs used their allocated presentation time—which was fifteen minutes for each country—to present specific proposals on areas where there was still debate and contention. CSOs demanded responses from AICHR commissioners on specific submissions, and in some instances, illuminating exchanges occurred. For example, in response to the submission from representatives of the Women's Caucus that "public morality" should be removed as a limitation on rights, the Malaysian commissioner told NGOs that Malaysia, as well as Singapore and Brunei, possessed legal systems that included ideas of public morality as a limitation on the exercise of freedoms and that because of this, public morality must remain as a limitation in the declaration.[100] On the question of including indigenous rights in the declaration, the Lao PDR representative was reported as saying that "the concept was not appropriate for countries that have no indigenous peoples, including Lao PDR."[101] On the question of whether rights to sexual orientation and gender identity should be included, the AICHR representative from Malaysia stated that LGBTIQ rights were incompatible with the legal systems of ASEAN countries that applied Sharia law.[102]

At the national level, in some countries (Thailand, Indonesia, the Philippines, Singapore, and Malaysia) individual commissioners held a number of meetings with CSOs on the declaration.[103] CSO submissions to commissioners generally exhorted the same basic principle: that the declaration should enshrine the human rights principles found in the UDHR, the ICCPR, the ICESCR, and the other major human rights treaties.[104] In Brunei, Vietnam, Cambodia, Laos, and Myanmar, there was virtually no engagement between AICHR and CSOs on the declaration. Indeed, in these countries, the identity of the AICHR country representative was not widely known. Few CSOs within these countries contributed submissions on the declaration. As the Malaysian Bar Association noted: "Discussion of the draft AHRD between AICHR representative and civil society of each ASEAN country has not been consistent or widespread, depending very much on individual initiatives, and varying from country to country."[105]

When meetings between commissioners and CSOs did occur, it is difficult to say what effect they had. For example, after the first CSO-AICHR consultation, the Philippines' commissioner announced that she had become convinced that the public morality limitation should be removed from the draft; the Malaysian representative undertook to include the rights and concerns of indigenous peoples in the draft; some commissioners undertook to adopt in the declaration the formulation of the right to self-determination as it is included in Article 1 of the ICCPR (with the proviso that the right to self-determination would not be applicable to the territorial jurisdiction of the state); and many AICHR representatives agreed that the limitation of rights provision in the declaration should follow international standards.[106] Yet none of these undertakings was realized in the final declaration. One reason for this is that after January 2012, AICHR was no longer in control of the drafting process. After a draft of the declaration was leaked to the public, the task of drafting the final declaration was taken out of the hands of AICHR and given to the ASEAN secretariat. This means that during consultations that occurred after this point, those who were responsible for actually drafting the declaration were not the ones engaging in the debate, argumentation, and justification about how it should be framed, what rights it should include, and what limitations it should exclude.

The draft leaked in January 2012 contains some instructive insights into the different priorities and concerns of ASEAN states. The draft was the creation of a group, comprised of one representative from each ASEAN member state, which had been established to assist AICHR in creating the declaration.[107] The draft was sufficient to confirm the fears of civil society activists that the declaration would reflect a "lowest common denominator" approach to articulating rights in Southeast Asia. It contained one hundred clauses, most of which were bracketed, indicating that agreement had yet to be reached on the final form of those particular clauses.[108] Contentious clauses were footnoted, indicating which country was proposing the clause or had reservations about its form or inclusion. It is notable that Thailand, Indonesia, and the Philippines (referred to as "ThaiIndoPhils" in the draft) presented a united position on almost all clauses, and this position was, by and large, a progressive and liberal one. Little can be learned from the draft on the stance of Singapore, Myanmar, Brunei, and Malaysia, although we know that Malaysia and Brunei objected to expanding the prohibition on discrimination to include "sexual identity." Vietnam and Laos, however, provided some illuminating contributions. In the section on civil and political rights, Vietnam objected to the inclusion of the word "freely" in the clause "Every citizen has the right to participate freely in the government of his or her country."[109] Laos also proposed a limitation clause, which stated: "The exclusive insistence on rights can result in conflict, division, and endless dispute and can lead to lawlessness and chaos. Nothing in this Declaration may therefore be interpreted as implying for any State, group or person any right to engage in any activity or to perform any act aimed at the destruction of any of the rights and freedoms set forth herein."[110]

Because the drafting group alone had prepared the draft, and because AICHR and the ASEAN Senior Officials Meeting (SOM) had not reviewed it before it was leaked, its significance should not be overstated. Nonetheless, CSOs interpreted the leaked draft to indicate that concessions to regional exceptionalism may have been winning out over the imperative toward universalism. From January 2012, therefore, most of the submissions put forward by CSOs cautioned against a failure to meet "international standards" in the ASEAN Human Rights Declaration. A submission by the International Commission of Jurists (ICJ), for example, stated that the ICJ "shared the apprehension expressed by numerous human rights stakeholders that the outcome of this drafting process may be a document with provisions falling below international human rights standards and even unduly limiting rights that have been set out in international human rights instruments to which ASEAN members are parties."[111] The ICJ reminded AICHR that it must uphold the principle of universality of human rights embodied in those instruments.[112] But in the end, the result was disappointment. "We see our expectation on AHRD becoming smaller and smaller in the due course of drafting process," said Febionesta, the director of Jakarta Legal Aid. "We doubt that AHRD will be at par with the international human rights standard as AICHR's earlier promises. For Indonesia, there is no point of return. The country should stand firm with its civil society to only accept AHRD at par with the international standard. Period."[113]

Human Rights in the Absence of Democracy

In the 1993 Bangkok Declaration, Asian leaders did not resile from the principles of the Universal Declaration on Human Rights.[114] But they insisted that all countries have the right to determine their political systems, to control and freely utilize their resources, and to freely pursue their economic, social, and cultural development. They stressed that "the promotion of human rights should be encouraged by cooperation and consensus, not through confrontation and the imposition of incompatible values."[115] This attitude still prevailed in Southeast Asia at the time ASEAN leaders embarked upon the drafting of the ASEAN Charter. The charter reflects what Singapore's senior minister, Lee, described as "the Asian will to differ" on questions of democracy, human rights, tradition, and development: "We are all in the midst of very rapid change and at the same time we are all groping towards a destination which we hope will be identifiable with our past. . . . It can be seen as a working out of collective rights to a cultural heritage. It is the exercise of the internationally recognized right to determine one's own system of culture and politics."[116]

But without some form of participatory politics (democracy in its broad sense), the form and content of the ASEAN Charter, the AICHR, and the AHRD cannot be said to be the will of the people of Southeast Asia. The framers did not hear the different voices of rights-holders or consider their views about how regional institutions should protect rights. Groups with diverse interests and opinions did not take part. Those in authority did not consult with civil society groups in clear and transparent processes, respond fairly to these groups' concerns, consider their ideas about how to realize their own and communal interests, or explain decisions publicly. Also, the framers did not clearly keep in mind a conception of the common good of the regional society. In sum, citizens had insufficient opportunity to formulate freely their understanding of rights, express the social values that they wished to guide governance, or articulate their views about the appropriate limits of state power. As a result, key stakeholders consider these institutions to lack legitimacy and to possess very limited potential as instruments of human rights change.

CHAPTER 3

The ASEAN Human Rights Declaration

The text of the ASEAN Human Rights Declaration (AHRD) reveals how the absence of democratic processes during its drafting constrained regional dialogue on the meaning and value of rights. It also reflects the tension between the aspirations of the more liberal and democratic ASEAN states, which have to different extents embraced the discourse of international human rights, and those states that are not liberal democracies. By examining in more detail what is in the declaration, what is missing, and how its framers put it together, we can better understand why key stakeholders largely dismissed the result. And by considering this human rights instrument in light of the Universal Declaration of Human Rights (UDHR) and other relevant regional instruments, we can better assess the view that the ASEAN declaration did not meet international standards.

The Power and Potential of Human Rights Instruments

One of the tenets of international human rights law is that even when international human rights instruments do not provide mechanisms for enforcement, they can still enable and facilitate nonstate actors' efforts to change government behavior.[1] This is because human rights instruments set normative standards, which domestic and international actors invoke to pressure or shame states into reforming their practices. The utility of human rights instruments, however, depends on a variety of factors, one obvious one being the political character of the state in question. For example, in circumstances where civil society actors cannot agitate for change, or where governments do not need to be responsive to the public because they do not face elections, the effectiveness of international human rights instruments as tools of change is severely circumscribed.

The effectiveness of international human rights instruments also depends on perceptions about their legitimacy. For example, if the instrument does not reflect authoritative global norms and standards, such as those set out in the UDHR, then civil society actors may be reluctant to invoke it. On the other hand, if the instrument does not reflect the cultural, social, and economic particularities of the particular state in which rights will be operationalized, governments will find it easy to dismiss the instrument as an irrelevant imposition of foreign priorities and ideologies.

The ASEAN Human Rights Declaration and the Universal Declaration of Human Rights

On several occasions, members of the ASEAN Intergovernmental Commission on Human Rights (AICHR) informed audiences that they aimed to draft a human rights declaration "that met international standards for the protection of human rights" and that also contained an "added value" for Southeast Asia.[2] The ASEAN Human Rights Declaration (AHRD) states that ASEAN member states affirm all the civil and political rights, and all of the economic, social, and cultural rights, in the UDHR, as well as the specific rights listed in the AHRD.[3] From this, we can assume that the declaration was intended to meet the standard of the UDHR in relation to the protection of all rights listed there and that any divergences between the two texts were not intended to have significance.[4] Articles 3 and 5 of the declaration, concerning the right to recognition before the law[5] and the right to an enforceable remedy,[6] mirror Articles 6 and 8 of the UDHR. Article 4, which has no counterpart in the UDHR, draws special attention to the rights of women, children, the elderly, persons with disabilities, migrant workers, and vulnerable and marginalized groups as an "inalienable, integral and indivisible part of human rights and fundamental freedoms."

Nonetheless, despite the declaration's stated intention to include all of the rights in the UDHR, there are some potentially significant differences between the AHRD and the UDHR, both in relation to civil and political rights and in relation to economic, social, and cultural rights.

Many of the civil and political rights in the AHRD are copied directly from the UDHR; the prohibition on torture, for example, is a direct replica of the provision in the UDHR.[7] In relation to certain other rights, the AHRD actually expands and clarifies rights. In relation to the prohibition on slavery and servitude, for example, along with the general prohibition on these things, the declaration includes references to "smuggling or trafficking in persons, including for the purpose of trafficking in human organs."[8] In other cases, the AHRD adopts a slightly different expression than the one used in the UDHR, but the difference is inconsequential. For example, the provisions on freedom of movement in the AHRD and the UDHR are identical, save that the AHRD is more gender inclusive, adding "or her" to the UDHR's "his."[9] In relation to some articles, however, the AHRD's provisions are different from the UDHR provisions in small but not necessarily trivial ways. In relation to several articles, the AHRD modifies the UDHR by adding the phrase "in accordance with state law."

In relation to the right to seek and to enjoy in other countries asylum from persecution, for example (UDHR, Article 14), the AHRD also includes this right but adds a phrase at the end: "in accordance with the laws of such State and applicable international agreements."[10] In relation to the right to a nationality (UDHR, Article 15), the AHRD adds the phrase: "as prescribed by law" (AHRD, Article 18). The AHRD's right to freedom of thought, conscience, and religion, which includes a strong statement that "all forms of intolerance, discrimination and incitement of hatred based on religion and beliefs shall be eliminated,"[11] does not contain the UDHR's expansive right to change religion or to manifest religion in teaching, practice, worship, and observance.[12] The UDHR provisions would have troubled some followers of Islam in countries such as Malaysia, Brunei, and in parts of Indonesia. Islam does not permit Muslims to change religion; the manifestation of religions other than Islam is controversial in Islamic society.[13] In a final example, the UDHR contains the right to peaceful assembly and association.[14] The ASEAN declaration contains a right to freedom of assembly but not, oddly—or perhaps ominously—a right to freedom of association.[15]

In relation to economic, social, and cultural rights, the right to found a family, guaranteed in the UDHR to men and women of full age without limitation due to race, nationality, or religion,[16] is circumscribed in the AHRD by the addition of the phrase "as prescribed by law" and does not contain the UDHR's prohibition about discrimination.[17] The right to work in the UDHR is more expansive than in the AHRD. The UDHR provides for the right to equal pay for equal work, without discrimination; it also provides that everyone who works has the right to remuneration that will give him and his family an existence worthy of human dignity and that it will be supplemented, if necessary, by other means of social protection.[18] The AHRD merely states that every person has the right to work, to the free choice of employment, to enjoy just, decent, and favorable conditions of work and to have access to assistance schemes for the unemployed.[19] On the other hand, the AHRD includes a clause *not* found in the UDHR, one that relates specifically to the problem of child labor, prevalent in Southeast Asia: "No child or any young person shall be subjected to economic and social exploitation. Those who employ children and young people in work harmful to their morals or health, dangerous to life, or likely to hamper their normal development, including their education should be punished by law. ASEAN Member States should also set age limits below which the paid employment of child labour should be prohibited and punished by law."[20]

Other rights included in the declaration but not in the UDHR are the rights of those suffering from communicable diseases, including HIV/AIDS,[21] and the right to reproductive health, within the broad "right to health."[22] The right to development, discussed below, is also present in the declaration.[23]

Self-Determination and Indigenous Rights

Two rights that are notably *not* present in the AHRD are the right to self-determination and the rights of indigenous peoples. These rights are not contained in the UDHR or in the regional human rights instruments of Europe or the Americas.[24] However, the right to self-determination is found in Article 1 of both the ICCPR and ICESCR, as well as in the United Nations Charter, Articles 1(2) and 55.[25] In relation to the rights of indigenous peoples, it is notable that all ASEAN states voted in favor of the adoption by the United Nations of the Declaration on the Rights of Indigenous Peoples,[26] which provides that indigenous peoples may "freely determine their political status and freely pursue their economic, social and cultural development."[27]

The traditional understanding of the principle of self-determination is a right of states to determine, without external interference, their own political status.[28] The principle is most commonly invoked in the context of decolonization. At first blush, therefore, we might assume that self-determination would be a principle that appealed to ASEAN states, with their diverse political systems and histories of colonialism. Why were governments within Southeast Asia averse to including these rights in the declaration?

It is possible that some ASEAN governments perceived self-determination as suggesting a right to secession, and hence as a threat to unity, stability, and order.[29] Within many Southeast Asian states, there are groups who deny, on historical, cultural, sociological, anthropological, economic, or political grounds, that they belong to the state where they reside. Many of these groups have sought recognition and/or independence for decades, often through violent conflict.

One notable example is Myanmar. In Chapter 6, I draw attention to the civil conflict within Myanmar and to the efforts—in some cases, the violent ongoing struggles—of several ethnic groups for self-government. Under the 2008 constitution, ethnic groups are arranged into states, which possess some powers of self-government.[30] But several states are dissatisfied with the degree of independence they have been given and in some states, such as Kachin and Shan, conflict between ethnic armies and the Burmese military has actually increased since the transition to democracy began. Myanmar's government, which has long struggled to forge unity and cooperation among the various ethnic groups in the country, and which still fears the balkanization of the union, would be hardly likely to endorse a regionally mandated concept as potentially unsettling as "the right to self-determination."

Such a right is equally unappealing to the government of the Philippines. In October 2012, the Philippines announced a peace agreement between the republic and the Muslim Moro peoples of Mindanao, in the southern part of the country. The decades-old conflict between the government of the Philippines and the Moro people has its origins in the nation's colonial history. In 1946, when the United States granted independence to the Philippines, it incorporated into the new republic two previously independent Muslim sultanates. These sultanates specifically stated, in the 1935 Dansalan Declaration, that they desired to be excluded from the proposed republic. The Dansalan Declaration predicted that if incorporation proceeded, the result would be unrest, suffering, and misery.[31] And so it proved to be. The Mindanao conflict has taken various forms since 1946: agitation within parliament for self-government; calls for secession; armed struggle by the Muslim Independence Movement and later the Muslim National Liberation Front (MNLF); and calls for a jihad (holy war) to defend the Moro homeland. In 1972, there was full-scale civil war in the southern Philippines. The Moro people's long-standing demand has been for full political autonomy from the Philippines or a separate Islamic state. The 2012 agreement paved the way for the establishment of a new autonomous region, the "Bangsamoro new autonomous political entity" to replace the Autonomous Region in Muslim Mindanao (ARMM), which

President Benigno Aquino III called a "failed experiment."[32] In March 2014, with Malaysia acting as mediator, the Philippines government signed a peace agreement with the largest separatist group, the Moro Islamic Liberation Front (MILF).[33] However, the deal with MILF was criticized for not encompassing other Moro Muslim factions[34] including original MNLF members and Bangsamoro Islamic Freedom Fighters (BIFF).[35] In September 2014, the Aquino administration submitted a draft bill for the Bangsamoro Basic Law (BBL) aiming to establish the basic government structure of the new Bangsamaro Autonomous Region.[36] In January 2015, Congress suspended deliberations over the BBL, following clashes between government and MILF forces.[37] Arguments over the constitutionality of certain parts of the BBL plagued deliberations in the Senate, and by the May 2016 election the bill had still not passed.[38] Newly elected president Rodrigo Duterte, who was born in Mindanao and has Moro family members, urged Congress to approve the BBL as part of a broader goal of changing the system of government to a federation.[39] At the time of writing, the fate and form of BBL and the autonomous Bangsamoro political entity remain unclear.

In the Cordillera region of the Philippines, the indigenous inhabitants, the Igorot peoples, have long called for the right to maintain control over their land and resources, practice and develop their own cultures, and determine their own path of development. But there has been deep disagreement among the Igorot people themselves about precisely what political form self-determination should take. The militant Cordillera Peoples Liberation Army has called for the establishment of an independent "Cordillera Nation." The Cordillera People's Alliance has called for the establishment of a "Cordillera Autonomous Region" within the Republic of the Philippines. At the core of both sets of demands is the right to recognition of indigenous control over ancestral lands and a degree of territorial sovereignty, together with self-rule, which would enable collective control, management, and development of indigenous territories and resources. The government of the Philippines proposed two Organic Acts to recognize the right of self-determination of the Cordillera indigenous peoples, but both were defeated in plebiscites held in 1990 and 1997 for a number of reasons: mistrust in the national government; fear of discrimination by nonindigenous residents; and the view that the Organic Acts did not truly recognize indigenous rights, largely because both acts contained a clause limiting the actual exercise of regional autonomy where it is in the interests of the republic's "national interest, security and development."[40]

In 2012, the Congress of the Philippines deliberated on House Bill No.

5595 and Senate Bill No. 3115, a third Organic Act that would create the Cordillera Autonomous Region and provide measures allowing the regional government to control its resources and obliging the national government to augment yearly revenues.[41] But one commentator noted that "[an autonomous government] is inherently a power of the central government, given to [the region], which means at any time, that power can be taken back by the state. . . . Don't expect to be liberated from the central government. That will never happen."[42] After House Bill No. 5595 failed to pass, a similar House Bill, No. 4649, was crafted in 2014 and continues to be debated.[43] In September 2016, Cordillera elders called on Cordillera politicians to not refile the bill at the House of Representatives, arguing that it "does not embody the substance of genuine recognition of the collective rights of the Cordillera indigenous peoples over their ancestral lands and right to self-determination" and instead calling for the crafting of a new bill.[44] Under President Duterte's current mandate to establish a federal system of government, it is unclear whether Cordillerans will establish an autonomous region *within* a federal state or as a *separate* federal state.[45]

Finally, there is the case of Indonesia. Since gaining independence from the Dutch after World War II, Indonesia has engaged in several internal armed conflicts with ethnic groups, who have all claimed a right to independence from the Republic of Indonesia. These include: the Aceh/Sumatra National Liberation Front; the movement of the Republic of South Moluccas; the Independence Movement of West Papua; and the Fretelin of East Timor. East Timor gained independence from Indonesia in 1999, following a UN-sponsored referendum. The Free Aceh Movement signed a peace accord with Indonesia in 2005, in the wake of the Asian tsunami.[46] The largely Christian inhabitants of the Moluccas, which were part of the Netherlands East Indies but only formed part of Indonesia after decolonization, continue to agitate for independence from Indonesia.[47] West Papua also continues to call for independence and for the reversal of the 1969 UN resolution concerning the handover of then West New Guinea—now Papua and West Papua—from the Netherlands to Indonesia.[48]

During the drafting process for the AHRD, the AICHR representative from Laos stated that the right to self-determination was "not appropriate for countries that have no indigenous populations, such as Laos."[49] This statement is not a reflection of reality. Laos and Vietnam classify indigenous populations as "minorities." Laos, together with Vietnam, Indonesia, and most other countries in Southeast Asia, still possess autochthonous populations.[50]

These populations exist in relative poverty and are politically underrepresented at local, regional, and national levels. Because they are often geographically located in remote and regional areas, they are vulnerable to the effects of development projects and natural resource exploitation (logging, damming, and mining), which impact heavily (and largely negatively) upon them.[51]

How the Preamble Evolved

In early drafts of the AHRD, the Preamble contained broad statements about the nature and value of rights.[52] In the final declaration, these sorts of clauses are found in the body of the declaration proper, in the first "General Principles" section of the declaration. In the final declaration, the Preamble simply reaffirms adherence to "the purposes and principles of ASEAN as enshrined in the ASEAN Charter, in particular the respect for and promotion and protection of human rights and fundamental freedoms, as well as the principles of democracy, the rule of law and good governance" and "a commitment to the Universal Declaration of Human Rights, the Charter of the United Nations, the Vienna Declaration and Programme of Action, and other international human rights instruments to which ASEAN Member States are parties."

It is perhaps significant that the "object" clause in the Preamble of the AHRD changed significantly throughout the course of the drafting. The original preamble, in the January 2012 draft declaration, included a broad and ambitious "purpose" clause, which envisaged the declaration as "a foundational instrument to manifest common values, commitments and aspirations in the field of human rights promotion and protection for the peoples of ASEAN, and as a shared vision of ASEAN for the fulfilment of the goals and objectives set forth herein, including establishing a framework for human rights cooperation through various ASEAN conventions and other instruments dealing with human rights."[53]

The final draft of the declaration is much less ambitious: "CONVINCED that this Declaration will help establish a framework for human rights cooperation in the region and contribute to the ASEAN community building process."[54]

Unlike the UDHR, which begins with only one general article, a philosophical statement about the universal nature of rights, the ASEAN Human Rights Declaration contains many more broad "general principles."[55] The following sections consider the significance of these.

Article 1: "Free and Equal in Dignity and Rights . . ."

Article 1 of the AHRD mirrors Article 1 of the UDHR.[56] Both provide that "all persons are born free and equal in dignity and rights. They are endowed with reason and conscience and should act towards one another in a spirit of humanity."

The drafters of the UDHR drew their text from the 1948 Pan-American Declaration of Human Rights and Duties,[57] which was itself drawn from the French 1789 Déclaration des Droits de l'Homme et du Citoyen.[58] The 1993 Vienna Declaration and Programme of Action reaffirms Article 1 of the UDHR in its own Article 1: human rights and fundamental freedoms are the birthright of all human beings; their protection and promotion is the first responsibility of government. Parliamentarians from Malaysia, Thailand, Indonesia, Singapore, and the Philippines drafted the preamble to the 1993 Kuala Lumpur Declaration directly after the Vienna World Conference on Human Rights, stating that "all human beings are created by the Almighty, and possess fundamental rights which are universal, indivisible and inalienable" and that "the peoples of ASEAN are born free and equal with full dignity and rights and are endowed with reasoning and conscience enabling them to act responsibly and humanely towards one another in a spirit of brotherhood."[59]

Neither ASEAN's human rights commissioners nor the drafting working group debated or discussed Article 1 to any significant extent, and Article 1 was one of the few that CSOs did not query or quibble with, accepting its inclusion in the form proposed in the various drafts of the AHRD. Article 1 was subject to only one amendment throughout the drafting process of the declaration. In the January 2012 draft, Article 1 begins with the word "Everyone." Representatives from Thailand, the Philippines, and Indonesia jointly suggested changing the word "Everyone" to "All persons." This amendment does not appear to have been the subject of debate or controversy: in the June 23 draft, in the September draft, and in the final version, Article 1 begins with "All persons."[60]

This is not, perhaps, as minor a change as one might think. The American Declaration on the Rights and Duties of Man begins its statement about "the freedom and equality of all" with the phrase "all men." In the drafting of the American Convention, the words "all men" were changed to "All persons." Clearly, "All persons" is the more inclusive in gender terms, but there is perhaps a more significant difference between "all men" and "all persons." "All men" denotes "all mankind" or "all human beings": it is a general reference to humanity. The concept of "person" is a legal concept—a person is someone who is recognized under law and who is accorded a particular bundle of rights. From this perspective, the shift from "all men" to "all persons" in the American instruments can be viewed as a consequence of the shift from a nonbinding declaration to an enforceable convention. On the other hand, Article 1 of the UDHR begins with the words "All human beings."[61] When the UDHR was finally transformed into the two conventions, the broader references to "human beings" and to "everyone" were preserved.[62]

Representatives of Thailand, the Philippines, and Indonesia, supported by some CSOs, suggested that "all persons" be substituted for "everyone" in the AHRD.[63] From this, one might assume that "all persons" was not substituted because it was (potentially) a more legally restrictive phrase than "everyone" but because "all persons" conveys a stronger aura of legality, which might imply more enforceable protection of rights than the less specific "everyone." The change from "everyone" to "all persons" was not the subject of discussion in either of the two regional consultations or among civil society groups who prepared submissions on the declaration.

Article 1 also makes the claim that human beings are (1) rational, (2) of equal moral worth, and (3) born equal in dignity and rights. It thus affirms the principle of universality: all human beings have rights simply by virtue of being born human. What does this acknowledgment mean, given the region's long-standing resistance to a Western-dominated discourse of rights, the contentious debate about universality during the 1993 Vienna World Conference on Human Rights, and the profound diversity of religious beliefs within Southeast Asia?

A shared "philosophy of life" can provide a common platform for a statement about human rights, as Jacques Maritain noted when the UDHR was drafted.[64] But the belief about the nature of human beings that Article 1 of the AHRD articulates may not be fully congruent with the various other philosophical beliefs held by the peoples of Southeast Asia. To illustrate: Article 1 may sit uneasily with the Confucian idea that individuals do *not* exist as free, autonomous, independent selves, with rights that attach to them simply because they are born human, but instead exist in a context of social relationships that define the rights and obligations owed.[65] It may also jar with the Buddhist idea that no one is born equal (because of past karma) and that one's duty is to strive toward a more equal existence in the next life.[66] It may conflict with the caste system within the Hindu tradition, which denies the equal worth of all human beings,[67] or with the differentiated legal rights that Islamic Sharia allots to women.[68] All of these religious beliefs profoundly shape the lives and value patterns of many Southeast Asians. If the philosophy articulated in Article 1 of the AHRD does not reflect the deeply held convictions of those subject to the declaration, what does this mean for the legitimacy of the regional human rights regime?

The drafters of the ASEAN Human Rights Declaration viewed questions about the metaphysical basis of human rights as being of limited importance and value.[69] This is not an indefensible position. After all, when the Universal Declaration of Human Rights was drafted, the conclusion to long and acrimonious disputes about the philosophical basis of human rights was simply to adopt what Jacques Maritain described as a "practical viewpoint and concern ourselves no longer with seeking the basis and philosophic significance of human rights but only their statement and enumeration."[70] Maritain's lead has been followed by several contemporary philosophers. Charles Beitz, for example, argues that what matters is how human rights operate as a discursive and political practice, and not as a philosophical doctrine.[71] Richard Rorty suggests that the metaphysical basis of human rights is less important than its rhetorical role in stirring sympathy for those who might be suffering.[72] Thomas Nagel suggests that the violation of basic human rights is devoid of philosophical interest: "The maintenance of power by the torture and execution of political dissidents or religious minorities, denial of civil rights to women, total censorship, and so forth demand denunciation and practical opposition, not theoretical discussion. One could be pardoned for thinking that the philosophical interest of an issue is inversely proportional to its real-life significance."[73]

Nonetheless, many other philosophers have considered it important to demonstrate that at the core of Asian philosophies and religions are values compatible with the modern doctrine of human rights. Within the Confucian tradition, for example, scholars have pointed to the fact that although "human rights" do not exist as a concept in Confucian thought (or as words in the Chinese language),[74] one can find in the works of Confucius and Mencius a focus on humanity and human dignity that is entirely compatible with the philosophy of contemporary international human rights.[75] In Thailand, scholars such as Sulak Sivaraksa have drawn on the central Buddhist notions of individual responsibility for enlightenment to formulate a new application of the doctrine of nonviolence that calls for respect for the autonomy of each person and a minimal use of coercion in human affairs.[76] R. Panikkar argues that the Indian view of social order captured in Hinduism provides an account of human dignity that conforms with human rights standards. He argues that the individual exists and has meaning within a social order, and this order defines the individual's entitlements and duties in relation to others within the order.[77]

Simon Jones describes these approaches as "continuous" strategies—they attempt to establish continuity between the theory of human rights and the various doctrines to which people are committed.[78] Onuma Yasuaki calls them a "theory of universal origin," a way for intellectuals and human rights advocates in diverse societies to argue, "Look, human rights are not alien. They are already in *our* religion (culture, customs, etc.)."[79] The argument is, in essence, that if *all* societies, in *all* ages, have seen the human person as holding a certain value and deserving respect, then we can take this as justification for a doctrine of human rights. The Western bias of human rights, and its basis in natural law, is removed. Some scholars, however, such as Alison Dundes Renteln, question the integrity of any hunt to find common values in all cultures. Renteln argues that it is not possible to pluck values from a complex culture and still have those values retain their original meaning. In Renteln's view, what matters within any particular culture is how values relate to one another and rank beside each other.[80]

It is also difficult to identify with precision what these things are that all cultures respect and value. The answer is more easily given in the negative, in terms of things that all cultures abhor. Charles Taylor identifies genocide, murder, torture, and slavery as things that all cultures condemn.[81] In a similar vein, Jack Donnelly suggests that there are certain things that simply cannot legitimately be done to human beings (such as chattel slavery and the caste system) and some things that seem to be accepted as binding by virtually all cultures (such as prohibition of torture and requirements of procedural due process in imposing and executing legal punishments).[82] These are the same types of things that Bernard Williams recognizes as "abuses of power that almost everyone everywhere has been in a position to recognise."[83]

Thomas Nagel believes that such things constitute a "core of inviolability" to which no cost-benefit analysis applies; they are wrong regardless of culture or circumstance and demand active opposition and rejection rather than esoteric debate.[84] These inviolable rights seem, for most who have written in this vein, to be the non-derogable rights listed in the International Convention on Civil and Political Rights: the right to life; freedom from torture, slavery, arbitrary arrest, and imprisonment; recognition before the law; and freedom of thought, conscience, and religion. But from an empirical perspective, it is difficult to argue that even these basic rights are universal, that is, that they have been accepted, at all times, by all cultures.[85]

Values assumed to be cross-culturally valid because they are found in every culture are often either very vague or very meager. Some scholars, for example, have found in the concept of "dignity" the necessary element of commonality to ground a universal system of value.[86] But attempts to give meaning to the word diminish its practical utility. In Pannikar's conception of the caste system, for example, dignity might derive from one's role in a social order, and one's rights might be those that attach to a person as ruler, wife, mother, or street sweeper. In such an order, there may be manifest dignity in a wife's fulfillment of sati after the death of her husband. But observers from other cultural backgrounds would find it difficult to see how in these circumstances the wife could be said to possess freedom and equality in the same way that her husband does. In the end, perhaps wisely, the drafters of the AHRD did not open up for debate the question of the cross-cultural relevance of human rights.

Article 2: Nondiscrimination

Article 2 of the ASEAN Human Rights Declaration again replicates the UDHR. It contains the essential principle of nondiscrimination, entitling everyone to all the rights and freedoms set forth in the AHRD, without distinction of any kind, such as race, gender, age, language, religion, political or other opinion, national or social origin, economic status, birth, disability, or other status. But both the declaration's drafters and the public debated over protections related to sexual orientation and gender identity.

In the January 8, 2012, draft declaration, the prohibited grounds of discrimination included "sexual identity," which in the text was enclosed in brackets, signifying that at that stage there was lack of agreement among the drafters on the inclusion of this ground. The June 2012 draft declaration makes no reference to rights of sexual orientation or gender identity, indicating that by June 2012 the question had been resolved. Article 2, and the issue of whether sexual orientation and gender identity should be included as a prohibited ground of discrimination, represented one of the few occasions on which the declaration became the subject of broad debate in the public arena.

Nongovernmental organizations whose work focused on sexual orientation and gender identity (SOGI) played a leading role in this debate. These NGOs participated in the ASEAN Civil Society Conference, held in April 2012, and agitated there among other CSOs for recognition of SOGI rights in the declaration. After the April 2012 conference, one of the key regional CSOs, the ASEAN People's Forum, agreed to press for the inclusion in the declaration of equality rights relating to sexual orientation and gender identity.[87] AICHR representatives of Thailand, the Philippines, and Indonesia supported the inclusion of SOGI in Article 2. However, AICHR representatives from Malaysia and Brunei, states with majority Islamic populations and that apply Sharia law, and some prominent social and religious actors within these countries, strongly objected to the inclusion of rights of sexual orientation and gender identity. Singapore's AICHR representative did not support the inclusion of SOGI rights.

The exchange of viewpoints illustrates the sort of regional dialogue about rights that can lead to new understandings about the scope and value of rights. The International Gay and Lesbian Human Rights Commission began the public debate by publishing online some of the reasons that in their view justified inclusion of SOGI rights in the declaration:

> In Brunei, Burma, Malaysia and Singapore colonial laws that criminalize SOGI are used to harass, extort money and demand sexual favours, arrest, detain and persecute LGBTIQ persons. In the Philippines and Indonesia, anti-trafficking or pornographic laws are used to conduct illegal raids at gay establishments and detain LGBTIQ people. The anti-kidnapping law in the Philippines is used to forcibly break apart lesbian couples in legitimate and consensual relationships. In Cambodia, a lesbian was imprisoned following a homophobic complaint by the family of her partner because of their relationship. In Thailand, the negligence of the state is clearly manifested in the refusal to investigate the killings of fifteen lesbians and gender-variant women. The existence of the pornographic law in Indonesia, which haphazardly included SOGI as pornography, is used by several internet providers to block websites of legitimate LGBTIQ organization[s] such as the International Gay [and] Lesbian Human Rights Commission (IGLHRC) and the International Lesbian, Gay, Bisexual, Transgender and Intersex Association (ILGA) websites. In Malaysia, Seksualiti Merdeka, an annual sexuality festival[,] was disrupted and banned by the police as the festival was deemed a "threat to national security." Basic human

rights, such as right to healthcare, housing and education, are denied on the basis [of] SOGI. This has contributed to the steep rise in HIV infection amongst most at risk populations: men who have sex with men and transgendered people. Archaic laws that criminalize SOGI make it even more difficult in implementing life-saving interventions to at-risk groups.[88]

This statement was picked up by the media in several states across the region and formed the subject of much online discussion. The vice president of the Muslim Lawyers Association of Malaysia, Azril Mohd Amin, responded to the suggestion that SOGI rights should be included in the ASEAN Human Rights Declaration in the following way:

Were ASEAN to endorse such rights in the final declaration, Malaysia as a Muslim-majority country would have to reiterate her strong objections; as such a policy clearly contradicts the principles enshrined in the religion of Islam. . . . The 12 September 2012 Regional Consultation is expected to submit a revised draft of an ASEAN Human Rights Declaration for Leaders' signing at the 21st ASEAN Summit to be held in November 2012. In it, you will see the disregard for medical opinion, the politicisation of all gender issues, and demands for recognition for public behaviour that has never been publicly endorsed in most previous cultures, and certainly not in any major religion. You will see the immense pressure on ASEAN governments, particularly on the Malaysian government, to subscribe and submit to the "Yogyakarta Principles" of 2006, in fear of the upcoming 2013 United Nations' Universal Periodic Review (UPR) of Malaysia's Human Rights situation, which will inevitably be a review of Malaysia's LGBT policy and rights. If Malaysians and their friends do not take a firm stand against deviation from the teachings of all major and revealed religions, they may well suffer the punishment of others who have disregarded the Quranic principles at some point on the stage of human organisation. . . . What is to be done?[89]

The juxtaposition of these two alternate views served an important public purpose in identifying the parameters of the debate on whether discrimination on the basis of SOGI should be recognized in the AHRD. The difficulty was that ASEAN's human rights commissioners, who were "accountable to their appointing governments," did not act, in meetings and consultations about the AHRD, as independent agents who were interested in furthering debate and testing ideas through reasoned discourse. During the second regional consultation on the AHRD, in Manila in June 2012, commissioners again raised the issue of including reference to sexual orientation and gender identity. NGOs who attended the conference reported that Malaysia's commissioner, Muhammad Shafee Abdullah, said: "I cannot use my personal decision since together with Brunei and Singapore, we have strict instructions from the government to oppose LGBT rights inclusion in the declaration."[90]

The second difficulty was that commissioners gave too little time in the drafting process to exploring complex questions of religion, sexuality, and morality. During the Manila consultation, for example, a member of a Malaysian Muslim youth group, who had been invited to the consultation by the Malaysian government, had a heated exchange with Ging Cristobal, an LGBT activist from the Philippines. The Muslim youth group member stated: "Even if we agree that LGBT persons should not be discriminated against, they are abnormals and should not be in the declaration and should be deleted." Cristobal responded that "this is clearly what inequality and discrimination looks like—maligning LGBT persons by claiming we are 'abnormals' and by denying our rightful space in the declaration."[91]

The mistrust between civil society and the governments of the region surfaced when Yuyun Wahyuningrum, senior advisor on ASEAN and human rights at the Human Rights Working Group (HRWG), suggested that AICHR commissioners (or their governments) had deliberately invited to the consultation civil society representatives whose views were in violent opposition to one another so that they would be able to point to the lack of consensus that exists among civil society itself, and civil society's disorderliness, as evidence that their views should be discounted.[92]

The truncated conversation that occurred in relation to recognition of SOGI rights, to which this chapter returns in the discussion on the "public morality" limitation, shows that not all debate leads to consensus. Nonetheless, discussion brings, if not agreement, the kind of understanding of the other's views that eventually, one hopes, leads to respect and to tolerance. For example, Wahyuningrum, who supported the inclusion of SOGI rights in the declaration, does not view it as a defeat that they were not ultimately included. She considers it progress that in the course of the drafting of the declaration, states such as Malaysia, Brunei, and Singapore were forced to acknowledge the position of proponents for SOGI rights and to listen to their arguments.

We thus return again to the importance of free inquiry and debate and to the civil liberties that are necessary in order for these things to occur. Free inquiry and debate will not necessarily lead to consensus on questions about the relative importance of values such as individual autonomy, liberty, and social cohesion. On the issue of sexual autonomy, liberals might follow Nagel's simple proposition: "it is essential that we learn to live together without trying to stifle one another's deepest feelings."[93] For others, the answer may be more complex, and the scales may be tilted in favor of social cohesion over individual self-expression. Nonetheless, these sorts of conversations are a necessary step toward clarifying the positions of people who fundamentally disagree on important issues and helping the respective parties understand where the differences lie. The debate itself works toward ensuring that the common public life reflects the views of all its members, so that all members stand a chance of achieving self-realization as part of a community. One of the central difficulties of the Article 2 exchange was that SOGI activists attempted to put forward rational arguments for recognition of their rights, but these were met with arguments from religion, which proponents did not think required justification. This too I will discuss in the context of the "public morality" clause.

Article 6: Duties

> The enjoyment of human rights and fundamental freedoms must be balanced with the performance of corresponding duties as every person has responsibilities to all other individuals, the community and the society where one lives. It is ultimately the primary responsibility of all ASEAN Member States to promote and protect all human rights and fundamental freedoms.

The January 9, 2012, working draft of the declaration contains ten alternative formulations of what became Article 6, suggesting that it caused significant difficulties for the working group. Several of the draft provisions were along the following lines: "Everyone must respect the human rights and fundamental freedoms of others as it contributes to the State, society and their own development. Duties and responsibilities are implicit in the understanding of good citizens and responsible members of the ASEAN Community."[94]

The Preamble to the January draft of the declaration also contains a reference to duties, emphasizing "the interrelatedness of rights, duties and responsibilities of the human person and the ASEAN common values in the spirit of unity in diversity in the promotion and protection of human rights, while ensuring the balance between such rights, duties and responsibilities, and the primary responsibility to promote and protect human rights and fundamental freedoms, which rests with each Member State."[95]

The June 2012 draft contained what was to become the final formulation of the duties provision and remained unchanged.

Civil society organizations objected very strongly to any reference to "balancing" rights with duties. The HRWG, for example, argued that "the notion of 'balancing' duties against human rights is alien to the concept of 'inalienable' human rights."[96] In her statement to the Bali Democracy Forum on November 7, 2012, the High Commissioner for Human Rights, as well as (again) criticizing civil society's exclusion from the drafting process for the ASEAN Human Rights Declaration, specifically stated that "the balancing of human rights with individual duties was not a part of international human rights law, misrepresents the positive dynamic between rights and duties and should not be included in a human rights instrument."[97]

The idea of "duties" has a pedigree in international human rights instruments.[98] In the lead-up to the drafting of the UDHR, for example, the importance of including duties was emphasized by participants from China, Latin America, the Soviet Union, and France.[99] The result was the provision in Article 29(1) of the UDHR that states: "Everyone has duties to the community in which alone the free and full development of his personality is possible." Regional human rights instruments such as the American Declaration of the Rights and Duties of Man,[100] the American Convention on Human Rights,[101] and the African Charter on Human and Peoples' Rights (Banjul Charter)[102] also contain references to duties. Indeed, nearly all of the human rights instruments created since World War II have provided express or implied recognition of duties. Twenty-five years ago, Jordan J. Paust noted a shift from theoretical inquiries about whether duties existed in international human rights law to questions about what sorts of duty correspond to what sorts of rights in what contexts, how competing rights should be accommodated, and how these ultimately affect public responsibility.[103]

The idea of duties as an important and natural part of a theory of rights seems entirely unremarkable to modern philosophers of rights.[104] For example, Joseph Raz employs the notion of duties to identify whether something is a right at all. Raz argues that a person has a right if some aspect of her well-being (some "interest") is sufficiently important to justify holding another person or persons to be under a duty to respect and fulfill that right. A's right to free speech, for example, is sufficiently important from a moral point of view to justify holding other people (particularly the government) to have duties not to place A under restrictions or penalties in this regard.[105] Amartya Sen has explored the scope of duties in international human rights law, without questioning that the idea of duty belongs in the theory of human rights that he proposes. For Sen, all of us have a basic general obligation (a duty) to engage in an act of deliberative reasoning in order to work out what should be done, given the parameters of a particular case, to prevent the human rights of others from being violated or to aid their enjoyment of rights.[106] Thomas Pogge has offered a more specific and demanding idea of duty, arguing that every person has a responsibility not to cooperate in imposing an unjust institutional scheme upon others, one that might violate their rights in indirect ways, and that continued participation in an unjust institutional scheme triggers obligations to promote feasible reforms of this scheme.[107] In his (very brief) contribution to the UNESCO Committee on the Drafting of the UDHR, Mahatma Gandhi suggested that instead of a list of rights, it might be better for the committee to "define the duties of every Man and Woman and correlate every right to some corresponding duty to be first performed. Every other right can be shown to be a usurpation hardly worth fighting for."[108]

Some scholars, however, have drawn attention to the dangers of advancing a notion of duties within a framework of human rights. Ben Saul, for example, in his critique of the 1997 Draft Declaration of Human Responsibilities, created by the Inter-Action Council, argues that: (1) duties cannot be defined with sufficient clarity and precision to make them useful legal concepts; (2) duties involve subtle and particularistic matters of custom and lore, better suited to local systems of morality than codification at the international level; and (3) historically, the concept of human duties has proven open to abuse and manipulation.[109] This last argument is particularly telling in the context of Southeast Asia, where a very specific conception of duty has prevailed among governments in the region. This idea of duty was most clearly set out in the Singapore government's white paper titled *Shared Values*, published in 1991 (discussed in Chapter 1).[110] The white paper, presented as a pan-Singaporean national ideology, identifies five key values of Singaporean society.[111] The first value is "nation before community and society before self." This is projected as the foundational value upon which the other four values (family as the basic unit of society; community support and re-spect for the individual; consensus, not conflict; racial and religious harmony) are built. "Nation before community" means that no ethnic or religious group should place its own interests above those of other groups; all subgroups should support the national interest above all. "Society before self" means that individuals should pursue the common good and not selfishly prioritize their own interests and benefits. The white paper states: "If Singaporeans had in-sisted on their individual rights and prerogatives, and refused to compromise these for the greater interests of the nation, they would have restricted the options available for solving these problems."[112]

The white paper endorses a uniquely East/Southeast Asian version of communitarianism, one that preferences collectivism over individualism, es-pecially the individual's freedom.[113] The community is exalted in the forma-tion and shaping of the individual's values, behavior, and identity. For example, in the white paper, Singaporeans are exhorted to compromise their selfish individual interests, benefits, and rights for the common good and to perform their duties as members of their family and community. Personal rights and civil and political liberties are less important than fulfilling duties and respon-sibilities toward family and community. The Singapore white paper does not base a commitment to upholding rights on the needs and interests of each individual but on a calculus that relates the importance of a particular interest to the importance of every other interest, such as social stability or national security. In Malaysia, Mahathir Mohamad pronounced similar philosophies to the ones set out in the white paper about the duty of citizens to put the interests of the state before their individual desires. Consider the following speech: "For Asians, the community, the majority comes first. The individual and minority must have their rights but not at the unreasonable expense of the majority. The individuals and the majority must conform to the mores of society. A little deviation may be allowed but unrestrained exhibition of per-sonal freedom which disturbs the peace or threatens to undermine society is not what Asians expect from democracy."[114]

In the hands of some governments, the concept of duty becomes a justifi-cation for, as well as an instrument of, authoritarianism.[115] The fulfillment of duties frequently betokens social, economic, or political subordination and tends toward conservatism and the perpetuation of inequalities. The emphasis on duties that permeated the policies and rhetoric of leaders such as Lee Kuan Yew, Mahathir, and Suharto essentialized citizens as people who are obedient and devoted to the community and civic and national virtue as demanding an orientation away from "individualistic" demands such as freedom of expression or sexual liberty.[116] The political logic following from an emphasis on duty was a constraint of civil and political rights in the name of order, harmony, and control.

There is a clear strand of utilitarian thinking in this kind of philosophy about duties: an idea that individual rights might justifiably be "traded off" against a greater good. This is the very notion that the idea of rights was supposed to resist, in Ronald Dworkin's idea of rights as "trump cards," which protect the basics of our individual freedom and liberty against other imperatives.[117] Rights are supposed to impose limits on the sacrifices that can be demanded from individuals as contributions to the general good; rights are "designed to pick out those interests of ours that are not to be traded off against the interests of others," in Jeremy Waldron's words.[118]

In relation to ASEAN's communist members, Vietnam and Laos, the idea of balancing duties with rights is inherently problematic. In communist societies, the possession of rights is contingent on the performance of duties, as I explained in Chapter 1. Because of this element of contingency, many argue that in communist societies, rights are not the equal and inalienable entitlements that the UDHR envisions.[119] If the state can bestow or remove rights based on its assessments of citizens' contributions to the state, then entitlements are not held as *rights*.[120] Article 51 of the constitution of the Socialist Republic of Vietnam, modeled on Article 59 of the 1977 Soviet constitution, states: "The citizen's rights are inseparable from his duties. The State guarantees the rights of the citizen; the citizen must fulfil his duties to the State and society."

CSOs involved in advocacy around the ASEAN Human Rights Declaration were not opposed to a reference to duties. The draft declaration prepared by the ASEAN Working Group for a Human Rights Mechanism, for example, itself includes an article on duties.[121] It was the idea of "balancing" rights and duties that many found problematic.[122] CSOs feared that the conception of balance favored by Southeast Asian governments would be a balance between individual liberty and the duty of citizens to preserve the existing social order. CSOs feared that an individual's duty to ensure the cohesion and security of the state would prevail over individual liberty. In circumstances where the existing social order subjugates the rights of women, or ethnic minorities, or indigenous peoples, this was viewed as unacceptable.

The duties that Article 29 of the UDHR covers apply in a community where the free and full development of personality is possible.[123] This implies that the individual owes the community duties so that he or she can flourish within the community. We cannot owe duties to communities in which we are not free and equal members, in which our views about balancing rights, and the relationship between rights and duties, are ignored or subjugated. Put simply, civil society actors in Southeast Asia did not trust that the governments of the region would carry out any balancing between rights and duties in an even-handed way.

Article 7: "Indivisible, Interdependent and Interrelated"

> All human rights are universal, indivisible,
> interdependent and interrelated. All human rights
> and fundamental freedoms in this declaration must
> be treated in a fair and equal manner, on the same
> footing and with the same emphasis. At the same
> time, the realisation of human rights must be
> considered in the regional and national context
> bearing in mind different political, economic, legal,
> social, cultural, historical and religious backgrounds.

So reads Article 7, which closely follows the formulation of Article 5 of the Vienna Declaration: "All human rights are universal, indivisible and interdependent and interrelated. The international community must treat human rights globally in a fair and equal manner, on the same footing, and with the same emphasis. While the significance of national and regional particularities and various historical, cultural and religious backgrounds must be borne in mind, it is the duty of States, regardless of their political, economic and cultural systems, to promote and protect all human rights and fundamental freedoms."[124]

The phrase "indivisible and interdependent and interrelated" is ritually invoked in the statements, speeches, and reports of UN human rights actors and institutions. Only recently have scholars attempted to unpack the meaning and potential of the phrase.[125] Initially, the idea was born from the desire of developing nations to emphasize economic and social rights, in contradistinction to the perceived emphasis placed on civil and political rights, as well as to stress that social and economic rights are as essential to a life with dignity as rights connected to individual liberties. As the 1968 Proclamation of Tehe-ran states: "Since human rights and fundamental freedoms are indivisible, the full realization of civil and political rights without the enjoyment of economic, social and cultural rights is impossible."[126]

It is surely the case that economic and social rights, and civil and political rights, are interrelated. The work of Amartya Sen links rights of political par-ticipation to the fulfillment of economic and social rights: in democracies, the exercise of one's civil and political liberties (for example, to protest against the government's economic and social policies) assists political communities in avoiding the severest forms of economic deprivation (famines).[127] Sen argues that egregious social injustices are less likely to prevail in societies that prac-tice liberal democracy.[128] Viewed from the alternative perspective, jurispru-dence from the Inter-American Commission on Human Rights has established that there is a link between economic and social conditions and the ability to exercise rights of political participation: poor, less educated, and marginalized people are less able to access systems of power and more likely to be excluded from decision-making processes.[129] In this way, rights are clearly interdepen-dent and interrelated among civil and political rights (for example, in the way the right to freedom of expression supports the right to political participa-tion), among social, economic, and cultural rights (for example, in the way the right to food supports the right to work, and vice versa), and between civil and political rights and economic, social, and cultural rights (in the way, for ex-ample, that equality rights support the right to education).

All rights are clearly interdependent and interrelated, but are they all in-divisible? And if they are not, then are indivisible rights, without which other rights cannot exist, more important than other rights? And if some are more important, how much weight can we give to the statement that "all rights must be treated on the same footing and with the same emphasis?" These questions bring us to the vexed issue of whether or not there is a hierarchy of human rights. Is the right to life, protected in Article 11 of the AHRD, equally as important as the right to "freely take part in cultural life, to enjoy the arts and the benefits of scientific progress," protected in Article 33 of the declaration? It is certainly arguable that cultural life is extremely important, that it is essen-tial to self-identity and fulfillment, and even that it is necessary in order for an individual to realize his or her potential to lead a fully "human" life. But is it as important as being alive or not being a slave? Death or enslavement pre-cludes the possibility of enjoying *any other rights* at all. Is it helpful to the realization of *all* rights to argue that these rights are thus of a different and more important order than other rights and that their realization should be prioritized in government policy?

In relation to questions such as these, James Nickel has argued that indivisibility should be viewed differently from interdependence and interrelatedness. His argument is that indivisibility is a very strong form of interdependence, where one right cannot exist in the absence of another. Interdependence and interrelatedness mean merely that one right supports the other without being essential to its survival. He uses the analogy of human biology. The heart and the liver are indivisible: one cannot function without the other. A person's two hands, in contrast, are merely mutually supportive, not indivisible.[130]

In most countries in Southeast Asia, governments have very limited resources and the prioritization of some pressing social needs over others is inevitable. There may indeed be utility in counting some core rights as indivisible and prioritizing their realization over other rights, which are merely interdependent and interrelated. International customary law recognizes certain rights as peremptory norms of international law, from which no derogation is possible. International human rights treaties—and indeed the ASEAN Human Rights Declaration itself—implicitly acknowledge that there is a hierarchy of rights, in the sense that they demand immediate protection for some rights ("negative" civil and political ones) and provide that other ("positive" social and economic) rights may be realized progressively.[131]

The second sentence of Article 7 of the AHRD, about the realization of rights "in the regional and national context bearing in mind different political, economic, legal, social, cultural, historical and religious backgrounds," generated significant protests from civil society organizations. CSOs identified this sentence as one of the declaration's key shortcomings, which would "allow ASEAN member states to not respect human rights" and, in the words of Human Rights Watch Thailand, render the AHRD "a tragedy" for the six hundred million people of Southeast Asia.[132]

Yet by itself, the article is unobjectionable. Nothing of any consequence flows from the difference between Article 7 in the AHRD and Article 5 in the Vienna Declaration. True, Article 5 of the Vienna Declaration provides that *regardless* of historical or cultural background (which can be borne in mind), it is the state's duty to promote and protect all human rights and fundamental freedoms, while the AHRD does not make this clear and instead merely draws attention to the fact that different political, economic, legal, social, cultural, historical, and religious backgrounds should be borne in mind. But the AHRD contains an expansive provision about state responsibility in Article 6, when it states, "It is ultimately the primary responsibility of all ASEAN Member States to promote and protect all human rights and fundamental freedoms." Why then did Article 7 cause so much ire?

The response of civil society can only be explained in the context of the Asian Values debate and the secretive drafting process of the ASEAN Human Rights Declaration. The January 8, 2012, version of the declaration includes a preambular clause that states: "Reaffirming that the Declaration adheres to the purposes and principles of the ASEAN Charter, and international human rights standards, taking into account national and regional particularities." The phrase "taking into account national and regional particularities" echoes Article 8 of the 1993 Bangkok Declaration: "while human rights are universal in nature, they must be considered in the context of a dynamic and evolving process of international norm-setting, bearing in mind the significance of national and regional particularities and various historical, cultural and religious backgrounds."[133]

The word in the Bangkok Declaration that greatly troubled human rights activists and Western leaders at the time of the Vienna World Conference was "while": "*while* human rights are universal in nature, they must be considered in the context of a dynamic and evolving process of international norm-setting, bearing in mind the significance of national and regional particularities and various historical, cultural and religious backgrounds [emphasis added]."

After tortuous negotiation, in the Vienna Declaration, the qualifying "while" was placed in relation to the claim for *particularism*, rather than the claim for universalism, translating into an uneasy compromise between universalism and relativism.

The 1993 Kuala Lumpur Declaration on Human Rights, prepared by ASEAN member states *after* the Vienna World Conference on Human Rights, evades the universalist/relativist controversy, merely stating that "the peoples of ASEAN accept that human rights exist in a dynamic and evolving context and that each country has inherent historical experiences, and changing economic, social, political, and cultural realities and value systems which should be taken into account."[134]

Given this background, we can see more clearly the reasons behind the strong objection of CSOs to the inclusion of the phrase "national and regional particularities" in the January 2012 draft of the declaration. CSOs saw it as an attempt to revive the "Asian Values" debate and an opening to future concessions to relativism. The views of CSOs prevailed, in terms of removing the phrase "national and regional particularities" from the Preamble.

The contention surrounding Article 7 of the ASEAN Human Rights Declaration is again one that is a result of civil society's distrust of the governments of the region and the particular histories of authoritarianism and oppression that have shaped postcolonial Southeast Asia. For on one reading, the statement that human rights must be realized "in the regional and national context bearing in mind different political, economic, legal, social, cultural, historical and religious backgrounds" is entirely unremarkable. As long as one accepts that human rights are universal, indicating that there is at some level a common global standard in the way a right is understood, defined, and interpreted, then there is little problem in acknowledging that rights will be realized in different regional and national contexts, where different political, economic, legal, social, cultural, historical, and religious backgrounds exist. Indeed, the effective realization of rights *demands* that the different political, economic, legal, social, cultural, historical, and religious backgrounds of different societies must be considered. The action required to ensure that a woman living in a rural area of the Philippines can attain "the highest attainable standard of reproductive health"[135] is different than what is required to ensure this same right to a woman living in Singapore. CSOs feared that permitting the consideration of particular historical, political, and cultural elements in different societies would allow states to *defer* to culture, religion, and political background, in the interpretation and implementation of rights, in ways that denied that there was any common global standard in the way a right was understood and defined.

Article 8 Limitations: "Public Morality"

Article 8 contains a limitations clause, which provides that "the human rights and fundamental freedoms of every person shall be exercised with due regard to the rights and duties of others. The exercise of human rights and fundamental freedoms shall be subject only to such limitations as are determined by law solely for the purpose of securing due recognition for the human rights and fundamental freedoms of others and to meet the just requirements of national security, public order, public health and public morality and the general welfare of the peoples in a democratic society."[136]

It is not, in any substantive way, different than the limitations clause contained in Article 29(2) of the UDHR, which permits limitations on the basis of morality, public order, and the general welfare in a democratic society.[137] Nonetheless, some civil society organizations objected to the limitations clause on the grounds that it was placed in the "General Principles" section of the text, meaning (in the view of these organizations) that limitations could potentially apply to *all* rights, including rights that are non-derogable under international law. For this reason, some NGOs, some Western governments, and the UN High Commissioner for Human Rights were very critical of the limitations provision within the declaration.

Some were also highly critical of the inclusion of "public morality" as a limitation on the exercise of rights and freedoms. This criticism requires some explanation, as most international human rights instruments include a provision that permits states to limit certain rights and freedoms on the basis of public morality. The UDHR contains a provision very similar to that of the ASEAN Human Rights Declaration;[138] the European Convention on Human Rights permits limitations on certain rights (privacy, freedom to manifest one's religion or beliefs, expression, and assembly) on grounds of public morality;[139] the American Convention on Human Rights largely follows the European model; the Banjul Charter permits certain rights to be limited or circumscribed by reference to national law; and the Arab Charter permits limitations on rights to political participation and information on the basis of morality.[140] The constitutions of most ASEAN states, in one form or another, provide for the limitation of rights based on public morality.[141]

Nonetheless, several civil society organizations—particularly those representing women's organizations—argued against the inclusion of this limitation. They feared that states would use the public morality limitation to justify domestic laws and practices that subjugate women and sexual minorities. The Southeast Asia Women's Caucus on ASEAN (Women's Caucus) produced a submission that argued that in Southeast Asia, the "public morality" justification permitted the survival of cultural practices that were harmful to women such as female genital cutting as a sign of chastity (Indonesia); discrimination against married women who commit adultery (Philippines); traditional birth practices (Cambodia and Laos); and prohibition against same-sex relationships (Malaysia). The Women's Caucus argued that the interpretation of "public morality" was based on the perspective of the dominant patriarchal and religious hierarchies and that the experiences of women and girls were excluded from these popular understandings of public morality by the realities of patriarchy, family responsibilities, education, religion, land acquisition and trading systems, militarization, labor, and migration.

For these reasons, the Women's Caucus argued that "public morality" should not be permitted to limit rights and freedoms: to do so would further exclude and subjugate women and sexual minorities.[142] The Asia Pacific Forum on Women, Law and Development agreed that "morality clauses have the potential to undermine women's rights and should not be used in the AHRD."[143] The forum argued that "morality" reflected the dominant culture that tended to favor some, who were mostly men in power, and marginalize others, mostly women. They argued that in Southeast Asia, political and religious hierarchies made women the subject of patriarchal and heteronormative standards and excluded the narratives and perspectives of minorities, denying them access to the processes of deliberation and decision making within societies. They pointed, again, to the noninclusive, nontransparent way in which the declaration had been drafted.[144]

Where there is no common position on a particular moral issue within a state or region, bodies such as the European Court of Human Rights and the Human Rights Committee have deferred to states' views on the necessity of a public morality limitation. On matters of public morality, states are seen "by reason of their direct and continuous contact with the vital forces of their countries as being in principle in a better position than the international judge to give an opinion on the exact content of these requirements as well as on the "necessity" of a "restriction" or "penalty" intended to meet them."[145] The difficulty perceived by Southeast Asian critics of a public morality limitation in the declaration was that the diversity of opinion on issues of public morality within the region would provide states with wide latitude to determine themselves whether or not freedoms should be restricted in the interests of preserving the prevailing morality.

Within Southeast Asia, there is no common position on morality issues such as adultery, solicitation, obscenity, abortion, same-sex relations, censorship, and pornography. For example, in Indonesia, homosexuality is not illegal except under regional ordinances in South Sumatra and Palembang.[146] In Laos, adultery is punishable by imprisonment or "re-education";[147] for monks or novices who commit sexual acts, the punishment is imprisonment and a fine;[148] the dissemination of pornography and objects that are "contrary to fine tradition" carries a penalty of imprisonment and/or a fine.[149] Yet in Laos, same-sex relations are not prohibited. In Cambodia, the Law on Marriage and the Family prohibits marriage between persons of the same gender and prohibits men who are impotent to marry.[150] In the Philippines, homosexuality is not illegal, but attempts to legislate for protection from discrimination for sexual minorities have been resisted by the Catholic Church and thus far have been unsuccessful.[151]

Under Vietnam's constitution, the family is "the cell of society," and marriages must reflect "the principles of free consent, progressive union, monogamy and equality between husband and wife."[152] In January 2016, Vietnam abolished regulations that prohibit marriage between people of the same sex. Singapore's penal code no longer prohibits consensual anal and oral sex, but it retains a provision that criminalizes "outrages of decency" between male homosexuals.[153] Brunei's penal code criminalizes obscene acts and songs,[154] uttering words with deliberate intent to wound religious feelings,[155] and "unnatural acts."[156] There is no antidiscrimination protection in Brunei. In Myanmar, same-sex relations are criminalized under the nation's colonial penal code, and although it is not strictly enforced, activists say the law is still used by authorities to discriminate and extort.[157]

In Malaysia, the constitution declares Islam to be the religion of the federation.[158] The Malaysian government uses Islam as a justification for the criminalization of anal and oral sex, for which the penal code provides a maximum penalty of twenty years in prison, with fines and lashes.[159] In addition, states within Malaysia have enacted Islamic Sharia laws, promulgated by local fatwas, which apply to all Muslims. These laws also criminalize certain sexual acts (such as sodomy) and punish them by imprisonment and whipping. The Sharia penal law in the Malaysian state of Syriah, for example, prescribes penalties for sodomy (*Liwat*) and lesbian relations (*Musahaqat*) with fines of RM5,000, three years' imprisonment, and six lashes of the whip.[160]

Malaysia's role in preserving the "public morality" limitation within the AHRD merits special attention. Reports from the Second Public Consultation on the ASEAN Human Rights Declaration were that the Malaysian representative to AICHR, Datuk Seri Muhammad Shafee Abdullah, strongly defended the public morality limitation in the declaration on the basis that Malaysia's own constitution permitted limitations on the grounds of public morality. He argued that it would therefore be inconsistent if the regional instrument did not permit similar limitations. In a public statement issued on November 19, 2012, the Women's Caucus claimed that while representatives of some of other ASEAN nations seemed prepared to abandon a "public morality" limitation, Malaysia insisted on preserving it.[161]

In Malaysia, the government's view is that the character of Malaysian society as Islamic precludes tolerance of homosexuality because homosexuality is profoundly at odds with Islam, to the extent that tolerance of homosexuality threatens the shared morality upon which the survival of Malaysian society depends. Homosexuality is forbidden in Islam: it is seen by some Muslims as a crime worse than murder.[162] The Human Rights Committee of the Malaysian Bar Council has reported, "The LGBTIQ community is frequently perceived as breaching social codes, fomenting dissent and advocating 'deviancy' and in particular the perception that they are not 'normal.'"[163]

In July 2012, Malaysia's prime minister, Datuk Seri Najib Razak, gave a public address in which he stated that "LGBTs, pluralism, liberalism—all these 'isms'—were against Islam and it is compulsory for us to fight these." He said that the government supported human rights but that "it must do so within the boundaries set by Islam," and he told Muslims to avoid discord that could threaten those who safeguard Islamic principles.[164] That same day, Malaysian opposition leader Anwar Ibrahim, who was convicted in 1998 under Malaysia's sodomy laws and spent six years in prison, released a statement averring that "vice activities" such as homosexuality, free sex, and gambling were prohibited in the Quran and Hadith; Islamic law did not distinguish whether these activities were carried out in the public domain or in private places; and the government had a responsibility to enforce these types of laws where they were committed by individuals in the public domain.[165] Both Razak and Ibrahim, in their views on homosexuality, follow in the footsteps of former prime minister Mohammad Mahathir, who throughout the course of his twenty-two-year-rule placed sexual freedom at the core of what Malaysia stood against in terms of the West: "Our minds, our culture, our religion, and other things will become the target. In the cultural and social fields they want to see unlimited freedom for the individual . . . they accept the practice of free sex, including sodomy, as a right . . . the cultures and values which they will force us to accept will be hedonism, unlimited quest for pleasure, the satisfaction of basic desires, particularly sexual desires."[166]

Where religious beliefs form the foundation of the state's idea about what public morality consists of, it is particularly difficult for proponents of new ideas to open up areas for debate and discourse. Specifically, religious arguments present difficulties for those who would try to champion individual liberties in the face of what appears to be a moral consensus because an appeal to a deity *is* a principled moral reason for holding a particular moral viewpoint, and it is often offered by religious authorities against whose teachings criticism is discouraged, if not forbidden.[167]

We can see conflict between a religious view that lays claim to representing a "public morality" and individual claims about the right to liberty in matters of sexuality in almost all societies within the region. In the Philippines, for example, over 81 percent of the population claims to belong to the Roman Catholic faith.[168] During the period of the drafting of the ASEAN Human Rights Declaration, there was intense public debate in the Philippines around the passage of House Bill 5043, the Reproductive Health and Population Development Bill. The bill aimed to improve reproductive health choices through compulsory sex education in school and by enabling access to contraception, reproductive health services, and "post-abortive" health care for women. Proponents of the bill argued that these measures were necessary in order to realize women's autonomy and liberty. They also argued that the measures would serve the interests of the state in curbing population growth, particularly among the poor.

The position of the Catholic Church in the Philippines is that legislation should be consistent with traditional church teachings on sexual morality and family planning. The Catholic Bishops Conference of the Philippines has consistently rejected the bill, *not* on the basis that it contradicts specifically Catholic religious teachings but on the basis that it contradicts "the fundamental ideals and aspirations of the Filipino people." In this regard, the bishops cite Article 12 of the constitution of the Republic of the Philippines: "The State recognizes the sanctity of family life and shall protect and strengthen the family as a basic autonomous social institution. It shall equally protect the life of the mother and the life of the unborn from conception."

In their 2010 encyclical, the bishops declared "it would be morally corrupt to disregard the moral implications of the RH bill," which "is a major attack on authentic human values and on Filipino cultural values regarding human life that all of us have cherished since time immemorial." They argued that the bill "does not respect moral sense that is central to Filipino cultures. It is the product of the spirit of this world, a secularist, materialistic spirit that considers morality as a set of teachings from which one can choose, according to the spirit of the age. Some it accepts, others it does not accept. Unfortunately, we see the subtle spread of this post-modern spirit in our own Filipino society."[169]

In relation to the claim of the bill's proponents that it would empower women, the bishops stated:

Advocates also assert that the RH Bill empowers women with owner-ship of their own bodies. This is in line with the post-modern spirit declaring that women have power over their own bodies without the dictation of any religion. How misguided this so-called "new truth" is! For, indeed, as created by God our bodies are given to us to keep and nourish. We are stewards of our own bodies and we must follow God's will on this matter according to an informed and right conscience. Such a conscience must certainly be enlightened and guided by reli-gious and moral teachings provided by various religious and cultural traditions regarding the fundamental dignity and worth of human life.[170]

The idea that access to technologies of reproductive choice contravenes not merely Catholic morality but the morality of the nation is a powerful ideological argument, one that is difficult for religious people, or patriots, to refute. Nonetheless, there were dissident voices within the Catholic Church.[171] In 2007, during a symposium on population and development, three Jesuit priests, Fathers Gernilo, Carroll, and Echica, argued that there was space within the Catholic Church to accommodate use of artificial contraception and that, in the context of a conjugal relationship, sexuality need not be sub-ordinate to the procreative value of sex. These priests acknowledged the real-ities of the lives of working Filipinos, many of whom live in poverty, in circumstances where feeding and raising many children is a terrible struggle and where many men work as contractual laborers, making only periodic returns to the family home and thus making natural family planning impos-sible. These views emanated from what one researcher called "a more acute consideration of the circumstances in which married couples must decide on their reproductive well-being in light of their financial and other non-doctrinal considerations."[172] On December 13, 2012, the reproductive health bill was passed, and in March 2013 the bill's implementing rules and regula-tions were passed into law. That same month, religious groups challenged the constitutionality of the act in the Supreme Court. In August 2014, the Su-preme Court upheld the constitutionality of the act.[173]

Article 9: Particularization

> In the realisation of the human rights and freedoms
> contained in this Declaration, the principles of
> impartiality, objectivity, non-selectivity, non-
> discrimination, non-confrontation and avoidance of
> double standards and politicisation, should always
> be upheld. The process of such realisation shall take
> into account peoples' participation, inclusivity and
> the need for accountability.

The principles listed in the first part of Article 9 are the same as those listed in Articles 3 and 7 of the 1993 Bangkok Declaration.[174] They reflect the view held by some Asian governments, at the time of the 1993 Vienna World Confer-ence, that Western states were guilty of hypocrisy in their exhortations to other states about human rights. Asian governments argued that it was not so very long ago that the West was plundering colonial possessions, practicing slavery, and denying the vote to women and people of color. It seemed outra-geous to Asian governments that the West should now try to call Asian gov-ernments to account under the authority of this new secular religion of "human rights."

The final form of this article in the ASEAN Human Rights Declaration was the result of two important and very late changes. First, when the article was originally drafted, and right up until September 2012, it included the word "paramount" before the word "principles." That is, Article 9 provided that: "the *paramount* principles of impartiality, objectivity, non-selectivity, non-discrimination, non-confrontation and avoidance of double standards and politicisation, should always be upheld [emphasis added]". During the Manila consultations, civil society organizations objected to the inclusion of the word "paramount" on the grounds that it implied that these consider-ations were capable of overriding other principles (such as the universality of all human rights). The word "paramount" was removed.[175]

Second, the final sentence of this article was not originally included in the drafting and was only added after the Manila consultation. The sentence, em-phasizing participation, inclusivity, and accountability, speaks to precisely the concerns about participatory democracy with which this chapter has been concerned.

Solidarity Rights: The Environment, Development, and Peace

The ASEAN Human Rights Declaration contains three "solidarity" rights: the right to a safe, clean, and sustainable environment,[176] the right to development,[177] and the right to peace.[178] The wording of these rights in the declaration largely tracks their formulation in international human rights treaties and declarations. Civil society organizations and the governments of Southeast Asian nations were largely in agreement about the inclusion of these "solidarity rights." This is unsurprising. The environment, development, and peace represent genuinely cross-border "regional" issues, where the actions of individual states impact regional neighbors and where the effects in terms of human rights of environmental degradation, war, and poverty are obvious to citizens and governments alike. For example, the haze arising from forest fires in Indonesia in 1997 affected the health of people as far afield as Thailand, Malaysia, Singapore, the Philippines, and Irian Jaya.

Deforestation, overfishing, and the pollution of urban air and waterways threaten not just the communities in states where these activities occur but also neighboring states. Large-scale development projects such as dams, in places like the Lower Mekong, affect communities along the river in Laos, Cambodia, Vietnam, and Myanmar. Conflict in nations such as Myanmar spills across the border to Thailand.

Furthermore, environmental, development, and peace concerns have been prominently articulated in Southeast Asian regional instruments. The 1967 Bangkok Declaration, announcing the establishment of ASEAN, put peace as the raison d'être of the association's existence.[179] The first Article of the 2008 ASEAN Charter confirms that the purpose of ASEAN is to "maintain and enhance peace, security and stability and further strengthen peace oriented values in the region."[180] Of the fourteen "Principles" set out in the ASEAN Charter, eight are concerned with the preservation of peace, largely through respect for sovereignty. Concerns with development and the environment are also prominent in the charter. The Preamble to the ASEAN Charter resolves "to ensure sustainable development for the benefit of present and future generations and to place the well-being, livelihood and welfare of the peoples at the centre of the ASEAN community building process," and Article 1(9) of the charter lists as one of the "purposes" of ASEAN as promoting "sustainable development so as to ensure the protection of the region's environment, the sustainability of its natural resources, the preservation of its cultural heritage and the high quality of life of its peoples."

It is interesting to note, from the working papers of the drafting group of the ASEAN Human Rights Declaration, that some debate surrounded the issue of *where* in the declaration certain solidarity rights—such as the right to peace—should be located. Some representatives proposed putting the right to peace in the declaration's "General Principles," before the right to life, indicating that they perceived peace as an individual right. Others within the drafting group argued for inserting the provisions near the right to development, aligning it with other collective rights. In the end, as we have seen, the right to peace was placed with collective rights. But the text of the AHRD nonetheless states that peace is a right *of every individual.*[181]

The Declaration's Potential to Effect Change

The ASEAN declaration maps the specific needs of the association's diverse and developing nations, and it provides scope for ASEAN states to elaborate and specify the precise content of rights within their borders in the future. In relation to several key points, the views of the more liberal ASEAN states prevailed as the commissioners drafted the declaration, and, overall, the document evinces a clear intent to avoid some of the serious concessions to relativism that marred the Bangkok Declaration. However, detailed examination of selected articles reveals the limitations of the declaration and the qualifications that undermine its legitimacy and potential. As we have seen, these were so serious that Indonesian civil society organizations publicly demanded that their government refuse to ratify the AHRD,[182] and the High Commissioner for Human Rights, Nava Pillay, called for a delay of the signing until broad public consultations could be carried out.[183]

The ASEAN Human Rights Declaration has a modest purpose: to create "a framework for human rights cooperation in the region" and to "contribute to the ASEAN community building process."[184] It may yet serve these purposes, if governments of the region interpret the declaration sympathetically and use it as a tool to guide regional human rights policy decision making. The stronger purpose of human rights tools is their potential to be instruments of change in the hands of activists. But while the region's human rights activists eschew the declaration on the grounds that it does not meet global standards and was not brought into being through a transparent and inclusive process, it is unlikely the declaration will serve as an instrument of change.

Debates such as occurred during the drafting of the declaration are a necessary step toward clarifying the positions of people who fundamentally disagree on important issues and helping the respective parties understand where the differences lie. The debate itself works toward ensuring that the common public life reflects the views of all its members so that they stand a chance of achieving self-realization as part of a community. In this sense, we see that at the heart of civil society's concerns about permitting states in Southeast Asia to limit freedoms on the grounds of public morality lies a concern about the regional absence of democracy, in its broad deliberative sense—about the lack of real freedom within societies in Southeast Asia for people to voice their concerns about liberties and restraints and to participate in dialogue and debate about what their society is and what they would like it to be.

Dialogue and debate that occur at the regional level are particularly important. If the work of the state is to balance people's wish to pursue their own ends with the goal of social solidarity and the formation of a common good, then the experience of one's neighboring states in striking this balance is highly relevant, particularly if these neighbors share similar histories, emphasize religious values in similar ways, or face similar political, economic, or social challenges. Regional human rights arrangements provide the distance necessary to make objective judgments about the balance between liberty and social stability, yet in a context of cognizance of local conditions. A state may have, for example, neighbors who have found it possible for a government to support solidarity and a richer public life without unduly restricting an individual's opportunities for self-creation. These regional instances stand as points of resistance to the inherent conservatism of states, their propensity to maintain the status quo, their interest in the preservation of power, and their eye to the appetites of the majority, all of which inhibit a government's willingness to open a particular contentious issue to broad dialogue and debate. Engaging regional views permits the inflection of the dialogue—particularly where some members of the region are democracies that encourage free and fair debate between diverse participants. As we saw in Chapter 2, the kind of comparative dialogue that I am describing did not take place in relation to the drafting of the declaration.

The absence of a common understanding of democracy is perhaps the most obvious limitation on the evolution of a regional human rights community. Without democratic conditions permitting free discourse, there is a diminished ability for actors to forge shared understandings around human rights concerns.

PART II

APPLICATIONS:

ASSESSING THE REGIONAL DYNAMICS OF HUMAN RIGHTS COMMITMENT AND COMPLIANCE

IN THE FIRST half of this book, I showed how the democratic deficit in Southeast Asia limits the legitimacy and potential of the region's human rights institutions. In the second half, I explore whether ASEAN's regional human rights institutions may yet have the power to influence the human rights behavior of member states in relation to specific human rights issues. I test the regime's influence in relation to the rights of women (Chapter 4); the issue of trafficking in persons (Chapter 5); and Myanmar's treatment of its minority Muslim population, the Rohingya (Chapter 6).[1]

Investigating how the embodiment of regional rights norms affects the status of women and trafficked persons lets us see whether, when a regional human rights entity promotes norms, states exhibit a greater propensity to commit to those norms than when they are part of a global normative order. It also lets us determine whether a regional entity promotes greater levels of compliance with those norms, as evidenced by rule-consistent behavior. I selected these specific issues for several reasons.

First, at the simplest level, in Southeast Asia there are only a limited number of rights that have been the subject of both regional and global approaches. Women's rights and trafficking in persons are both issues with which all ASEAN states have engaged (though not all to the same extent) at both the regional and the global levels.

Second, although the rights of women and trafficking in persons are highly particularistic issues, occurring in specific economic and cultural contexts of disempowerment, discrimination, and deprivation, they are both linked to a broader concern about women's rights, in the sense that both issues have at their core ideas about physical and material security, capacity for self-direction (autonomy), and equality. It is easier to draw conclusions about the relative responsiveness of states to different levels of governance where the rights in question are somewhat similar or related. This is because the kinds of variables that influence the effectiveness of implementation (such as domestic governance issues concerning capacity or the degree of state sensitivity to international approbation on the issue) are more likely to be similar for both rights.

Third, although both issues share a similar concern with the integrity of the human person, they are different in the sense that women's rights are fundamentally matters of domestic politics. No direct benefits flow to states from multilateral coordination in relation to promoting and protecting the equality rights of women. There are no pragmatic or utilitarian reasons to explain why states decide to take joint action on the issue of women's rights at the regional *or* global level. On the other hand, human trafficking is an issue with obvious interstate ramifications. It is a problem that can readily be framed as a security issue, concerning international crime, the protection of borders, and illegal migration. Multilateral approaches are the *only* logical method of addressing the problem. I examine the extent to which this factor determines the legitimacy and effectiveness of global or regional approaches.

Finally, women's rights and human trafficking both illuminate the role of culture and the challenge emanating from claims of cultural relativism, which, as we have seen, are ongoing issues in the debate about human rights in Southeast Asia.

The final chapter of this book takes up the global and regional dynamics of influence from a different perspective. I examine ASEAN's role in purveying human rights norms in circumstances where Myanmar's military is accused of committing crimes against humanity against the country's Muslim minority population, the Rohingya. I look at what power the regional organization had to constrain or condition the behavior of Myanmar's leaders during the period of the country's uncertain democratic transition and the concurrent evolution of ASEAN into a more rules-oriented, democratically conscious, and human rights–aware regional grouping.

The question at the core of these chapters is: Given what we know about these human rights mechanisms and stages, does the global or regional level of engagement offer better prospects for positively influencing the behavior of states in Southeast Asia? There are dangers, however, in attempting to artificially distinguish between and isolate regional and global norms. Global and regional levels of governance inevitably influence one another. These final chapters show how the form of regional texts and the shape of regional institutions are inevitably marked by global influences and how the nature and design of a regional system, including its evolution and purpose, cannot be considered in isolation from developments at the global level. The global influence on regional developments may be positive (as in the case of the drafting of the ASEAN Human Rights Declaration, where the pull toward universal standards served as a counterweight to the insistence by some states of relative standards) or negative (as we see in the chapter on human trafficking, where the domestic policies of states are driven by the need to maintain levels of aid and support from the United States).

CHAPTER 4

The Rights of Women at the Global, Regional, and Local Levels

The Global Level: CEDAW

In 1979, the UN General Assembly, by a vote of 130–0, adopted the Convention on the Elimination of All Forms of Discrimination Against Women (the Convention).[1] The aim of the Convention is radical: to bring about "a change in the traditional role of men as well as the role of women in society and in the family" in order to achieve "full equality between men and women."[2] Only in the final years of the 1970s could almost all of the world's governments have accepted such an ambitious enterprise, as Beth Simmons argues: the Cold War, which for more than thirty years had stymied the evolution of multilateral human rights endeavors, had been mitigated by détente; women's groups were in ascendancy during the UN "Decade for Women" (1975–85); and religious fundamentalism, as a political force, was (temporarily) absent.[3] Today, the Convention remains the centerpiece of global efforts to obtain equality for women.[4]

The strength and scope of the international regime to protect the rights of women were considerable. The Convention's antidiscrimination provision prohibits "any distinction" on the basis of sex that has the "effect or purpose" of impairing or restricting the exercise or enjoyment by women of human rights "in the political, social, cultural, civil or any other field" (Article 1). The Convention's most notable provisions are contained in Article 2, which as well as prohibiting discrimination places an obligation on states to "take all appropriate measures, including legislation, to modify or abolish existing law, regulations, customs and practices which constitute discrimination against women."[5]

Article 5(a) requires parties "to modify social and cultural patterns of conduct of men and women, with a view to achieving the elimination of prejudices and customary and all other practices which are based on the idea of the inferiority or the superiority of either of the sexes or stereotyped roles for men and women." Article 9 provides equal rights in relation to nationality; Article 15 accords women equality with men before the law; and Article 16 sets out a range of measures required to ensure equality in marriage and family relations, such as equal rights for men and women to enter marriage; choose a spouse; end marriage on equal terms; decide on the number and spacing of children; and exercise equal rights in relation to the care and guardianship of children.

The Convention's monitoring body, the United Nations Committee on the Elimination of All Forms of Discrimination Against Women (CEDAW Committee), has stated that Articles 2 and 16 are core provisions of the Convention, in relation to which reservations are impermissible.[6] CEDAW has also stated that states' parties should move toward withdrawing *all* reservations, particularly to Articles 9, 15, and 16 of the Convention. Particular attention has been drawn to the importance of withdrawing reservations to Article 16.[7]

The Convention provides for optional jurisdiction of the International Court of Justice, but general oversight of compliance is provided by the CEDAW Committee, which publishes "General Recommendations" that clarify and in some cases broaden the scope of the Convention. For example, the Convention itself does not explicitly mention a prohibition on violence against women.[8] But General Recommendations 12 and 19 provide that "discrimination includes gender-based violence, that is violence that is directed at a woman because she is a woman or that affects women disproportionately" and that "includes acts that inflict physical, mental or sexual harm or suffering, threats of such acts, coercion and other deprivation of liberty."[9] In 1999, an Optional Protocol, to which reservations are not allowed, gave individuals and groups a right to complain about their government's violation of the treaty provisions and enables the CEDAW Committee to commence an inquiry procedure where there is reliable information of "grave or systematic violations."[10]

Since the Convention opened for signature, international instruments focusing on women's rights have multiplied. Women's rights are prominent in the 1993 Declaration and Programme of Action adopted at the 1993 Vienna World Conference on Human Rights.[11] That same year, the UN General Assembly passed the Declaration on the Elimination of Violence Against Women.[12] In

1994, a Special Rapporteur on Violence Against Women was appointed by the UN Commission on Human Rights. The United Nations sponsored a series of World Conferences on Women, held every five years, which became platforms for activism on women's rights around the world.[13] The 1998 Rome Statute of the International Criminal Court includes crimes against women as crimes against humanity, war crimes, and, in some instances, genocide.[14] In 2008, the Security Council passed resolutions 1325 and 1820 on women, peace and security.[15]

The sum of these efforts, argue many scholars, signals "a sustained feminist presence in the international realm, and one that has challenged the depiction of international law as concerned exclusively with a narrow range of matters related to affairs among states."[16] The architecture of women's rights at the global level is built upon the common understanding that inequality between men and women is a great evil and should be abolished and that culture is not a justification for tolerating inequality. The 1993 Declaration on the Elimination of Violence Against Women, for example, states at Article 4: "States should condemn violence against women and should not invoke any custom, tradition or religious consideration to avoid their obligations with respect to its elimination."[17]

ASEAN States and CEDAW

Cambodia, Indonesia, Laos, the Philippines, and Vietnam were among the Convention's first signatories, although Cambodia did not accede until 1992.[18] Laos and the Philippines ratified the Convention in 1981; Vietnam in 1982; and Indonesia in 1984. Thailand acceded to the Convention in 1985, and Singapore and Malaysia did so a decade later, in 1995. Myanmar acceded in 1997. Brunei was the last of the ASEAN states to join the Convention, acceding in 2006. CEDAW's Optional Protocol, which permits the CEDAW Committee to receive communications from individuals where domestic remedies have been exhausted, has been ratified by Cambodia, the Philippines, and Thailand.[19]

Given the radical nature of CEDAW and its potential to unsettle cultural practices, coupled with the reluctance of some ASEAN states to sign other major international human rights treaties, it is somewhat surprising that all ASEAN states have ratified CEDAW. This is especially so, perhaps, bearing in mind that Malaysia and Singapore acceded to CEDAW at the height of the Asian Values debate.[20] You will recall from Chapter 1 that this was a time when the leaders of both Singapore and Malaysia were extolling neotradition-alist ideas of "the family," particularly "the Asian family," based on conserva-tive interpretations of Islam and Confucianism that imply a subordinate role for women and emphasize conventional authority relations and traditional gender roles.[21]

How do we explain the ratification of CEDAW by ASEAN states? We can see that ratification occurs in temporal clusters around three points. The first is the period when CEDAW opened for signature, which was the middle of the UN Decade for Women (1975–85), immediately before the Second World Conference on Women, which was held in Copenhagen in 1980. Half the ASEAN states signed the Convention at this point, and all (except Cambodia) ratified soon after the Copenhagen conference. The second is the time of the Third World Conference on Women, which took place in Nairobi in July 1985. Thailand's accession to CEDAW took place on August 9, 1985, one month after the Nairobi conference. The third is around the time of the Fourth World Conference on Women, which took place in Beijing in 1995. Malaysia and Singapore acceded to CEDAW within months of this conference taking place. Myanmar acceded two years later.

Several scholars have noted that world events such as the women's confer-ences provide excellent opportunities for states and other international actors such as transnational nongovernmental organizations to persuade other states to ratify human rights treaties or to make proclamations that affirm the state's reputation as a rights-respecting actor in the international community.[22] Ac-cession to human rights treaties in anticipation of conferences, or announce-ments at the conference itself that accession will occur, enables a state to present itself favorably to its peers. The role of civil society (which was prom-inent in the women's conferences) amplifies the reputational stakes by draw-ing attention to a state's shortcomings, by encouraging ratification, and by disseminating information to the international community and to domestic audiences. In this way, civil society brings national constituencies into the calculation of the benefit that states might expect to gain from accession to a human rights treaty.

The temporal clustering also makes it possible to draw conclusions about diffusion—particularly regional diffusion. There is often a tendency for states to follow other states in ratification as part of a "contagion" effect.[23] Contagion operates in the sense that one state's ratification increases the probability that another state within a particular spatial clustering will ratify within a fairly circumscribed period of time. It is reasonable to assume that the fact that half of the ASEAN states ratified CEDAW within its first five years acted as a spur to the remaining ASEAN states.

We find no correlation between level of economic development and speed of ratification. Malaysia and Singapore, which are two of ASEAN's more developed states, were among the last to ratify. There is, however, a degree of correlation between the political systems of particular ASEAN states and alacrity in ratification of CEDAW. Brunei, an Islamic sultanate, was the last to ratify the Convention. It is notable that ASEAN's two communist states, Vietnam and Laos, were among CEDAW's first signatories. In Vietnam and Laos, the "woman question" in the classic works of Engels helped shape a state ideology of feminism that has been generally overlooked. In the 1970s and early 1980s, in these two countries, women were more prominent in terms of political representation, decision making, and participation in the workforce, than in other ASEAN states.[24] In Vietnam and Laos, before the economic "renovation" that began in 1986, there was accessible childcare; women were paid a subsidy to raise children; and there was considerable flexibility in the employment market because of the goal of full employment. In relation to Vietnam, William Turley writes, "undoubtedly, women's relative position improved under communism, with a reduction of early forced marriages, the public condemnation of wife-beating, free childcare and the recognition of housework."[25]

How can we tell whether ratification is a "tactical concession" to win international approbation or evidence of a state's genuine desire to work toward the realization of rights?[26] We can glean part of the answer by considering the nature and extent of states' reservations to the Convention. We can assume, for instance, that genuine commitment is diminished to the extent that reservations undercut the purpose and effect of the treaty. In relation to CEDAW, all states except Laos, Cambodia, and the Philippines have entered reservations with respect to the jurisdiction of the International Court of Justice. ASEAN states with Islamic populations (Malaysia, Brunei, and Singapore) have entered general reservations regarding provisions of CEDAW that may be contrary to religious beliefs. Malaysia and Singapore have entered reservations in relation to granting women equal rights with men with respect to the nationality of their children (Article 9[2]). Singapore has reserved the right not to apply the provisions of Article 2 (the cornerstone antidiscrimination provision, which exhorts states to embody the principle of equality) or Article 16 (relating to marriage). Thailand withdrew its reservation to Article 16 in 2012 after being urged to do so during its appearance at the Universal Periodic Review in October 2011.[27]

Malaysia has been particularly obdurate in relation to reservations. At the time it acceded to CEDAW, Malaysia indicated it does not consider itself bound by several provisions: Article 2(f) concerning state obligations to modify or abolish existing laws, regulations, customs, and practices that constitute discrimination against women; Article 5(a), the key provision concerning state obligations to take measures to modify social and cultural patterns with a view to achieving the elimination of prejudices; Article 7(b), which obliges states to take appropriate measures to eliminate discrimination against women in political and public life by providing them with the right to participate in the formulation of government policy and implementation and to hold public office and perform all public functions at all levels of government; Article 9, which provides that state parties shall grant women equal rights with men to acquire, change, or retain their nationality, particularly in marriage; and Article 16, which provides women with equal rights to enter marriage; to possess the same rights and responsibilities during marriage and at its dissolution; to have the same rights and responsibilities with regard to guardianship of children; and to possess the same personal rights as husband and wife, including the right to choose a family name, a profession, and an occupation. In 1998, Malaysia withdrew its reservations to certain clauses in Articles 2, 8, and 16. In 2003, Malaysia's National Human Rights Commission, SUHAKAM, engaged in a series of roundtable discussions with government agencies, CSOs, and the general public about the removal of remaining reservations. SUHAKAM's 2005 report recommended removal, justifying its reasons with reference to principles of equality in the Quran and Sunnah.[28] In 2010 Malaysia removed its reservations to certain clauses in Articles 57 and 16. However, reservations remain to Articles 9(2), 16(1)(a), 16(1)(c), 16(1)(f), and 16(1)(g).[29]

Conscientious adherence to reporting obligations could provide another form of evidence about genuine commitment versus tactical concession. ASEAN states have been tardy in submitting their initial and then four yearly reports to CEDAW (Lao PDR failed to submit its initial report until twelve years after ratification[30] and Brunei submitted a combined first and second report in 2013).[31] Yet this should not be overstated. Capacity to comply with reporting is an issue for many states, particularly developing ones, and has been so since CEDAW's inception.[32]

What follows from a finding that for most ASEAN states, ratification of CEDAW was merely a tactical concession? Even tactical concessions have power because states can be forced to translate these concessions into actual reform.[33] Real reform will occur when civil society or the international community puts pressure on the state to adhere to the promise of change implied in accession to the treaty. Regardless of original intentions, by the mere fact of accession, states are forced to accept the validity of international human rights and may ultimately be cajoled or corralled into adjusting domestic law to bring it into conformity with international obligations. Between the stage of "tactical concession" and "behavioral change" is a stage where norms assume "prescriptive status."[34]

The national legal systems of ASEAN show varying degrees of evidence of the prescriptive status of Convention norms. As the CEDAW Committee frequently points out, the status of the Convention in the domestic legal systems of ASEAN states is unclear.[35] The constitutions of Cambodia, Laos, Indonesia, the Philippines, and Vietnam recognize treaty law. Nonetheless, in Cambodia and Laos, I have found no cases where the Convention has been invoked in judicial proceedings as an actionable source of rights. Most judges, it seems, believe that implementing legislation is required.[36] This is not the case in Indonesia and the Philippines. In 1988, Indonesia informed the CEDAW Committee that the Convention had been cited before the courts.[37] The Convention has also been cited in several cases before the Supreme Court of the Philippines.[38] In Malaysia, the position seems to be changing. In July 2011, in a case involving a woman who had her job offer retracted by the Education Ministry because she was pregnant, the High Court of Malaysia held that the Convention had "the force of law."[39]

This case is worth considering in some detail, as it provides an illustration of precisely what we are looking for in relation to the move to prescriptive status of international norms in domestic law in Southeast Asia: a correlation between accession to the Convention, the activation of domestic pressure groups, and rights improvement—evidence, in fact, "of the importance of rhetorical entrapment in explaining eventual rule-consistent behaviour."[40] Moreover, it is an example taken from Malaysia, which, as we saw in Chapter 2, can be characterized as a "partial democracy." The spiral model is most likely to work its way to a positive conclusion in a country that is transitioning to, backsliding from, or in a state of partial democracy because these are the circumstances where pressure "from below" is most likely to be exercised, as Simmons predicts. In repressive autocracies, fear will often prevent mobilization, whereas in stable democracies, generally responsive government reduces the motivation for mobilization.[41]

The facts of the Malaysian case, *Chayed bin Basirun & Ors v Noorfadilla bt Ahmad Saikin* (*Noorfadilla*), are these. In 2009, Malaysia's Ministry of Education withdrew an offer of employment that had been made to Noorfadilla Binit Ahmad Saikin after Noorfadilla informed the ministry that she was three months pregnant. The ministry explained its decision on the following basis: (1) the period between the time of delivery and "full health" was too long (an estimated two months); (2) pregnant women were frequently unable to attend work for various health reasons; and (3) immediately after the birth, Noorfadilla would be unable to work and her replacement would require training.

Article 8(2) of Malaysia's 1953 federal constitution prohibits discrimination against citizens on the ground of religion, gender, race, descent, or place of birth.[42] "Gender" was added as an amendment to the constitution in 2001, following lobbying by SUHAKAM, the Ministry of Women, Family and Community Development, and women's NGOs. These groups argued that the amendment was necessary in order to ensure Malaysia's compliance with its obligations under the Convention, which it had ratified some six years earlier.[43] In the *Noorfadilla* case, which was decided in the High Court of Malaysia, Justice Zaleha held that the Convention was relevant to the interpretation of Article 8(2) of the constitution.[44] In her decision, the judge referred to the Convention definition of discrimination (Article 1); the obligation of states to take measures to eliminate discrimination against women in the field of employment (Article 11[1][b]); and the obligation of states to take measures to prohibit dismissal on the grounds of pregnancy (Article 11[2][a]).[45] Justice Zaleha also referred to the "Bangalore Principles," which emanated from a high-level judicial colloquium, the Domestic Application of International Human Rights Norms, held in India in 1988. Noting that the Chief Justice of Malaysia had participated in the colloquium, Justice Zaleha drew attention to the inclusion of "equality" as one of the Bangalore Principles to which judges should adhere in carrying out their duties.[46]

The court also referred to several cases from other jurisdictions: the Australian case *Minister for Immigration and Ethnic Affairs v. Teoh*,[47] in which the Australian High Court held that statutes are to be interpreted and applied, as far as language permitted, so as to conform with the established rules of international law, particularly conventions to which states are a party; and the Indian case *Vishaka v. State of Rajasthan AIR*,[48] in which the court had interpreted the Indian constitution in light of the government's support of the Beijing Statement of Principles of the Independence of the Judiciary and the Fourth World Conference on Women in Beijing. The court's conclusion, in the *Noor-*

fadilla case, was that Noorfadilla had suffered discrimination on the basis of pregnancy and that this was a prohibited form of gender discrimination.

The Malaysian government initially appealed the decision. However, it withdrew its appeal in July 2013 at the urging of the Malaysian Bar Council and CSOs. In the wake of the announcement that the appeal was withdrawn, the Bar Council and CSOs called upon the government to enact specific anti-discrimination laws, pointing out that the CEDAW Committee had advised the Malaysian government to do this in its 2006 report.[49]

The approach taken in *Noorfadilla* is notably different from that taken by the Federal Court of Malaysia in the case of Beatrice Fernandez, which was decided seven years earlier. In the *Fernandez* case, a flight attendant was forced to resign after becoming pregnant.[50] The court held that the constitutional amendment prohibiting discrimination on the grounds of gender had not yet taken effect but that *in any event* it would not have found that an employment provision allowing for termination on grounds of pregnancy was discriminatory: "just as it cannot reasonably be argued that the provision of the law giving maternity leave only to women is discriminatory as against men."[51] The court held that guarantees of equality under the constitution only related to infringements perpetrated by the state, not by other individuals or private companies. This was because (in the court's view) constitutional law deals only with the contravention of individual rights by the state itself or its agencies: "The very concept of a 'fundamental right' involves State action. It is a right guaranteed by the State for the protection of an individual against arbitrary invasion of such right by the State. Where the invasion is by another private individual, the aggrieved individual may have his remedies under private law, but the constitutional remedy would not be available."[52]

Perhaps the most marked difference between the *Fernandez* case and the *Noorfadilla* case is the openness of the court in *Noorfadilla* to the idea of employing, as Anne-Marie Slaughter puts it in her discussion of transnational judicial networks, "the common values that all judges share in guaranteeing litigant rights while also safeguarding an efficient and effective system."[53] The court in *Fernandez* was entirely dismissive of counsel's attempts to rely on comparable discrimination cases from other jurisdictions, such as India.[54]

Litigation is not the only method for drawing international law into the domestic arena and instigating discourse with government on rights issues. Consider the example of polygamy, which is permitted for Islamic men in Malaysia, Indonesia, Brunei, and Singapore under provisions of the Quran and provides that a husband has a right to four simultaneous marriages.[55] In

July 2013, in an attempt to address the plight of the "25,000 single women under 60 still eligible for marriage" in Kelantan State in Malaysia, the Kelantan government introduced an "ideal polygamist" program, by promoting happy polygamous marriages and providing rewards for men who treat their wives well.[56]

The international Islamic feminist organization Sisters in Islam (SIS) has a long-standing objection to the practice of polygamy on the grounds that it undermines women's equality and dignity. In relation to the "ideal polygamist" program, however, Sisters in Islam did not call for a prohibition on polygamy. Instead, they interrogated the program based on concepts of fairness and justice that exist within Sharia law itself. SIS pointed out that Section 23 of the Kelantan Islamic Family Law Enactment (2002) lists four requirements that a husband has to satisfy in order to get permission from the Sharia court to commit polygamy: (a) the proposed marriage is just or necessary; (b) the husband has the means to enable him to support his wives and dependents; (c) the husband is able to treat all his wives fairly, and (d) the proposed marriage does not cause *darar syarie* (harm to a wife's religion, life, body, mind, dignity, or property). SIS raised the question of whether fairness should be judged from the husband's point of view, the wives' point of view, or that of the children.[57] Relevant in the debate was Malaysia's statement before the CEDAW Committee in 2006, where it advised that polygamy required the permission of the Sharia court, which would only be granted "if it is satisfied that the proposed marriage is just and necessary, having regard to such circumstances as sterility, physical infirmity, physical unfitness for conjugal relations, wilful avoidance of an order for restitution of conjugal rights or insanity on the part of the existing wife or wives."[58]

The advocacy of SIS attempts to insert the Convention idea of equality into the Sharia idea of justice in order to construct the notion that polygamy is incompatible with both sets of ideas.[59] In publicizing the issue and in public discussions, SIS fleshed out the Convention idea of equality with reference to specific examples of how the practice of polygamy actually operates: for example, by coercing women into accepting polygamous relationships or into consenting to become additional wives; by keeping women powerless in what invariably becomes "an emotionally charged shift in the terms of the marriage contract"; by denying women dignity by placing them in circumstances where they are highly likely to be degraded or belittled; and by contributing to women's economic and psychological powerlessness, exacerbating inequality.[60] Crucial to the process SIS instigated of engaging state and religious institutions on the issue was broad-based consultation among all those who have a stake in and influence on the development of national laws and policies.[61] What mattered to SIS and women's advocates was that parties were drawn into a principled argument based on some shared understandings (for example, that the goal is a just and fair result for all involved) on the basis that the parties are open to being convinced by the better argument.[62] Arguing or justification represents a discursive opening that can lead parties to recalculate their interests and review their ideals.

In 2013, the sultan of Brunei announced the introduction of a new penal code, based on a strict interpretation of Sharia law, which includes stoning as a punishment for adultery. The first phase took effect in May 2014, but implementation of the second and third phases has been significantly delayed.[63] Civil society organizations, including Islamic women's groups based in Southeast Asia and the Middle East, argued that stoning is a violation of CEDAW (as well as being a human rights violation on other grounds) because it affects women disproportionately and because it is justified by rules and practices that impair or negate women's ability to exercise their human rights.[64] In relation to the sultan's edict, women's groups made two principal demands of the government of Brunei:

(1) that Brunei submit its long-overdue report to the UN CEDAW Committee in fulfillment of its state obligations under CEDAW, to which it has been a state party since 2006; and

(2) that Brunei sign and ratify the ICCPR and the UN Convention Against Torture and Other Cruel, Inhuman or Degrading Treatment or Punishment (United Nations Convention Against Torture).[65]

The women's groups and human rights activists aimed to draw Brunei into a dialogue with critics and external actors. They wished to force Brunei to explain and justify its policies and laws before the CEDAW Committee, where it would be called on to withdraw its reservations to the Convention and explain its failure to undertake the legislative changes necessary to comply with its Convention obligations. In essence, their aim was to have Brunei called upon to justify its interests and preferences, which would then open these to the discursive challenge of other actors, whose perception of the situation would be different than the one held by the sultan and his family. Engagement in the treaty monitoring process would amplify the voices of those calling for change. The fundamental question would become how Brunei constitutively identifies itself: as an Islamic state or as a human rights–respecting member of the community of nations. In his speech introducing the new penal code, the sultan stated that the new law "does not in any way change our policies . . . as a member of the family of nations."[66] There is in this statement an expression of understanding about what is at stake.

The difficulty in employing CEDAW in Brunei to effect change via discursive processes lies in the fact that Brunei is not a democracy. One consequence of this is that CSOs and the media within Brunei do not operate with the freedom to openly criticize or challenge government policy. In Brunei's 2014 CEDAW Committee session, only three CSOs presented pre-session reports and none of these were domestic, Brunei-based organizations.[67] There was no overt domestic criticism of government policy following the CEDAW Committee hearing. The *Brunei Times*, the country's major English-language newspaper, reported only on the positive comments that had been made to the committee by Brunei's own delegate.[68] In any regard, the sultan of Brunei has no political incentive to respond to domestic criticism, even if it exists. Because popular elections are not held in Brunei, there is no political incentive for change.

The situation is entirely different in Indonesia. Indonesia in recent years has recast its identity as a rights-respecting nation and a moral leader within ASEAN (see the discussion in Chapter 3). Because of this, Indonesia is particularly sensitive about protecting its rights credentials and easily drawn into argumentation. For example, in Indonesia, policies of decentralization, in place since 2004, have granted progressively greater degrees of autonomy to provinces and districts, particularly in the area of religious and traditional or adat law. Some of these laws and policies discriminate against women. In Aceh Province, for example, Law No. 11 of 2006 establishes the Ulama's Consultative Assembly, a Sharia court, and Sharia police. In June 2013, Indonesia's National Commission on Violence Against Women (Komnas Perempuan) identified fifteen regulations and bylaws passed by the Ulama Assembly that discriminate against women.[69] Punishments for violating these regulations can include beating, caning, being bathed in sewage water, and forced marriage.[70] Although Indonesia's federal government possesses the power to strike down discriminatory provisions inconsistent with the Convention, it has not done so.[71]

In its 2012 response to the CEDAW Committee's urging that Indonesia strike down laws in the provinces that "severely discriminate" against women, Indonesia took umbrage, writing to the committee at the conclusion of the session (an unusual step) in the following terms: "the term 'severely discriminate against women' is not accurate, as such laws and policies are only in a limited number and have impact in the enjoyment of certain women's rights, while at the same time, in the same provinces or districts, there are more laws and policies which are aimed to empower women and protect women's rights."[72]

What is notable about this response is that Indonesia finds it necessary to justify its position on the meaning of "severely discriminate against women." As international norms become generally more accepted, arguments about their meaning and scope increase. When human rights norms are no longer completely denied (evidenced, for example, by a state ratifying a human rights convention), critics have an opening to challenge them further, for example, by asking why, if human rights are accepted, the state systematically violates them. Further arguments then ensue. The state might respond that violations did not occur or that they are less significant and systematic than represented. Arguments become more specific, detailed, and legalistic.[73]

Despite the opportunities presented by international human rights law via litigation or lobbying and discursive engagement before the CEDAW Committee, the end game remains the enactment of domestic legislation to protect rights. To return then to the prescriptive status of the Convention norms: in 2006, both Vietnam and Laos passed legislation aimed at implementing the Convention;[74] in 2008, the Philippines enacted the Magna Carta for Women Act;[75] and in 2015, Thailand enacted the Gender Equality Act.[76] In 2006, the CEDAW Committee urged Cambodia to pass comprehensive gender equality legislation, which at the time of writing it has yet to do. Malaysia, as we have learned, has not passed implementing legislation for CEDAW and neither has Brunei, Myanmar, or Singapore. In Indonesia, a federal bill on gender equality, drafted to conform to the provisions of CEDAW, has been under consideration since 2012. Debate on the bill stalled after opposition from major Islamic organizations, which formally objected on the grounds that some articles opposed Islamic values.[77]

On the general issue of violence against women, there is significant evidence of the prescriptive status of the norm in most ASEAN states. All ASEAN states endorsed the United Nations Declaration on the Elimination of Violence Against Women.[78] All states have passed laws prohibiting violence against women, including violence that occurs within the home. Myanmar's draft National Law on Protection and Prevention of Violence Against Women was finalized in January 2017.[79] This would tend to confirm the observation of Keck and Sikkink (and others) that norms concerning bodily integrity are particularly effective transnationally and cross-culturally.[80] A report by the United Nations Entity for Gender Equality and the Empowerment of Women (UN Women) points out that the Philippine and Indonesian laws refer explicitly to the Convention (and other international human rights instruments) as the normative framework in the statement of objectives and that the language in the Lao legislation also reflects the Convention commitments.[81] Concordance between international norms and prescriptive status in domestic law is not perfect. For example, neither Indonesia's nor Malaysia's domestic violence laws include an offense of marital rape. In 2006, before the CEDAW Committee, Malaysia stated that marital rape could not be an offense because this would be inconsistent with Sharia law.[82]

To sum up, in Southeast Asia, as in many other regions, there is a significant gulf between the provisions of the Convention and the actual realization of women's rights to equality. Practices such as female genital cutting, female infanticide, child betrothal, and early marriage persist. More quotidian and more pervasive examples also exist: the disparity in wealth and income between men and women and disproportionate numbers of men and women in positions of power in government and business. The reason this state of affairs persists, despite the global pressure toward gender equality, is that the values that underpin the Convention run contra to long-standing and deeply embedded cultural norms. These norms are perceived as providing structure, order, and stability to society and are very resistant to change. Indonesia, for example, in explaining to the CEDAW Committee why the practice of child marriage persists, argued that the most significant reason was "the prevailing sociocultural norms of society which encourage the belief that marriage at a later age amounts to shameful conduct and therefore should be prevented."[83]

Culture and tradition are of course intertwined with religious beliefs. In the Philippines, the teachings and practice of Catholicism foreground marriage stability over sexual rights and the rights of the fetus over women's right to bodily integrity. In Thailand, being born a woman is still viewed in Buddhist belief as the result of previous bad karma. Buddhist texts such as the *Pali Canon*, the *Anguttara Nikaya III*, and the *Jatakas* portray the character of women as venal, duplicitous, and subintelligent.[84] In Singapore, Confucianism historically attributes an exalted position to men and an inferior status to women (*nan sun nu bei*).[85] In Islam, as we have already seen, it is impossible to escape the way that religion imbricates itself in the discourse on rights. As a delegate from Thailand explained to the CEDAW Committee, "The issue of Islamic law was a sensitive one. The situation was unique because Islam was considered to be not only a religion but a way of life, and the laws related to marriage were considered to be the laws of God, which could not be replaced by the laws of man."[86] In Malaysia, Brunei, Indonesia, and Singapore and in countries with minority Islamic populations, such as the Philippines and Thailand, women's sexual freedom, reproductive autonomy, and marriage equality are constrained on the basis of incompatibility with Islam. Generally, evidence from Southeast Asia supports the idea that strongly religious societies have a marked tendency to resist embracing norms of female equality associated with secularism.[87]

Nonetheless, the global ideal of equality between men and women, as captured in CEDAW, has in some cases provided civil society with an effective means of agitating for change. In relation to some aspects of women's rights (violence against women) there has been significant advancement. Yet the translation of global norms to domestic law is incomplete, and to the extent that opportunities for engagement and participation are denied to affected actors (as in Brunei), the potential for the global regime to effect change is stymied. Things remain at the stage of either "tactical concession" (of which Brunei is an example) or "prescriptive status" (which is closer to the position in which Indonesia finds itself and toward which Malaysia is moving).

The Emerging Regional Order

In December 1975, leaders and government representatives from ASEAN nations met in Jakarta to discuss a regional response to the United Nations International Women's Year Conference, which took place in Mexico in June of that year.[88] The world conference approved a ten-year "World Plan of Action" to advance the status of women around the world and to achieve equality, development, and peace, and urged cooperation at the regional and subregional levels in order to achieve these goals.[89]

The ASEAN Women's Leaders Conference was opened by Roesiah Sardjoro, secretary-general of Indonesia's Department of Social Affairs, who began by quoting the aim of the World Plan of Action: "to launch an international action program including short and long term measures aimed at achieving the integration of women as full and equal partners with men in the total development effort and at eliminating discriminations against women, at achieving the widest involvement of women at strengthening international peace and eliminating racism and racial discrimination."[90]

The response from ASEAN ministers from Singapore, Malaysia, and Indonesia was hostile. The ASEAN secretary-general, Umarjadi Mjotowijono of Indonesia, stated:

> The fact should not be overlooked that the situation and conditions in the ASEAN region differ from those in the advanced industrial countries. Whereas in developed countries the striving is towards greater equality of opportunity and treatment of women in economic and social life, and towards the elimination of persistent discriminatory practices, in the ASEAN region the first priority should not be to raise the status of women but efforts in the first place should be directed towards the improvement [of] the standards of living of the ASEAN peoples which represent the chief guarantee of the political and regional independence of ASEAN.[91]

The position of Singapore was that "Singapore women have no need for militant women's liberation movements . . . a quiet but effective transformation has taken place resulting in a gradual and steady integration of women in the whole process of modernization." Malaysia's concern was that "the best traditions of our social and cultural values that give special meaning to our quality of life in our countries and a recognition of the uniqueness of womanhood" should not be "eroded or destroyed in our pursuit for progress."[92] Doubts about the legitimacy of the women's movement did not emanate only from states. Many women's rights activists across Southeast Asia were also worried about the divisive effects of recognizing the primacy of women's issues over class-based problems.[93] They argued that the "woman question" was "vague, abstract, and does not have a material base," a "middle class perception with which the majority of women find no identification."[94]

On this last point, consider, for example, the vexed question of how to deal with gender-specific violations perpetrated by "private" agents (for example, in family situations, within the home). Many Western feminists argue that the corpus of human rights must be expanded to include the experiences of women wherever they occur, even in what has been traditionally seen as the "natural," private, invisible domain outside politics and the public sphere.[95] Yet for women's rights activists in Southeast Asia, this led to some troubling questions. As several anthropologists have noted, the concepts of "public" and "private" are products of liberal modernity in the West. In many traditional cultures, there is no clear notion of a distinction between the public and private realms.[96] Is there utility for women in developing nations in agitating for extension of rights to a private, domestic realm that does not exist for them? Does conflating women with "the private" threaten to embed the very assumptions about the public/private divide that are being challenged? The CEDAW Committee's stance on other cultural issues has not always met with the wholehearted support of feminists, particularly feminists writing in the global South. To many, it has seemed that inordinate attention has been given to certain "traditional practices" (polygamy, female genital cutting, suttee, foot-binding) to the detriment of other more quotidian but equally damaging issues, such as economic disadvantage and the absence of education for girls.[97] In this context, the suspicion has arisen that the women's human rights movement, as part of the broader human rights movement, is an example of Western feminist universalizing—a(nother) "tool of the West and its self-serving Enlightenment project."[98]

At least until the end of the twentieth century, there was ambivalence about the women's rights project in Southeast Asia. At the regional level, this ambivalence is reflected in the tone of the Declaration on the Advancement of Women in the ASEAN Region, which was completed and adopted by ASEAN heads of state in July 1988.[99] The declaration contains only one reference to the principle of equality. In Article 1, it lists as one of its objectives: "to promote and implement the equitable and effective participation of women whenever possible in all fields and at various levels of the political, economic, social and cultural life of society at the national, regional and international levels."

The declaration makes no reference at all to cultural impediments that might prevent women from achieving equality and no reference to women's "rights." Instead, the declaration recognizes the "multiple roles of women in the family, in society and in the nation and the need to give full support and provide facilities and opportunities to enable them to undertake these tasks effectively."[100] It advances as its reason why ASEAN states should pay attention to women's issues the following: "To enable women in the region to undertake their important role as active agents and beneficiaries of national and regional development, particularly in promoting regional understanding and cooperation and in building more just and peaceful societies."[101] The declaration also refers to the role of women in strengthening "national and regional resilience"[102] and "strengthening solidarity in the region and international women forum by promoting harmonization of views and of positions."[103]

Between 1988 and 2004, during which period ASEAN's membership doubled, the ASEAN Committee on Women (ACW) worked to advance the aims of the declaration, chiefly through holding meetings and workshops. It also devised a "Work Plan for Women's Advancement and Gender Equality." One of the fruits of these efforts was the publication of a series of reports on progress in achieving the goals of the declaration. The first report was published in 1996 with data from seven ASEAN countries; the second report was published in 2001 with data from all ten ASEAN countries.[104] The ACW was also responsible for producing the 2004 Declaration on the Elimination of Violence Against Women in the ASEAN Region (DEVW).[105]

The DEVW, adopted eleven years after the signing of the United Nations Declaration on the Elimination Violence Against Women,[106] is markedly less utilitarian in tone than the 1988 Declaration on the Advancement of Women. The DEVW states in Article 2 that its purpose is to "promote an integrated and holistic approach to eliminate violence against women by formulating mechanisms focusing on the four areas of concerns of violence against women, namely: providing services to fulfil the needs of survivors; formulating and taking appropriate responses to offenders and perpetrators; understanding the nature and causes of violence against women; and changing societal attitudes and behaviour."

At Article 5, the declaration links nondiscrimination and women's economic independence and empowerment to the prevention of violence. The Preamble to the declaration notes that violence is an obstacle to the achievement of equality, development, and peace. As I noted in the preceding section, within three years of the adoption of this declaration, all ASEAN states (except Myanmar) passed legislation criminalizing violence against women. Most of this legislation was enacted shortly after the adoption of the regional declaration (the Philippines, Laos, and Indonesia in 2004; Cambodia in 2005; Thailand and Vietnam in 2007). Malaysia and Singapore, however, passed domestic violence legislation in 1994 and 1996, respectively, closer in time to the adoption of the UN Declaration on the Elimination of Violence Against Women. What we see, in relation to the issue of violence against women, is a broad alignment between global, regional, and local ideas about the moral imperative of preventing violence against women. This follows, it should be noted, the demise of the "Asian Values" debate at the end of the 1990s and the admission to ASEAN of communist states Laos and Vietnam (countries with strong histories of promoting women's rights under Marxist principles of equality between the sexes).

The ASEAN Commission on the Promotion and Protection of the Rights of Women and Children (ACWC), inaugurated in 2010, has as its aim "to promote and protect the human rights and fundamental freedoms of women and children in ASEAN."[107] The ACWC has adopted as its first task advancing the issue of preventing violence against women and children.[108] Despite some excitement at the reference to the ACWC's apparent "protection" function, it is clear that the ACWC is a consultative body. Its mandate and functions, listed in Article 5, all concern the promotion of the rights of women and children and the commission's role in coordinating action among ASEAN states.[109] Similar to AICHR, ACWC has no investigative, evaluative, or enforcement powers or any early warning mechanisms. ACWC can provide advice to ASEAN sectorial governments upon request and advocate on behalf of women and children to improve their human rights situation.[110]

The ACWC oversaw the drafting of the Declaration on the Elimination of Violence Against Women and Elimination of Violence Against Children in ASEAN (DEVWC), which was adopted by ASEAN leaders at the October 2013 Summit in Brunei.[111] The DEVWC acknowledges the commitment of ASEAN states to international instruments such as the United Nations Declaration on the Elimination of Violence Against Women but does not include the strong and specific definition of violence that we find in Articles 1 and 2 of the UN declaration.[112] Nor does the ASEAN instrument set out in the body of the text the various rights to which women are equally entitled (life, equality, liberty, and security).[113] There are other small but not necessarily trivial differences between the two instruments. The Preamble to the DEVWC employs the language of CEDAW, obliging ASEAN member states to take all appropriate measures to modify social and cultural patterns of conduct with a view toward eliminating prejudices and customary practices based on the idea of the inferiority or superiority of either sex.[114] In the UN declaration, this same obligation is placed in the declaration proper, under Article 4. Like the UN instrument, the DEVWC lists the various methods that should be pursued to eliminate violence against women and children, largely by strengthening and enacting effective legislation, policies, and measures to prosecute perpetrators of violence, protect women and children, and provide them with access to remedies.[115]

In sum, there is a degree of concordance between global, regional, and local norms on violence against women in Southeast Asia. Furthermore, in the work of the ACWC, we see the beginnings of a regional approach to managing the issue. However, we do not find the same robust regional response, or similar agreement, in regional understandings about the meaning of women's equality.

Particularly troubling in ASEAN is the way we see, in the Ha Noi Declaration on the Enhancement of Welfare and Development of ASEAN Women and Children (2010), the rights of women aligned with the rights of children. The Ha Noi declaration references ASEAN states' commitments to the Women's Convention and the Convention on the Rights of the Child and recognizes in its Preamble "a need to continue to tap on the strength of these groups [women and children] as well as to empower those who are in vulnerable situations."[116] The 2012 ASEAN Human Rights Declaration, as we have seen, contains Article 4, which discusses the "inalienable, integral and indivisible rights" of women, who are placed beside other "vulnerable and marginalised groups" such as "children, the elderly, persons with disabilities, [and] migrant workers."[117]

The conflation of women's rights and children's rights in ASEAN institutions and declarations is problematic for the advancement of women's equality. Children depend on adults and lack capacity. Women have special attributes that require particular attention, such as historical subjugation and reproductive capacities, but these are of an entirely different order than the attributes and hence the needs of children. Merging the rights of children with the rights of women perpetuates the idea of women's biologically determined dependency and the role of women in society as being primarily concerned with home and childcare. It is too early to say how the ACWC will proceed to fulfill its mandate and whether or not, in practice, it will distinguish women's issues from children's issues and work to promote policies directed toward substantive equality for women.

Why was a separate regional institution to oversee women and children's rights created at all, in light of the global trend toward mainstreaming women's issues? In an influential article published in *Human Rights Quarterly* in 1990, Charlotte Bunch argued that "woman-centred" strategies had failed and that the separation of "women's rights" from "human rights" had led to the marginalization and devaluation of women's issues. Bunch argued that the effects of this were both material (at the global level, the Human Rights Commission had more power to hear and investigate cases than the Commission on the Status of Women, "more staff and budget, and better mechanisms for implementing its findings")[118] and ideological ("human" rights were considered more important than "women's" rights, based on an idea that the rights of women are of a lesser order than the "rights of man").[119] In the wake of Bunch's article and in the shadow of gender-specific events such as "ethnic cleansing" in Bosnia and Rwanda in the early 1990s, a project of "gender mainstreaming" was advocated as a new global strategy for promoting gender equality.[120] At the core of gender mainstreaming was the idea that equality between the sexes should no longer be addressed as a separate "woman's issue" but must be a part of all UN activities.[121] The Commission on Human Rights defines mainstreaming as "the placing of an issue within the pre-existing institutional, academic and discursive framework."[122] For many feminists, however, mainstreaming means more than that. The goal of Bunch and her colleagues was to impact and ideally transform the mainstream: to rebuild the concept of human rights from a feminist perspective, so that it took greater account of the realities and concerns of women's lives.[123] The "women's rights are human rights" movement was to a degree successful in bringing women's rights into the fold of broader human rights. Yet the second part of the post–Beijing World Conference project—the goal of reimagining the human rights project to account for the perspective of women, while at the same time recognizing difference, specificity, and context—was only ever imperfectly realized.[124]

Regional Legitimacy

From this study of local, regional, and global influences on women's rights, we can draw several tentative conclusions about the conditions under which a regional system for the promotion and protection of human rights possesses legitimacy.

First, leaving aside the specific issue of violence against women, we see among ASEAN states tactical concessions to global international norms relating to women's rights. The most plausible explanation for these concessions, given the temporal and spatial dimensions of ASEAN states' ratification of the Convention on the Elimination of All Forms of Discrimination Against Women, centers on socialization (primarily through the World Conferences on Women) or diffusion (through the regional "neighbor" effect). We do not yet see a full-blown translation of these concessions into prescription (domestic law reflecting genuine commitment to international norms). What we can see, however, are examples of the way that domestic groups have employed commitments to the Convention in order to move states along the path to prescription. The examples provided of activism in Malaysia, Indonesia, and Brunei usefully illustrate the dynamics at play in different political contexts. In Malaysia, litigation and lobbying around international norms have proven to be effective strategies for engaging government in accepting the validity of a particular norm (the Malaysian government, under pressure, withdrew its appeal in the *Noorfadilla* case). In Indonesia, a state that prides itself on its democratic credentials, discursive processes of argumentation are more evolved and directed toward exploring the meaning of norms in particular contexts (what does it mean to *severely* discriminate against women?). In Brunei, where there is no political opposition, civil society activity is curtailed, and religious norms are dominant, the government is reluctant to engage in discussion or argumentation at all—the state is still in the "denial" stage. Simmons argues that "the findings are remarkably robust: international legal commitments improve the legitimacy of women's demands for equality and help to elicit social change."[125] She notes, however, that ratification makes little difference in countries where the conditions do not exist for "mobilisation" or litigation: "CEDAW effects could never be shown to exist in countries with established, stable official religions or in countries with nonperforming judicial systems."[126] In ASEAN, Brunei—at present—stands as an example of this.

Second, regional instruments and institutions in Southeast Asia, at present, only weakly reflect a commitment to the idea of women's equality. This ambivalence, I argue, stems from several factors. The first has to do with the historical development of ASEAN's women's rights institutions. States were advised in 1975 after the First World Conference on Women to devise a regional response to the issue of promoting and protecting women's rights. ASEAN states reluctantly came together to do so. But at this particular stage of the economic development of ASEAN states, what mattered (to governments at least) was the equality and social welfare of *all* citizens. The idea of women's right to equality was resisted by governments based on the poor economic and social position of both men *and* women in Southeast Asia. Where governments were forced to pay attention to the issue, the advancement of women was couched in instrumental terms, concerned with the contribution that women's advancement could make to the well-being of *all* people within the region. This alignment sat neatly with national conversations orchestrated by many ASEAN states about "family" and "family values."[127] Yet it is important not to overstate ASEAN's singularity in this regard. Deep and unresolved tensions also undercut the global women's rights movement.

Third, civil society groups, which might have pushed states toward a regional consensus on equality issues, had (at least initially) reservations about the global women's movement and focused their energies locally. Regional networks of activists, of the kind I discuss in the next chapter, did not develop until the 1980s. What we do see, in more recent times, is a transregional movement by civil society groups such as Sisters in Islam. Its focus is not on specifying the meaning of women's rights in the regional context but on specifying the meaning of women's rights in the context of Islam. We also see that increasing levels of democratization in countries such as Malaysia are progressively widening the space for civil society activism, which is further encouraged by growing judicial sensitivity to global human rights developments.

Fourth, in relation to the most recent institutional developments, we can see the results of a certain pragmatism underpinning the drive to create a regional human rights institution. The fact that all ASEAN states had acceded to the Convention on the Elimination of All Forms of Discrimination Against Women (though with reservations, as we have seen) and the Convention on the Rights of the Child prompted the push toward the establishment of an institution dedicated to promoting and protecting the rights of women and children. But as I have argued, the conflation of the rights of women and the rights of children has a deleterious effect on generating an autochthonous regional understanding about women's equality. It is unclear at the time of writing how the work of the ASEAN Commission on Women and Children will evolve. It is a positive sign, perhaps, that the Declaration on the Elimination of Violence Against Women and Elimination of Violence Against Children in ASEAN hints at an understanding that the needs of women and children are of a different order (we see this in the bifurcated phrasing of the title of the declaration).

Finally, related to this last point, it is noteworthy that the issue of violence against women has gained significant traction at global, regional, and state levels. This confirms the view that norms protecting the physical security of innocent or vulnerable actors have a particular purchase: as a norm, they possess an "oughtness" that sets them apart from other kinds of norms. Because of this, we see a stronger push to reach precise understandings about what constitutes "appropriate" or "proper" behavior in relation to the promotion and protection of this particular norm and more standard-setting taking place. Furthermore, greater disapproval and stigma attach to state failure to translate the norm into prescriptive form. Regional examples of how this should be done, in the form of domestic legislation, are highly relevant.

But overall, Southeast Asian states have not developed a distinct regional response to the meaning of equality between men and women and the abnegation of distinction based on gender. They have not designed specific ways, relevant to states in the region, how they might begin to modify social and

cultural patterns of the conduct of men and women with a view toward eliminating prejudices. We can conclude, then, that in relation to the issue of
women's rights, a particular legitimacy does *not*—given the particular stage of
the norm life cycle presently occupied by ASEAN states—attach to the regional approach in Southeast Asia. On the subject of women's rights, the
global regime currently has greater utility as an instrument of change.

CHAPTER 5

Trafficking in Persons

The issue of trafficking in persons provides another opportunity to assess empirically the relative legitimacy and effectiveness of global and regional rights regimes. The 2000 United Nations Protocol to Prevent, Suppress and Punish Trafficking in Persons, Especially Women and Children ("the Trafficking Protocol")[1] deals with the violation of a range of individual civil liberties (the prohibitions against slavery, servitude, and compulsory labor; liberty and security of the person; and, potentially, life). There seems to be, at least at the level of rhetoric, a global consensus that trafficking is a moral evil and that states have a duty to prevent it. Addressing the problem of human trafficking requires collaboration between countries of origin (from which victims are transported), countries of transit (through which victims are trafficked), and countries of destination (where exploitation occurs). Unilateral action to address the problem and its consequences will be ineffective. The issue lends itself, therefore, in a practical way, to intergovernmental cooperation.

In particular, the issue is one that would seem to lend itself to intergovernmental cooperation among states within a particular geographic region. Institutions situated at the regional level are more likely to possess knowledge of the economic geographies that influence trafficking flows; more likely to be in a position to foster cooperative efforts at borders and in relation to the return of trafficked persons; and better able to frame the issue in a way that establishes links between trafficking and high-priority regional issues such as transnational crime, increasing the political palatability of state responses. Furthermore, we might anticipate that regional arrangements would have a comparative advantage over global schemes given the sheer number of states participating in the global regime and the diverse forms the problem takes in different geographical regions.[2]

In this chapter, we see that ASEAN's efforts to prevent trafficking in persons are the result of precisely the sorts of processes that make regional-level governance of human rights issues effective: moral consciousness-raising, argumentation, and persuasion among regional peers, by national and regional actors, both governmental and nongovernmental, coupled with the alignment of interests among states that share instrumental reasons for advancing a particular joint project. What emerges is a specifically *regional* understanding of the problem of trafficking that is particularly well suited to promoting the internalization of norms about preventing trafficking. The 2004 ASEAN Declaration Against Trafficking in Persons, Particularly Women and Children and the ASEAN Convention Against Trafficking in Persons, Particularly Women and Children (ACTIP) are reflections of this regional vision. The Convention entered into force on March 8, 2017, with ratification by six ASEAN states.[3]

This chapter is also about how global mechanisms of influence might (under certain conditions) distort and delay the internalization of human rights norms. Different modes of influence (persuasion, material inducement, fines) implemented at the *global* level do not necessarily complement processes of socialization at the regional level. I argue that interaction between different mechanisms of influence can have negative effects and that global attempts to influence state responsiveness on the issue of human trafficking in Southeast Asia, predominantly the actions of the United States under the Trafficking Victims Protection Act, provide an example of this.

The Global Regime to Prevent Trafficking in Persons

The extent of trafficking in persons in Southeast Asia is difficult to assess. There are several reasons for this: the borders of many Southeast Asian states are porous and trafficking may go undetected; citizenship and birth records do not exist in parts of Southeast Asia, making it difficult to identify trafficked persons; and trafficked persons may be reluctant to file reports with the police because the result can be deportation.[4] The extent of internal trafficking is even more difficult to assess than that of cross-border trafficking.[5] The United Nations reports that in 2012 there were 10,000 cases of trafficking in persons in South Asia, East Asia, and the Pacific.[6] It appears that since 1997 and the Asian financial crisis, trafficking has increased.[7] Although charting the geography of interstate trafficking flows is complicated, the overall pattern seems to be that people are trafficked from Laos, Cambodia, Vietnam, Indonesia, the Philippines, and Myanmar into the relatively rich and developed countries of Malaysia and Singapore, and (sometimes) further abroad to Australia, Europe, and the United States.[8] China and Thailand are countries of both origin and destination, as well as places where internal trafficking occurs.[9]

The centerpiece of the global effort to end human trafficking is the Trafficking Protocol.[10] The main elements of the protocol are as follows. First, the protocol depicts human trafficking as a complicated form of organized crime, systematically run by subnational and transnational corporate agencies.[11] Indeed, the protocol only applies to trafficking conducted by "an organized criminal group."[12] Second, in relation to the prevention of trafficking, the protocol places significant emphasis on border control.[13] Third, the protocol attempts to distinguish human trafficking from practices such as people smuggling and illegal migration by emphasizing the elements of coercion and exploitation inherent in human trafficking.[14] The protocol provides that consent is irrelevant in circumstances where coercion is present.[15] Finally, although the Trafficking Protocol encompasses all forms of exploitation, there is an emphasis placed on sexual exploitation.[16]

The United States Trafficking Victims Protection Act (2000) (TVPA)[17] was passed less than one month before the General Assembly adopted the UN Protocol on Human Trafficking. Like the Trafficking Protocol, the TVPA has two primary purposes: combatting human trafficking (largely through the prosecution of traffickers) and protecting the human rights of trafficked persons.[18]

The TVPA contains a set of minimum standards for combatting trafficking, which require the government of a country to prohibit severe forms of trafficking in persons and to punish acts of trafficking by making trafficking a criminal offense; provide adequate punishment; prescribe appropriate sentences in cases of sex trafficking involving children or that include aggravated circumstances, such as rape, kidnaping, or death; prescribe "sufficiently stringent" punishment for severe forms of trafficking to deter others from committing the crime and to reflect the serious nature of the crime; and make "serious and sustained efforts" to eliminate trafficking.[19] In order to determine whether a government's implementation efforts are "serious and sustained," the TVPA delineates seven criteria. The first three criteria measure government efforts in the areas of prosecution, protection, and prevention. The remaining four criteria measure the degree of international cooperation, including investigation of severe forms of trafficking, extradition of traffickers, monitoring of immigration and emigration, and investigation and prosecution of public officials involved in trafficking.[20]

The Office to Monitor and Combat Trafficking in Persons, located within the U.S. State Department, publishes an annual "Trafficking in Persons" (TIP) report, in which countries are ranked into "tiers" of compliance with the TVPA: Tier 1 (fully compliant); Tier 2 (not fully compliant but making efforts to ensure compliance); Tier 2 watch list (where a country is not compliant and the problem of trafficking is significant or increasing, and where a country makes a commitment to take additional steps to combat trafficking the following year but cannot provide evidence of doing so); Tier 3 (not compliant).[21] There is a two-year time limit for countries on the Tier 2 watch list: at the end of this two-year period, the Tier 2 watch list countries that have not made significant efforts to address human trafficking are classified as Tier 3.[22]

In contrast to the Trafficking Protocol, which under the Organised Crime Convention has no machinery for oversight or enforcement,[23] the TVPA provides for a program of unilateral sanctions against countries deemed noncompliant with the minimum standards.[24] Sanctions for failure to meet TVPA standards can include the denial of nonhumanitarian aid, non-trade-related assistance, certain development-related assistance, and aid from international financial institutions, specifically the International Monetary Fund and multilateral development banks such as the World Bank.[25] In applying the U.S. Minimum Standards, the State Department considers whether countries are of origin, transit, or destination for trafficking; the extent to which government actors are involved or complicit in the trafficking; and what measures would be reasonable given a country's resources and capabilities.[26] The object of the TIP reports is to pressure governments to institute policies and strategies to reduce the trafficking of persons, using the threat of U.S.-imposed sanctions and the shame attached to international disapprobation that follows a low ranking in the TIP reports.

Anne Gallagher, international expert on the law of human trafficking, argues that there is no substantive difference between U.S. standards relating to trafficking in persons and those that have emerged from the United Nations.[27] The indicators for both are largely the same (criminalization of trafficking, number of prosecutions, number of "victims" repatriated, and their conditions of care). Nonetheless, Gallagher champions the Trafficking Protocol and is, by and large, highly critical of the U.S. approach. In 2007, Gallagher produced a "Shadow Report on Human Trafficking in Lao PDR: The U.S. Approach v. International Law." In it, she argues:

the U.S. government, through its annual TIP report, has developed a unilateral assessment system based on standards derived from its own national legislation and reflecting its own understandings of the problem and its own views on the best solutions. Part One of this study has demonstrated that such an approach is conceptually faulty, politically divisive, and ultimately unpersuasive. It hampers international norm development and thereby directly serves the interests of those States that wish to weaken and disengage from international rules, systems and processes.[28]

While recognizing that there may be some role for unilateral assessments of states' efforts in some cases, Gallagher nonetheless contends that "the impetus for development of an effective national response to trafficking must come from within. Unilateral assessments that do not derive their legitimacy from internationally agreed standards will therefore never be as significant or as legitimate as a judgment made on the basis of commitments voluntarily accepted by Lao PDR and endorsed by the international community of States. This is the value and the strength of international law."[29]

The fundamental distinction Gallagher perceives between the U.S. approach and the UN approach lies in the idea that greater legitimacy attaches to the Trafficking Protocol than to the TVPA by virtue of the fact that the former was negotiated and agreed upon in a multilateral forum and then voluntarily accepted by states. Over the past decade, however, the U.S. approach and the UN approach to the issue of trafficking in persons have been conflated, both in perception and in the way that anti-trafficking measures are undertaken by UN agencies and NGOs. The TIP reports exhort states to subscribe to the Trafficking Protocol, giving the impression that the objectives of the two regimes are identical. At the same time, measures taken to prevent trafficking, under the auspices of the United Nations, are often funded by the United States, meaning that in general, greater attention is paid to the issue of trafficking for the purposes of sexual exploitation than, for example, trafficking for exploitation of labor.[30]

Response of ASEAN States to the Global Regime

The engagement of ASEAN states with the UN regime for combatting human trafficking has been equivocal.[31] Brunei has still not signed the Trafficking

Protocol. Indonesia and Vietnam ratified the protocol relatively late, in 2009 and 2012, respectively. Thailand did not ratify the protocol until 2013. Singapore did not ratify until September 2015.[32] Although the other ASEAN states have ratified or acceded to the protocol, only the Philippines and Cambodia have accepted Article 15(2), which provides for the submission of disputes to arbitration or, failing that, to the International Court of Justice.

One explanation for the reluctance of ASEAN states to engage with the international regime is the disjuncture that exists between the global conception of the problem of trafficking and the dimensions and scope of the problem as it exists in Southeast Asia. Let us consider this further.

First, the Trafficking Protocol emphasizes the nature of trafficking as an organized transnational crime. The idea of trafficking in the protocol is usually described along the following lines:

> Over the last ten years, the issue of illegal migration has been increasingly linked to organised criminal groups that now largely control the smuggling and trafficking of people. People traffickers and smugglers make high profits while risking relatively short prison sentences in comparison with drug dealers. They are connected to other transnational criminal networks involved in narcotics, arms trafficking, money laundering and counterfeit documentation and dispose over the necessary funds to purchase modern equipment and corrupt police and other government officials. Their activities rely on complex infrastructures and are taken more and more seriously by states.[33]

But there is scant evidence that trafficking in Southeast Asia is practiced predominantly as a systematic, patterned, and organized form of crime. Indeed, recent ethnographically oriented research points in precisely the opposite direction.[34] Molland's work, for example, carried out along the Thai-Lao border, reveals that much trafficking is *not* the prerogative of organized and calculating criminal groups[35] but takes place on an opportunistic basis, by friends, acquaintances, and sex workers themselves, who recruit among their peers on visits back to their village communities.[36] The research of Derks and colleagues, carried out in the Mekong region, also concludes that trafficking is a "cottage industry" involving family members, neighbors, and friends and that no specific studies have revealed the "criminal networks" of human traffickers.[37] The work of Bouhours and his colleagues, in Cambodia, also casts doubt on claims about the high prevalence, profitability, or role of organized crime in human trafficking. Bouhours points out that incarcerated traffickers in Cambodia are poor, uneducated individuals, and 80 percent of them are women: "Their activities are unsophisticated and conducted by sole operators or small casual or informal networks. Pushed by a lack of legitimate opportunities and pulled by the presence of illegitimate opportunities, they engage in trafficking for very modest gains."[38]

Second, the Trafficking Protocol emphasizes the presence of coercion as the element that distinguishes trafficked persons from migrants or participants in people-smuggling schemes.[39] Yet in Southeast Asia, the circumstances of poverty that cause people to move or make them susceptible to being moved involuntarily (trafficked) severely complicate notions of consent. There is a significant body of research demonstrating that in many cases, at least initially, the "victim" of trafficking in Southeast Asia is a willing participant in a scheme that promises benefits, which might be economic (work, food, housing) or social (in the form of *chiwit thyansamay*, the "taste for modern life").[40] Molland argues that while there does appear to be some cases of abduction, more commonly what occurs is deceptive recruitment, primarily about conditions of work (which are sometimes more restrictive than described) and earnings (which can be less than described).[41] In this way, much trafficking in Southeast Asia is conflated with or hidden within the broader (and more difficult to prevent) phenomenon of illegal migration.[42]

Third, it is not at all clear that in Southeast Asia the majority of trafficking occurs for the purpose of prostitution or sexual exploitation. The evidence would seem to show that in Southeast Asia, exploitation of labor is at least as prevalent as sexual exploitation.[43] For those migrating from Lao PDR, for example, the largest site of exploitation seems to be labor outside of the sex industry.[44] Even in Cambodia, where there is significant evidence that trafficking does occur for the purpose of work in the sex industry, there is also evidence that equally as many (mainly men) are trafficked into other industries, such as "factories, the agricultural sector and fishing industries where they work in circumstances of actual or potential exploitation, for legal and illegal work, legal and illegal marriages, organ trade, camel racing and bonded labour."[45]

Finally, the Trafficking Protocol places an emphasis on maintaining the integrity of borders. Yet many of Southeast Asia's borders were imposed (sometimes arbitrarily) by colonial rulers. Prior to this, they were "frontier" areas, where neighbors and family traveled and traded without restriction.[46] In many cases, the traditions of unfettered trade and exchange have continued because states lack either the incentive or the capacity to stem unofficial cross-border commerce.[47] In Hekou, for example, where the Nanxi River and the Red River merge, and China and Vietnam meet, tens of thousands of undocumented Vietnamese women, many of them under the age of eighteen, enter China illegally by boat.[48] In the Isaan region, where the Mekong River marks the border between Thailand and Laos, government regulations on both sides make legal migration a lengthy, expensive, and difficult process, unfamiliar to many people and avoided by most.[49]

The inadequacy of the global regime in reflecting the particularities of the practice of trafficking in Southeast Asia might plausibly explain the reluctance of states to subscribe to the protocol. Yet, as the following section shows, the majority of ASEAN states have passed, or are in the process of passing, legislation aimed at addressing trafficking in persons. This legislation, without exception, draws heavily on the text of the protocol and the TVPA. This raises two central and related questions. First, why, over the period of a decade, despite the disjuncture between the practice of trafficking and the global anti-trafficking architecture, have the ten member states of ASEAN passed broadly similar legislation, consonant with international norms, directed at preventing human trafficking and protecting the human rights of trafficked persons? Second, what is the effect of global norms in these circumstances? Is the result compliance (rule-consistent behavior)? If not, then what is the explanation for this?

Domestic Response of ASEAN States to Trafficking in Persons

Except for Laos, every ASEAN state has passed specific legislation relating to human trafficking.[50] In all cases, the legislation includes provisions for the protection of victims of trafficking, as well as for the prosecution of perpetrators. All legislation references, to different extents, the Trafficking Protocol definition of "trafficking in persons." In 2003, the Philippines passed the Anti-Trafficking in Persons Law of the Philippines, which sets the issue of trafficking within a human rights framework and provides a broad definition of "trafficking," deeming the issues of "consent" irrelevant.[51] In February 2013, President Aquino signed the expanded Anti-Trafficking in Persons Act,[52] which strengthens powers to prosecute those who engage or attempt to engage in human trafficking and provides increased protection for the rights of trafficked persons.[53] In 2004, the Government of Brunei announced the passage of the Trafficking and Smuggling Persons Order.[54] The means for procuring trafficking as set out in Section 4 of the Brunei legislation (threat, use of force or other forms of coercion, etc.) is identical to the means set out in the Trafficking Protocol.[55] In 2005, Myanmar's Anti-Trafficking in Persons Law was decreed. Again, Myanmar's legislation sets out in identical form the prohibited means of procuring persons for the purpose of exploitation.[56] Myanmar's anti-trafficking law also replicates the definition of "exploitation" contained in the Trafficking Protocol.[57] In 2007, the Malaysian House of Representatives passed the Anti-Trafficking in Persons Act, which adopts the Trafficking Protocol language regarding means of trafficking[58] and the Trafficking Protocol definition of exploitation.[59] The Malaysian act deems consent to be irrelevant and provides some measures for the care and protection of trafficked persons.[60]

In June 2008, Thailand introduced the Anti-Trafficking in Persons Act,[61] which replaced the 1997 Measures in Prevention and Suppression of Trafficking in Women and Children Act.[62] Thailand's 2008 act extends protection to male victims of trafficking and significantly strengthens the protection for victims of trafficking. The Thai legislation does not mirror the protocol language as precisely as does the legislation of Myanmar, Brunei, and Malaysia. However, the Thai legislation does contain the essential elements of the protocol's definition of trafficking.[63] The same may be said of Cambodia's Law on the Suppression of Human Trafficking and Commercial Sexual Exploitation, passed in 2008.[64] In March 2011, Vietnam's National Assembly passed the Anti-Human Trafficking Law and introduced a $13.5 million, five-year anti-trafficking plan.[65] In 2012, Singapore's government implemented a National Plan of Action designed to combat human trafficking and in 2014 passed the Prevention of Human Trafficking Act.[66] Laos, at the time of writing, is drafting specific anti-trafficking legislation.[67]

Bilaterally, there are a host of agreements and Memorandums of Understanding between ASEAN states on the issue of trafficking: between Lao PDR and Vietnam;[68] between Cambodia and Thailand;[69] between Lao PDR and Thailand;[70] between Cambodia and Vietnam;[71] between Myanmar and Thailand;[72] between Thailand and Vietnam;[73] and between Myanmar and China.[74] Not all of these agreements include the definition of trafficking contained in the Trafficking Protocol, but most provide details about the way in which trafficked persons should be treated (for example, referring to the provision of medical and psychological care) and make reference to the process for their return home (for example, within a certain time frame). No ASEAN-wide extradition treaty exists, although Cambodia and Thailand have signed one between themselves.[75]

It is helpful to recap briefly, at this point, some of the various theories about why states commit to international human rights norms and then translate their commitments into domestic laws and policies. The assumption of compliance scholars such as Risse, Ropp, and Sikkink, and many others, is that states do not of their own accord effect measures to protect international human rights—states must be coerced, persuaded, or socialized by the international community into doing so.[76] Theories about why states commit to international human rights cluster around three main ideas. First, many scholars, following the "spiral theory of human rights" described by Risse, Ropp, and Sikkink in *The Power of Human Rights*, argue that states act instrumentally in committing to international human rights norms, rationally balancing the costs and benefits of material and/or social sanctions and rewards.[77] Following this, tactical concessions by states (such as treaty ratification) provide domestic and international actors with the leverage and lobbying power to pressure states to give norms prescriptive status.[78] In this way, then, eventually, the passing of domestic legislation will follow ratification. Below, I argue that the first stage of this process—tactical concessions motivated by sanctions and rewards—explains why ASEAN states passed domestic legislation to prevent trafficking. As I will show, however, this stage is not necessarily followed by compliance.

There are two other ways in which human rights change is commonly held to occur. One is where there is a community of states that practice certain patterns of behavior, and states within that community behave in ways that the community deems appropriate. Where the adoption of international human rights norms is part of this pattern, then states will, like their peers, also adopt human rights norms.[79] This is connected to (but distinct from) the third process of human rights change. This is where interaction, social learning, and deliberation about human rights norms occur between and among a group of states. The result is that states gradually redefine the way they think about themselves and reshape their interests and preferences.[80] One theory about the comparative effectiveness of regional human rights systems posits that within a regional system of states or as a result of regional-level interaction, these last two processes take place, and the result is a deeper level of commitment and better level of compliance because norms are developed and articulated by (and between) a small number of states that share similar backgrounds, histories, borders, and concerns. We see this occurring, I argue, in relation to the response of ASEAN states to the issue of trafficking in persons.

Responding to Pressure

The most plausible explanation for why ASEAN states transposed international norms into domestic legislation centers on the influence and effect of the TVPA in encouraging the passage of domestic legislation and in generating policy measures. The history of Indonesia's anti-trafficking measures provides an illustration of the way the TVPA operates in this regard. In 2001, the United States published its first Trafficking in Persons Report, placing Indonesia in the Tier 3 category. Indonesia remained in the Tier 3 category in the 2002 report. On December 30, 2002, through Presidential Decree Number 88, Indonesia announced a National Plan of Action (NPA) to end human trafficking. The NPA references the specific criticisms made of Indonesia in the 2002 TIP (for example, "that there is currently not a comprehensive and specific trafficking law in Indonesia") and lists among its objectives: "the passage of laws to punish trafficking and traffickers and to protect victims of violence, witnesses, and migrant workers." The NPA recognizes "the need to ratify the Convention against Transnational Organized Crime of 2000 and two associated international protocols related to trafficking in persons in order to meet international standards" and the need to "synchronize international standards on trafficking with national laws through revision of the Criminal Code, Criminal Procedural Code, Marriage Law, Immigration Law, and the Law on the Human Rights Tribunal."[81] The NPA adopts a definition of human trafficking that conforms to the definition contained in the UN Protocol to Prevent, Suppress and Punish Trafficking in Persons. Following these efforts, in the 2003 TIP, Indonesia was placed in the Tier 2 category.[82]

By 2006, however, Indonesia had still not passed comprehensive anti-trafficking legislation and, in the view of the United States, had not provided evidence of increasing efforts to combat trafficking.[83] In 2006, Indonesia was downgraded to the Tier 2 watch list. Following this, in April 2007, Indonesia's president signed into law a comprehensive anti-trafficking bill. In the 2007 TIP, Indonesia was again returned to Tier 2. Observers within Indonesia are candid about the fact that Indonesia's response to human trafficking has been motivated by the need to escape sanctions from the United States, such as restrictions on funds not only for countertrafficking measures but also for nonhumanitarian and non-trade aid.[84]

There are many examples of this kind of responsiveness in Southeast Asia. In 2010, the Philippines was placed on the Tier 2 watch list, which, according to Philippines vice president Jejomar C. Binay, placed at risk "some $700 million worth of non-humanitarian and non-trade related aid from the US."[85] Increased efforts to prevent trafficking, including the Philippines' "Expanded Anti-Trafficking Act" (2013), were passed explicitly "to make the fight against human trafficking more effective, as the country remains in the United States State Department's radar as a venue that harbors the modern form of slavery."[86] Vice President Binay stated that the country was "increasing the number of anti–human trafficking monitoring teams in entry and exit points in the country, strengthening anti-trafficking legislation and speeding up prosecution for trafficking cases. With all these initiatives in play, Tier 1 classification [fully compliant with anti-trafficking standards] is more than possible. Indeed, it is only a question of time."[87]

The government discourse surrounding the introduction of the 2013 act was entirely focused on the potential for the new measures to change the Philippines' position in the TIP rankings. Introducing the bill, presidential spokesperson Edwin Lacierda said:

> It is Malacañang's [the Presidential Palace] hope that the new law would result in the United States' removing the Philippines from its anti-trafficking watchlist. This is a concern and a priority of our President and this measure will be enforced by the different agencies, especially by the Department of Justice as well as our police agencies. . . . Over a year ago we were taken out of that category—Tier 2. [But] we're still in the watchlist. We would like to improve our standing in the watchlist and we hope that, with this expanded coverage of anti-trafficking, we will be able to remove ourselves from the watchlist.[88]

In Thailand, the Thai minister of social development and human security, Santi Promphat, announced on April 3, 2013, the drafting of new anti-trafficking laws designed to respond to the fact that "the United States has placed Thailand in the Tier 2 Watch List for three consecutive years in the Trafficking in Persons Report of its Department of State, which could affect Thailand's image. The image of Thailand's exports into the American market could also be affected, especially seafood products, which have been determined as products that involve the use of child labor and illegal foreign workers, and human trafficking."[89] Writing specifically in relation to Southeast Asia, trafficking expert Anne Gallagher claims to have observed "multiple instances in which the open threat of a negative grade in the U.S. TIP Report provided the impetus for major reform initiatives, including the criminalization of trafficking."[90]

Although several ASEAN states appear to have passed reforms directly in response to U.S. pressure, there has been cavilling (which has been public, in the case of Singapore) about the lack of transparency and the subjective methodology employed to rank states into tiers of compliance and accusations that ranking are based less on empirical evidence than on the political preferences of the United States.[91] Myanmar, for example, despite passing significant legislation directed to addressing trafficking in persons in 2005, has been consistently ranked Tier 3. Myanmar finally achieved a Tier 2 watch list ranking in 2012, the same year that the United States dropped many of its sanctions against Myanmar, and after Myanmar agreed to a joint plan on trafficking with the United States.[92] Janie Chuang notes that Indonesia achieved a Tier 2 ranking in 2003, at around the same time that Indonesia became a key U.S. ally in the War on Terror.[93]

One of the criticisms of the TIP reports is that they place significant emphasis on the number of convicted traffickers, and an increase in the number of convictions from previous years is viewed as an indicator of a country's success in addressing the issue of trafficking.[94] For example, in 2004, Laos's anti-trafficking office reported five convictions for trafficking-related crimes. The 2005 TIP report placed Laos in the Tier 2 category.[95] The following year, Laos reported only one conviction for trafficking. Noting this, that year, the United States placed Laos in the Tier 3 category.[96] In 2007, however, the TIP report lauded the fact that the Lao government had demonstrated progress in its anti-trafficking law enforcement efforts, reporting 27 trafficking investigations that resulted in the arrest of 15 suspected traffickers, 12 of whom were prosecuted. Laos was returned to Tier 2. In relation to Thailand, the 2012 TIP report noted that the Royal Thai Police initiated 83 investigations of trafficking in 2011: 67 for sex trafficking and 16 for forced labor, involving 155 suspected offenders and representing an increase from 70 such investigations in 2010. However, it also noted that investigations led to only 67 prosecutions in 2011, compared to 79 prosecutions in 2010. The report also noted that there were 12 trafficking-related convictions in 2011, a decrease from the previous year's 18 convictions.[97] Thailand remained on the Tier 2 watch list in 2011.

The problem with what Anne Gallagher describes as a "success by num-bers" approach is that it "serves to discourage the development of longer-term capacities, systems and processes that are actually required for an effective criminal justice response. Conversely, it promotes a focus on the easy wins, the small players who can be identified and apprehended much more easily than those who are reaping the real financial rewards. The US standards are also silent on the issue of quality. All prosecutions seem to count, irrespective of their adherence to international criminal justice standards."[98]

International relations theorists have drawn on individual-level psychol-ogy (shame, social status, material reward) to explain what motivates mac-rolevel state practices. Although there have been questions and criticisms about how appropriate it is to employ theories about what motivates individ-uals to explain the behavior of states, most theories of human rights have done this, either explicitly or implicitly.[99] One argument is that there is likely to be greater compliance with human rights norms in cases where states are intrin-sically motivated because of congruence between human rights norms and their own interests, or between human rights norms and social norms that have significant legitimacy locally. If this congruence or local acceptance does not exist, the result is likely to be diminished incentive for compliance. From this perspective, let us consider the operation of the TVPA in relation to Southeast Asian states.

One of the primary ways that the TVPA operates as an external motivator is through material inducement and material disincentive. The problem with material rewards or punishment is that it has the potential to "crowd out" intrinsic motivation states may have to follow norms for nonmaterial rea-sons.[100] Incentive-based or punishment-based policies suggest to states that preferred behavior (preventing trafficking, protecting the rights of trafficked persons) is "not self-evidently appropriate or that the broader social environ-ment does not adequately value self-motivated rule adherence."[101] If action can be justified by both normative sentiments and externally imposed mate-rial incentives or disincentives, the result may be a negative effect on the in-ternalization of norms.[102] The reasons are as follows.

First, the purpose of a regime of penalties and incentives is twofold: to supply states with a rational reason for pursuing certain behavior; and to sup-ply a signaling effect, indicating that the proscribed behavior is abhorrent to a community of actors. In relation to the former, the inference that is generally drawn from the presence of material incentives or disincentives is that the reason for action is the material incentive rather than a state's moral character or principled beliefs. We see this clearly in the statements that have emanated from government representatives of the Philippines, Thailand, and Indonesia when they have supplied reasons for their actions in relation to anti-trafficking measures. References to the importance of protecting the human rights of trafficked persons (where any exist) are almost entirely drowned out by references to the importance of avoiding negative sanctions from the United States. At a minimum, this creates confusion: How can one tell whether a government is acting out of a principled belief about how it ought to behave or acting in pursuit of a material benefit? In relation to the "expressive function" of punishment (as a signal that the international community condemns the proscribed behavior), Ryan Goodman and Derek Jinks argue that this is diminished if penalties and rewards issue from actors who have insufficient social standing vis-à-vis the signaled actors—"a narrow band of donor countries, a remote foreign court, unrepresentative segments of civil society, a hostile country."[103] In relation to many Southeast Asian states, in relation to most human rights issues, the United States would fall within the category of actors with "insufficient social standing vis-à-vis the signalled actors."

Second, Goodman and Jinks argue that overjustification affects self-perception, causing actors to lose cognitive track of their motives for abiding by a norm. In these circumstances, actors are most likely to attribute their actions to material incentives. The result is that the strength of intrinsic motivation for observing a social norm is lost.[104] That is, states that comply (or would have complied) with a norm because it is an extension of their identity or internal value system lose track of this as the reason for compliance because of the presence of material reasons. This can delay the final stages of rule-consistent behavior or make it more shallow and difficult to sustain: "Accordingly, communicative exchanges within a domestic setting might shift toward the more limited agenda of powerful international institutions when those institutions promote human rights through material inducements. One concern is that, had actors been left to their own devices, a broader and stronger human rights agenda might have emerged."[105]

Third, and relatedly, the provision of material incentives often compromises a sense of self-determination and degrades intrinsic motivation for engaging in behavior.[106] Goodman and Jinks suggest that where international coercion through material incentives is considered controlling, actors resist even normative practices that they would otherwise agree with. We can see this in the attitude taken by Singapore to the requirements of the TVPA. Singapore, despite implementing policies designed to prevent trafficking, for many years refused to pass legislation for this purpose and publicly expressed resentment at U.S. attempts to influence the domestic agenda.

One might argue that this does not matter much. After all, if states are not intrinsically motivated to follow certain norms, then it is irrelevant how they are brought to include human rights norms on the domestic agenda. What matters is that they do *something*, regardless of why or whether it is the result of coercion. It might also be argued that even if states are initially spurred to action by crude measures of coercion and bribery, this may begin a process (of education and reflection) that ends in genuine acceptance of and respect for a particular norm.

My response to such arguments is that is *does* matter by what means states are led to adopt different norms because this affects how deeply and sincerely norms are promoted and acted upon. Granted, in circumstances where there is a blanket rejection of norms and denial that violations exist, coercion and bribery that result in even superficial change might be seen as better than no change at all. But where intrinsic motivation *does* exist, as I argue is the case in Southeast Asia in relation to the issue of trafficking in persons, coercive measures can lead to overjustification and problems with regard to self-perception and self-determination.

Let us turn then, finally, to my argument that an autochthonous regional conception of the importance of preventing trafficking in persons exists in Southeast Asia. What evidence is there to support the idea that if ASEAN states had "been left to their own devices, a broader and stronger human rights agenda might have emerged"?[107] What is the evidence that ASEAN states are sufficiently motivated to conform to norms about trafficking for nonmaterial reasons? In the following section of this chapter, I describe how ASEAN states do in fact possess intrinsic motivation for pursuing anti-trafficking norms, born out of long-standing and deeply held concerns about state sovereignty and the threat posed by the illegal traffic of persons across borders, and also, more recently, born out of the work of the region's national human rights institutions (NHRIs), which have focused on the human rights aspects of the practice of trafficking in persons. These reasons for actions are occluded by the discourse around the introduction of anti-trafficking measures, which focuses on immediate responsiveness to U.S. threats and TIP rankings.

ASEAN and Trafficking in Persons

In 2004, the same year that ASEAN states signed the Declaration on the Elimination of Violence Against Women[108] and agreed upon the Vientiane Action Program (which explicitly commits ASEAN to promote the awareness, education, and protection of human rights),[109] ASEAN states signed the ASEAN Declaration Against Trafficking in Persons, Particularly Women and Children.[110] As well as identifying trafficking in persons as a security concern, the declaration notes the link between social and economic rights, migration, and vulnerability to trafficking and, strikingly, draws attention to the "immorality and inhumanity of this common concern."[111] In that same year, the ASEAN Inter-Parliamentary Organization passed a "Resolution on the Role of Parliament in Combating Trafficking in Women and Children in the ASEAN Region," drawing attention to the fact that "the lack of education, unequal treatment and low status of women, poverty and unemployment of women, particularly in the ASEAN region, are major factors contributing to the causes of trafficking of women and minors."[112]

Seven years later, AICHR identified human trafficking as one of the thematic studies to be undertaken within the first five years of the commission and the ASEAN Commission on the Promotion and Protection of the Rights of Women and Children (ACWC) included a focus on victims of trafficking in its 2012–16 work plan.[113] In their 2007 joint communiqué, ASEAN leaders foreshadowed the development of an ASEAN Convention Against Trafficking in Persons, Especially Women and Children (ACTIP).[114] The ACTIP entered into force in March 2017.[115]

In this final section, I argue that a regional approach to the issue of human trafficking in Southeast Asia has been generated from the "top down" by states with similar concerns about sovereignty, territorial integrity, and threats to state security and from the "bottom up" by engagement between and among regional networks of NGOs and NHRIs. The driving factors behind these two interests in developing a regional approach to trafficking in persons are entirely different, and because of this, there is inconsistent and sometimes conflicting emphasis placed on different aspects of the issue of trafficking in persons: for example, on the protection of borders and the prosecution of the crime of trafficking instead of on the protection of the rights of trafficked persons. Nonetheless, divergent interests in eliminating trafficking are broadly congruous with a regional approach to the problem, and this explains why

ASEAN states have shown increasing willingness to cooperate among them-selves on the problem of trafficking in persons, even to the extent of appearing willing to subscribe to a legalized regime for addressing the issue. The back-drop to cooperative efforts is the imminent creation of a single ASEAN eco-nomic community.[116]

The ASEAN Economic Community (AEC) Blueprint envisages, by 2015, the following: (a) a single regional market and production base, (b) a highly competitive economic region, (c) a region of equitable economic develop-ment, and (d) a region fully integrated into the global economy. The AEC is expected to transform ASEAN into a region with free movement of goods, services, investment, and skilled labor and freer flow of capital.[117] As we have seen, one of the aims stated in the ASEAN Charter is to alleviate poverty and address the development gap between ASEAN states.[118] The AEC, arguably, will generate economic growth, resulting in more jobs, improved livelihoods, and an overall reduction in poverty. But it also has the potential to accentuate disparities within and between ASEAN countries and increase relative pov-erty and inequality, leading to cross-border migration and trafficking.[119]

First, let us consider the "top-down" perspective of states. Why is traffick-ing in persons an issue of joint concern to states in Southeast Asia? One part of the explanation centers on the particular notion of state security that pre-vails in the region. The idea of "comprehensive" or "overall security," originally coined by Japan in the 1970s, was adopted by Indonesia, Malaysia, the Philip-pines, and Singapore a decade later.[120] Within the framework of comprehen-sive security, national security depends not only on the absence of external military hostility but also on the presence of socioeconomic development.[121] Internal threats as well as external threats are recognized as having the poten-tial to destabilize the state and undermine sovereignty.[122]

As early as 1976, the idea emerged that the stability and internal and ex-ternal security of individual states were dependent on the stability of other states in the region, and that regional resilience and national resilience were interdependent. At the first ASEAN Summit, ASEAN's five members declared, "The stability of each member state and of the ASEAN region is an essential contribution to international peace and security. Each member state resolves to eliminate threats posed by subversion to its stability, thus strengthening national and ASEAN resilience."[123] The Treaty of Amity and Cooperation in Southeast Asia, agreed upon at this same meeting, requires ASEAN member states to "endeavour to strengthen their respective national resilience in their political, economic, socio-cultural as well as security fields in conformity with their respective ideals and aspirations, free from external interference as well as internal subversive activities."[124]

Transnational crime—specifically drug trafficking—was identified early on as a threat to comprehensive security and hence to national and regional stability.[125] Drug addiction and trafficking in drugs and crime were perceived as indicators of a state's inability to control its borders and thus as signs of a weak state where leaders were unable to maintain social order.[126] Later, in the 1980s, drug trafficking and drug use fed concerns about Acquired Immune Deficiency Syndrome (AIDS) and solidified the views of some ASEAN member states that AIDS was the result of homosexuality, prostitution, and heroin use.

In 1983, the Malaysian government officially declared illicit drug trafficking to be a threat to national security. In 1988, ASEAN issued a joint declaration in which it stated that the illicit drug trade was a problem that "could escalate to such a level where perpetrators can pose serious political and security threats to the region."[127] ASEAN ministers argued, "The management of such transnational issues is urgently called for so that they would not affect the long-term viability of ASEAN and its individual member nations."[128] In this context, the decision to expand the membership of ASEAN in the 1990s to include Myanmar and Laos, which were major cultivators of opium poppies, led to increased concern about drug trafficking. At a regional conference on transnational crime held in the Philippines in 1997, Philippines president Fidel Ramos declared, "Regional security continues to be assaulted by transnational crime and from time to time international terrorism."[129] At the 1997 meeting of ASEAN ministers, it was agreed that "sustained regional cooperation" was necessary in order to deal with "the problems of terrorism, narcotics, arms smuggling, piracy and human trafficking."[130]

The ASEAN Declaration on Transnational Crime, signed by heads of state in 1997, draws attention to "the pernicious effects of transnational crime . . . on regional stability and development, the maintenance of the rule of law and the welfare of the region's peoples" and recognizes the need for effective regional modalities to combat these forms of crime.[131] In 1999, ASEAN implemented a "Plan of Action to Combat Transnational Crime," which instituted the ASEAN Ministerial Meeting on Transnational Crime (AMMTC) and the Senior Officials Meeting on Transnational Crime, both bodies established to promote cooperation and coordination among ASEAN states in addressing human trafficking (as well as other transnational crimes).[132]

Although it had been mentioned earlier, it was not until the early 1990s that trafficking in persons came to be identified as another transnational crime that had the potential to threaten economic, political, and societal stability.[133] ASEAN's concern about human trafficking was threefold: first, it was seen as linked to drug trafficking (Thailand's government in particular viewed trafficking of drugs and persons from Myanmar as an immediate threat to its security); second, it had the potential to undermine orderly, legal migration and, hence, jeopardize relations between states, thereby threatening peace and security;[134] third, it was viewed as having the potential to undermine the moral foundation of the nation. In relation to this last point, in Indonesia, for example, the Islamic-based Justice and Prosperity Party (PKS) argued that trafficking "disgraced Indonesia's dignity and identity as a nation," giving the impression that Indonesia is "incapable to protect its citizens and is grouped with countries which have bad records on trafficking in persons."[135] An official at the Indonesian Ministry of Women Empowerment agreed: "Indonesia is committed to eliminate human trafficking, especially women and children. This is a matter of national dignity and human rights."[136] Trafficking implied that the state cannot protect its citizens, particularly its "most vulnerable" citizens (*especially* women and children).

The 1997 Asian financial crisis exacerbated poverty, intensified pressure for political change (most dramatically in Indonesia), and increased voluntary and involuntary irregular migration. Thailand, recently democratic, urged that a solution to these problems was a reconceptualization of security along the lines of "human security," which (it was argued) emphasized the needs of individuals and communities rather than the state and regime security.[137] The idea was that poverty, illiteracy, and economic dislocation led to violence, rebellion, and instability, all of which threatened the stability of the region as a whole. Economic development was viewed as the central plank of domestic stability. In 1998, at the ASEAN Post-Ministerial Conference (ASEAN-PMC) in Manila, a Caucus on Human Security was held, and the following year an ASEAN-PMC Caucus was established on social safety nets. Human security was taken up with alacrity by "track-two" regional processes such as ASEAN ISIS and the Council on Security Cooperation in the Asia Pacific: there were some thirty track-two meetings from 1998 to 2002 that had human security as the principal focus or a major theme. In the ASEAN Political-Security Community Blueprint (2009), human trafficking is identified as a "non-traditional security issue." The blueprint exhorts states to "further strengthen criminal justice responses to trafficking in persons, bearing in mind the need to protect victims of trafficking in accordance with the ASEAN Declaration Against Trafficking in Persons Particularly Women and Children."[138]

What I have described above shows the historical pedigree of the issue of trafficking in persons as a regional concern. There is ample evidence of state-led autochthonous regional conceptions around the importance of preventing trafficking in persons as part of a normative framework that involves the idea of transnational crime as a threat to the survival of the state.

The emphasis placed on securing the state by preventing crime and ensuring the integrity of borders does not necessarily translate into concern for protecting the human rights of trafficked persons. Indeed, the framing of trafficking as a transnational crime and security issue has the potential to undermine the rights of trafficked persons and elide key aspects of the reasons why trafficking occurs. The "national dignity" rhetoric, which emphasizes trafficked persons as rights-bearers *because* they are citizens of the state and holds the value of these persons to be their role as emblems of the dignity of the state, is deficient in its failure to appreciate the nature of trafficking as a rights issue involving the denial of individual autonomy and self-direction.

However, there is also evidence of regional-level concern about trafficking in persons as a distinct human rights issue, caused by economic and social inequity. This concern has been generated from the "bottom up" by the region's national human rights institutions, by institutions within different states that have a human rights focus, and by networks of civil society actors.

The 1999 Bangkok Declaration on Irregular Migration, which was agreed upon by ASEAN states (and others) at the conclusion of an international symposium on migration titled "Towards Regional Cooperation on Undocumented/Illegal Migration," acknowledges the links between migration, irregular migration, and human trafficking and notes the complexity of the issue of returning irregular migrants and the human rights dimensions of the problem of trafficking in persons and worker exploitation. It explicitly recognizes poverty as a root cause of trafficking and the need for international cooperation to promote sustained economic growth and sustainable development in the countries of origin as a long-term strategy to address irregular migration.[139] The declaration is of course not legally binding, and although the symposium recognized the need for a regional mechanism to deal with the problem of trafficking in persons and migration, the declaration does not refer to the creation of an institution to promote, monitor, or enforce its goals.[140] The Bangkok Declaration has been followed by many other Southeast Asian regional declarations and statements that profess a commitment to addressing trafficking in persons as a human rights issue.

It could be argued, of course, that such statements remain at the level of rhetoric; that ASEAN states are "mimicking" concern for norms prioritized by the international community;[141] or that these instruments reflect the views of international experts who are called in to advise on the drafting of regional statements and declarations.

However, the way these ideas have evolved belies this interpretation. Prominent in generating a human rights approach to trafficking has been the region's NHRIs. In Southeast Asia, NHRIs have been established in the Philippines (1987), Indonesia (1996), Malaysia (1999), Thailand (2001), and Myanmar (2011). NHRIs are independent institutions created by governments, with a mandate to promote and protect human rights. They are tasked with critiquing government laws, actions, and policies that might hinder the realization of human rights or might violate rights. Part of their role is to engage with the United Nations and to promote its treaties and policies; the other part is to engage with civil society and government within their own country. NHRIs are positioned, therefore, at the intersection between state, society, and the international community. NHRIs across the Asia Pacific are linked by a regional network, the Asia Pacific Forum of National Human Rights Institutions (APF). Southeast Asian NHRIs have formed their own subnetwork, the Southeast Asian NHRI Forum (SEANF).[142]

In 1999, the High Commissioner for Human Rights noted that NHRIs are "an underutilized resource in the fight against trafficking."[143] In 2002, Anne Gallagher, advisor to the High Commissioner on Trafficking, addressed the APF on the subject of "The Role of National Institutions in Advancing the Human Rights of Women: A Case Study on Trafficking in the Asia-Pacific Region."[144] The APF later established a Trafficking Focal Point Network between member institutions and the APF. In 2010, all of the then existing NHRIs in Southeast Asia signed a "Memorandum of Understanding Against Trafficking of Women and Children."[145] The memorandum begins with a statement about the principle of equal worth and dignity of women and children as members of the human family; adopts the definition of trafficking set out in the Trafficking Protocol; and makes detailed recommendations about the protection of victims, reparations, the provision of legal aid, and the development of victim-centered standards for dealing with trafficked persons. It exhorts states dealing with trafficking in persons to adopt "an inclusive perspective in its undertakings," be accessible to civil society, and be guided by the "best interest of the child" principle and the "right of a woman against discrimination and gender-based violence in all its forms, particularly trafficking and exploitation."[146]

The concern of the region's NHRIs for the issue of trafficking in persons was driven very much from the "bottom up." It is important to consider how this kind of concern arises. An example of the sorts of interactions that lead to the evolution of a human rights–based approach to trafficking in persons is the visit of the Human Rights Commissioners from SUHAKAM, the Malaysian Human Rights Commission, to Kajang Women's Prison, near the Malaysian capital of Kuala Lumpur in January 2003. During their visit, commissioners noticed that a large number of foreign nationals, mainly young girls, were being held in remand. In conversations with these girls, the commissioners heard that many of them had come into the country because they had been "lured and coerced with promises of jobs as home help, in supermarkets or restaurants, with lucrative incomes, but inevitably ended up in the pernicious flesh trade, often against their will."[147] Many of the girls were reluctant to tell their stories to officials for fear of being deported. Distressed by the plight of these women, the SUHAKAM commissioners formed a subcommittee to look into the issue and the following year organized a forum titled "Trafficking of Women and Children—A Cross Border and Regional Perspective." Prior to the forum, they held a series of roundtable dialogues on the issue of human trafficking, with personnel from the police, immigration officers, representatives of the Ministry of Home Affairs, the Ministry of Foreign Affairs, the Women Development Ministry, welfare officers, prison officers, representatives from the tourism ministry, NGOs, the Malaysian Bar Council, academics, human rights practitioners, and representatives from the embassies of Indonesia, Russia, Thailand, Cambodia, Vietnam, the Philippines, China, and Myanmar. Discussion at the forum noted the complexities of the causes of trafficking and made various recommendations: that Malaysia ratify the Trafficking Protocol (it would do so five years later); that the government should pass an anti-trafficking act (eventually passed in 2007); and that the role of NGOs "who operate at the grass roots level" in combatting trafficking should be recognized.[148] Of signal importance is the message contained in the final written report of the forum, where SUHAKAM refers to the need to harbor "the political will of the government and social will of the people/civil society" to protect "foreign victims of trafficking," as well as the state's duty to "reach out to victims and send the message that human freedom and dignity will be protected." The report includes a statement about the nature of human trafficking as a rights violation: "Traffickers violate the universal rights of all persons to life, liberty and freedom. It is an obstacle to the achievement of the objectives of equality and development. Trafficking of women and children impairs or nullifies the enjoyment by women and children of their basic human rights and fundamental freedoms."[149]

In June 2007, SEANF, then comprising the NHRIs of Malaysia, Thailand, Indonesia, and the Philippines, agreed to carry out a series of programs and activities in relation to five human rights issues of common concern, one of which was the issue of trafficking in persons. SEANF also agreed to prioritize encouraging other ASEAN countries to establish NHRIs so that they could more effectively engage with other institutions in cross-border issues of common concern. After Myanmar established its NHRI in 2011, it also joined SEANF. SEANF agreed to work cooperatively with CSOs, such as the Coalition Against Trafficking in Women in Asia-Pacific and the Global Alliance Against Trafficking in Women. Since 2009, AICHR has provided another forum for interaction between different actors around the problem of trafficking. In November 2013, AICHR hosted the "Regional Workshop on a Human Rights–Based Approach to Combat Trafficking in Persons, Especially Women and Children."[150] The workshop discussed the adoption of a legally binding ASEAN Convention Against Trafficking in Persons (ACTIP) and a "Regional Plan of Action to Combat Trafficking in Persons." The workshop also highlighted the need "to infuse the ACTIP with a human rights–based approach."[151]

In summary, what we see among the ASEAN states that have NHRIs, and perhaps more broadly across the region since the establishment of AICHR, is evidence of the emergence of a shared understanding of the problem of international trafficking and a shared approach to addressing the problem. Between some key actors within ASEAN states, we see increased levels of exchange (both formal and institutionalized, and informal and voluntary). We also see engagement between actors pursuing different policy approaches (border guards, prosecutors, police, and NGOs focused on the protection of trafficked victims).[152]

It remains to be answered why trafficking persists, in the face of what I argue is the apparent legitimacy of the regional anti-trafficking norm among both states and civil society actors in Southeast Asia, and despite a plethora of domestic legislation directed toward ending the practice of trafficking that exists across the region. There are several explanations. First, and most obviously, there is limited state capacity and resources, and the underlying causes of trafficking (poverty, domestic instability, and corruption) are intractable. Regional bodies such as the ASEAN secretariat have only limited capacity and resources to coordinate member states' actions. Second, there is also the influence of nonstate actors, such as the multinational companies that employ irregular migrants and trafficked persons. Third, there remain entrenched proclivities that augur against cooperative efforts, such as concerns about state sovereignty and patterns of noncooperative behavior that stymie the effectiveness of regional approaches.

Finally, what cannot be discounted in answering why trafficking persists is the distorting effect of the global regime to end trafficking, which undermines regional normative commitment and encourages states toward superficial and unilateral efforts to end trafficking. I contend that the global architecture to end trafficking in persons, particularly the TVPA, has made the progress of ASEAN states toward preventing trafficking in persons slower and more uneven than it would otherwise have been and has undermined an inchoate, genuinely autochthonous regional approach to the human rights problem of trafficking in persons.

Trafficking Law and Regional Circumstances

Given the nature and scope of the issue of trafficking in persons, as well as considerations of geography, sociocultural understandings between states, and levels of interaction between rule-makers and administrators in different states, the appropriate level for managing the issue of trafficking in persons is the regional one. Furthermore, we can see in Southeast Asia the emergence of a regionally based, multilayered response to the issue of human trafficking, where the parameters of the problem in Southeast Asia are defined not only as an issue of security but also as an issue of the violation of individual rights. This is taking place incrementally, through a process that engages many domestic institutions and the regional networks that operate between them and that, through interaction and engagement, generates a shared regional understanding about the nature of the problem and the parameters of a solution.

CHAPTER 6

ASEAN as a Purveyor of Human Rights in Myanmar

In March 2017, in his report to the Human Rights Council, the UN High Commissioner for Human Rights recounted events in Myanmar over the previous six months. He highlighted the plight of the Rohingya, Myanmar's minority Muslim population, at the hands of Burmese military and security forces. The High Commissioner spoke of mass killings, including the killing of babies, children, and elderly people. He described shootings, mass detention, the burning of entire villages, systematic rape and sexual violence, and the deliberate destruction of food and sources of food. In the High Commissioner's view, the intention of Myanmar's government was to expel the Rohingya from Myanmar altogether. He said that what was taking place amounted to the possible commission of crimes against humanity, warranting the attention of the International Criminal Court.[1] In September 2017, the High Commissioner described what was happening to the Rohingya as "a textbook example of ethnic cleansing."[2] By October 2017, more than six hundred thousand Rohingya had fled across the border to Bangladesh or died trying to.[3]

The immediate cause of the brutality, which Myanmar's government called a "clearance operation," was an attack by Rohingya militants on three outposts of the Border Guard Police (BGP) on October 9, 2016, which killed nine police officers. The attacks were purportedly carried out by a Muslim terrorist organization.[4] In response, the military and the BGP launched a joint operation to capture those involved and recover stolen weapons. They sealed off territory, denied access to humanitarian agencies and the international media, and conducted a counterinsurgency strategy that involved burning and destroying villages and food stocks, rounding up and detaining villagers, and shooting suspects on sight. The aim was to starve rebel forces of local support by cutting off food, funds, intelligence, and recruits. This was the "four cuts" strategy developed by the military during the long years of civil war against ethnic insurgents. It was a strategy of terror, involving torture and the rape of local women and girls.[5]

The broader backdrop to the events of 2016 was the historical persecution of the Rohingya by successive Burmese governments. Myanmar's Burman rulers viewed the Rohingya, with their dark complexions, Chittagonian dialect, and Islamic religious practices, as alien to Myanmar. To Myanmar's rulers, the Rohingya were "Bengalis," illegal economic immigrants who had come to Myanmar during the years of colonialism. In 1978, General Ne Win led an operation to purge the country of the Rohingya and 250,000 Rohingya fled to Bangladesh. In 1982, the military regime promulgated the Citizenship Act, which lists 135 ethnic groups as eligible for full citizenship in Myanmar. The list excludes the Rohingya. In 1991 the government led another campaign against the Rohingya and again there was an exodus across the border to Bangladesh. In 2012, rioting broke out in Sittwe, the capital of Rakhine, and in the northern township of Maungdaw following allegations that three Muslim men had raped a Buddhist woman. Reprisals against Muslims included widespread violence against local Muslim populations, which the police either ignored or participated in.[6] In 2014 a nationwide census was held, permitting the Rohingya to register only as "Bengali."[7] Without citizenship or status, denied rights of employment, education, and housing, and driven into camps rife with poverty and hunger, the Rohingya are particularly vulnerable to human trafficking.[8] They take the desperate passage across the Andaman Sea to Thailand or Malaysia, or overland through the jungle, at the hands of people smugglers.[9]

Myanmar's democratization, which began in 2010 with the first parliamentary elections after twenty-two years of direct military rule, did little to improve the plight of the Rohingya.[10] The 2008 Constitution of the Union of Myanmar, which provides the framework for Myanmar's transition to democracy, restricts key rights to "citizens."[11] The Rohingya, denied citizenship, are also denied the range of constitutional rights protections that are the preserve only of citizens. Constitutional rights specifically reserved for citizens include: rights of equality, liberty, and justice;[12] rights to ownership of private property, inheritance, and patents;[13] rights to political participation;[14] and freedom of conscience and freedom of religion, subject to public order, morality, or health.[15]

The Rohingya are denied the benefit of constitutional protection from discrimination on the basis of race, birth, and religion;[16] the right to freedom of expression and assembly;[17] the right to freedom of movement;[18] and the right to education.[19] Government policies, laws, and regulations that deliberately target the Rohingya, such as the regulation in Buthidaung and Maungdaw townships that restricts Muslim families to having only two children, are not unconstitutional.[20]

Myanmar's transition is defined by the continuation of a formal political role for the military in the administration of the state. The constitution provides that 25 percent of the members of state and federal parliaments must be serving army officers appointed by the commander in chief.[21] The commander in chief has a decisive say in the appointment of the president and two vice presidents. Certain key cabinet positions (such as Home Affairs and Defence) are confined to active military personnel. The army is fiscally and administratively autonomous. Article 445 of the constitution provides immunity for members of the former military government in relation to any act done in the execution of duty. Article 20(b) states that the Defence Service has the right to independently administer and adjudicate all affairs of the armed forces, and Article 343 provides that in the adjudication of military justice, the decision of the commander in chief of the Defence Services is final and conclusive.[22] The constitution cannot be amended without the support of 75 percent of parliament—that is, without the support of the military.

The general elections of 2015 resulted in a landslide victory for the party of former political prisoner and Nobel laureate Aung San Suu Kyi.[23] Suu Kyi was the daughter of General Aung San, who led Burma's fight for independence against the British. From 1988 Suu Kyi was at the center of the movement to bring democracy to Myanmar.[24] She endured intimidation, slander, and eighteen years of house arrest at the hands of successive military governments. She became known as "Burma's Gandhi" for her advocacy of nonviolent opposition to oppression. Suu Kyi's strategy, during the years of military rule, was to use the power of words to draw the world's attention to the suffering of her people.[25] In 2015, prevented from becoming president by a provision in the constitution that bars those whose spouses hold allegiance to a foreign power, Suu Kyi created a new role for herself as Special Counsellor of State. It was a role she said was "above the President."[26] In relation to the military, however, Suu Kyi's effective influence was limited.

Suu Kyi refused to champion the rights of the Rohingya or to denounce the human rights abuses perpetrated on them by the military. In 2016, as world leaders began to speak of a genocide in the making, critics drew sharp attention to Suu Kyi's lack of regard for the suffering of the Rohingya. Her response was that the situation in Myanmar was complex and that the world must give the country time.[27] As external criticism of Suu Kyi's silence grew louder, so did support within Myanmar for Suu Kyi and the military. There were rallies in honor of the military, and anti-Muslim violence spread from Rakhine to other parts of the country. In March 2017, the Special Rapporteur on Human Rights in Myanmar, Yanghee Lee, noted that "entrenched fear, hostility, and lack of empathy toward the Rohingya people are pervasive throughout the whole of Myanmar."[28]

This final chapter examines the role of ASEAN in addressing the situation of the Rohingya in 2016 and 2017. The ASEAN Charter, as we have seen, states that one of the association's purposes is to "strengthen democracy, enhance good governance and the rule of law, and to promote and protect human rights and fundamental freedoms, with due regard to the rights and responsibilities of the Member States of ASEAN."[29] The charter also provides that ASEAN and its members shall act in accordance with certain principles, one of which is "adherence to the rule of law, good governance, the principles of democracy and constitutional government."[30] The ASEAN Intergovernmental Commission on Human Rights has a mandate to promote and protect human rights and fundamental freedoms of the peoples of ASEAN,[31] and the ASEAN Human Rights Declaration upholds rights to life, liberty, and security of person and property. But ASEAN still cleaves to the principle of noninterference in the internal affairs of member states.[32] Noninterference is also one of the principles that guides AICHR,[33] which is an "intergovernmental" "consultative" body,[34] which must pursue "a constructive and non-confrontational approach and cooperation to enhance promotion and protection of human rights."[35]

My argument in this book is that regional human rights institutions hold unique potential to advance the realization of human rights because of the shared concerns and commonalities that define members of regional organizations, the closer economic and political links that enhance influence and pressure, and the deeper understandings that exist between smaller groups of members who interact more closely with one another. I have shown that in ASEAN's case this potential is to a significant extent unrealized because furthering human rights, normatively and practically, requires a community of democratic states. There are too few of these in Southeast Asia for there to exist a regional community of states willing to create and support effective institutions to protect human rights.

The previous chapter showed that there are some circumstances in which regional organizations nonetheless have the potential to advance the realization of human rights, even in the absence of a community of democratic states. This can occur, as in the case of regional responses to human trafficking, where there is a confluence of interests around pragmatic concerns such as security and border control, coupled with values-based motivation on the part of key actors within different states to protect individual or collective rights. The present chapter shows how in relation to the Rohingya crisis, Myanmar's regional peers, conscious of the cross-border implications of Myanmar's internal instability and the wish to prevent another humanitarian disaster on Southeast Asian soil, made efforts to curb the excesses of Myanmar's government. These efforts were only partially successful, but they had an impact that was not matched by the endeavors of the broader global community to shame, censor, and mold the behavior of Myanmar's leaders.

Myanmar: History and Transition to Democracy

Most accounts of postcolonial Myanmar present the nation's history as a sequence of defining historical moments: January 4, 1948, and independence from Britain; the coups of 1958 and 1962; the August 8, 1988, mass demonstrations and their suppression; and the "Saffron Revolution" of 2007.[36] Through these events, the country's history is most commonly portrayed as a dyadic struggle between democracy (represented by Aung San Suu Kyi and the National League for Democracy [NLD]) and authoritarianism (the generals of the Tatmadaw, Myanmar's armed forces).[37] The drama and tragedy of this struggle have, in many ways, shaped external attempts (by the "West," and less consistently by ASEAN) to influence the course of events in Myanmar.

This focus, however, risks ignoring deeper readings of the nation's political history, which emphasize intractable divisions between Myanmar's majority Buddhist Bamar population and ethnic minorities (the Arakanese, Chin, Kachin, Shan, Karenni, Karen, and Mon peoples) who inhabit Myanmar's outlier regions.[38] Praetorianism and the failure of representative democracy, which are the recurrent themes of Myanmar's postcolonial history, both derive from the core problem of attaining national unity in the face of ethnic diversity.[39] Democracy's other impediments—economic underdevelopment, the years of attempted socialism, the absence of the institutions of democracy (an independent judiciary, a free press)—exacerbated the destructive consequences of disunity.[40]

From 1962, Myanmar was ruled by successive military dictatorships. The subjugation of human rights in Myanmar in the period from 1962 to 2010 is documented in the reports of Special Rapporteurs, UN bodies, and international NGOs such as Amnesty International, Human Rights Watch, and Fortify Rights.[41] In 1992, the first Special Rapporteur on the Situation of Human Rights in Myanmar, Professor Yozo Yokota,[42] informed the UN General Assembly about war crimes and crimes against humanity carried out by the Burmese military, including extrajudicial and arbitrary executions; rape; torture; inhuman treatment; forced labor; arbitrary deprivation of liberty and property; denial of freedom of movement; lack of legal and due process rights; and limits to freedom of expression, assembly, and association.[43] In 1998, the Special Rapporteur stated that "these violations have been so numerous and consistent over the past years as to suggest that they are not simply isolated or the acts of individual misbehaviour by middle- and lower-rank officers but are rather the result of policy at the highest level, entailing political and legal responsibility."[44]

The fact that widespread human rights abuses took place is unsurprising. First, rule by force is itself a human rights violation. A political order not chosen by the people violates Article 21(3) of the Universal Declaration of Human Rights: "the will of the people shall be the basis of the authority of government."[45] Second, the suppression of dissent by the armed forces and the police involves the violation of rights to life, liberty, and freedom of speech and association. Myanmar's history is marked by the torture, murder, and imprisonment of those who spoke out against the regime. Third, the conditions of dictatorship, where rule is by fiat rather than through institutions established by law, are propitious for the abrogation of due process rights. Justice did not exist in Myanmar during the years of dictatorship. Fourth, there is little prospect for the realization of economic and social rights in the absence of the right to political participation: dictators have no need to be responsive to the people's demands for adequate food and housing.[46] Myanmar's generals stole the land of farmers, exploited the country's natural resources, and kept the profits for themselves, and when tragedy struck in 2008 in the form of Cyclone Nargis, they left the poorest and most vulnerable without aid or assistance.

During the period 1962–2010, Myanmar's rulers either denied that violations were occurring or justified violations on the grounds that they were a reasonable trade-off between rights and the preservation of national unity and peace. The government of Myanmar's response to the Special Rapporteur's Report in 1993 was: "The *Tatmadaw* has never, at any time committed such atrocities nor will it ever do so in the future. . . . Atrocities such as . . . rape of rural women, forced conscription and mass execution of villagers are being committed only by the insurgents time and again."[47] Myanmar's rulers argued that the ultimate welfare of the people depended on the attainment of peace and security and that in due course, rule would be returned to the people and attention would be turned to advancing human rights. The 2008 constitution was held out as the cornerstone of the promised new order.

In November 2010, Myanmar held its first parliamentary elections under the 2008 Constitution of the Union of Myanmar. These elections, in which the major opposition party, the NLD, did not participate, were won decisively by the military-backed Union Solidarity and Development Party.[48] What followed, under the presidency of former general Thein Sein, was a far-reaching agenda of legislative reform in areas such as human rights, press freedom, health care, and environmental protection. Thein Sein's government released political prisoners, eased press censorship, legalized trade unions, increased the pension rate, allowed public political gatherings, permitted the teaching of ethnic minority languages in schools across Myanmar, and intensified efforts to end long-running armed conflicts with ethnic minorities.[49]

Conflict with ethnic armies in the northern part of the country, however, continued. Myanmar's political transition did not provide ethnic minority states with political and economic autonomy in a genuinely federal state. Nor did it adequately protect minority rights, viewed by many in ethnic states as essential to prevent domination by Myanmar's Buddhist Bamar majority. In the absence of guarantees of autonomy and rights, armed groups such as the Kachin Independence Organisation (KIO) refused to surrender arms or submit to the control of the Burmese military. In Kachin State, government forces were accused of firing on unarmed civilians, including those sheltering in refugee camps; desecrating churches; abducting villagers suspected of belonging to the KIO; razing homes; pillaging properties; using antipersonnel mines; conscripting forced labor; enlisting children to serve as army porters; torture; and rape.[50]

There was also a rash of criminal prosecutions against individuals who criticized either the military or Aung San Suu Kyi's civilian government. Authorities used the 2013 Telecommunications Law, which criminalizes acts such as defamation and disturbing the peace, to stifle dissent.[51] In 2015, a student was arrested for a Facebook post that pointed out that Aung San Suu Kyi was wearing clothes of a color similar to those of the army.[52] By 2017, the euphoria that accompanied the early days of the transition had disappeared. Oppression, misinformation, and the potential for political violence hung in the air.

The Burmese Government's Response to the Crisis in Northern Rakhine State

In 2016 and 2017, Myanmar's political leaders attempted to discredit reports of human rights abuses, using the same strategies the country's military rulers had used against their political opponents during the years of dictatorship.

First, the government disparaged accounts of the atrocities as false or exaggerated.[53] Aung San Suu Kyi, through the Office of the State Counsellor, became an effective mouthpiece for the military. The State Counsellor's Office, through an "Information Committee" formed to disseminate news about military operations and their impact, released the same information as the Ministry of Defence.[54] In addition, the State Counsellor's Office published commentaries that referred to false news and stated that accusations about human rights abuses were an attempt to drive a wedge between the army and the people.[55] The state-run newspaper, the *Global New Light of Myanmar*, supported the government's position by reporting that security force activities in Rakhine State were carried out in accordance with international standards and that there was no room for suspicion or complaint about the government's way of handling the problems.[56] The paper reported Colonel Htein Lin, the minister for Security and Border Affairs in the Rakhine State Cabinet, saying that critics did not understand that the interests of the country must be prioritized over the interests of individuals, family, town, or race.[57] A foreign journalist writing for the *Myanmar Times* was fired after writing a story about rape by the military.[58]

Second, Myanmar's political leaders refused to allow UN investigators to visit northern Rakhine in the immediate aftermath of the clearance operation. This, again, was consistent with the regime's policy during the years of military rule. Myanmar's military leaders regularly denied UN investigators access to the country or to the parts of the country where abuses were allegedly being carried out. In the absence of independent evidence of human rights violations, the regime was able to claim that reports were false, based on fabrication and disinformation. In March 2017, when the Human Rights Council resolved to urgently dispatch an international fact-finding mission to investigate allegations of killing, rape, and torture,[59] Myanmar's ambassador to the United Nations rejected the move as "not acceptable."[60] Aung San Suu Kyi stated that the United Nations' decision to establish an independent international inquiry was "not in keeping with what is actually happening on the ground,"[61] and the Ministry of Foreign Affairs ordered its embassies not to grant visas to members of the UN fact-finding mission.[62] In September 2017, the fact-finding mission reported to the Human Rights Council that it had still not gained access to Myanmar and it requested more time to prepare its report.[63]

Finally, Myanmar's government formed its own inquiries in relation to Rakhine State. In the wake of the deadly sectarian violence in 2012, the government established a commission headed by former UN secretary-general Kofi Annan, with a mandate to advise on possible solutions to the situation. The commission's mandate excluded investigating human rights violations.[64] In the aftermath of the October 2016 violence, the president announced the creation of a thirteen-member commission led by Vice President Myint Swe, a former army general. The commission visited villages and security camps in northern Rakhine and interviewed security police, government staff, administrative organizations, villagers from different community-based organizations, and community elders.[65] The commission's interim report found that Islamic terrorists with overseas organizations had instigated the violence and that there was little evidence to support allegations of illegal arrests, rape, torture, and arson. The commission reported that where correct procedures had not been followed "in Bengali villages" legal action had already been taken and that, "as per the nature of these conflicts, illegal activities and fabricated rumours and news can appear occasionally."[66]

The army also established an investigation, led by Lieutenant General Aye Win of the Office of the Commander-in-Chief. The army's interim report, published in January 2017, stated that only a small number of minor offenses had taken place, such as military personnel using a motorbike without the owner's permission and beating villagers with bamboo sticks when they were tardy putting out a fire.[67] On May 23, 2017, the Tatmadaw True News Information Team published the final report, which stated that the events detailed in the Office of the High Commissioner for Human Rights' report were false.[68] Two other investigations also took place, the first under the auspices of the

Ministry of Home Affairs and the second by the Rakhine State Parliament. The Rakhine commission's chairman, M. P. Aung Win, claimed in an interview with the BBC that the rape of Rohingya women could not have occurred because the Rohingya were too dirty for local Buddhist men or soldiers to be interested in them.[69]

In January 2017, a Burmese policeman in Ko Tan Kauk village in northern Rakhine State recorded a video of fellow policemen carrying out a military operation in a Rohingya village.[70] The veracity of the video was not contested by the military or the government. The video shows the men of the village seated in rows on the ground, their hands behind their heads and their knees bent, while a group of policemen beat them with sticks and kick them in the back and in the face. At the very beginning of the video a young boy, appearing to be no more than seven or eight years old, is kicked in the back as he moves toward the lines of men with his hands raised above his head. There is no sense of crisis or urgency in the actions of the police: they carry out the beatings in a casual, matter-of-fact way, with some policemen ambling over to join them and wandering away again. Some of the policemen are aware that they are being filmed: one lights a cigarette and stares straight into the camera.[71] The casual brutality depicted in the video revolted viewers around the world. It also prompted a response from the State Counsellor's Office, which announced that four of the police officers shown in the video had been identified and arrested, including the one who filmed the video. The government did not admit the possibility that what had been captured on video might be happening in villages all over Rakhine State.

ASEAN's Relationship with Myanmar

Prior to Myanmar's transition to democracy, ASEAN made several attempts to persuade Myanmar's leaders to govern with decency. Initially, ASEAN hoped that membership in the association, awarded to Myanmar in 1997, would encourage the regime along a path of controlled liberalization through trade and interaction.[72] Between 1990 and 1997, ASEAN employed a strategy of "constructive engagement" with Myanmar, meaning a mode of dialogue and persuasion, and the pursuit of strategic and economic interests, with concomitant encouragement of "moderate" political reform.[73] The aim was to socialize Myanmar's elite toward good governance and (it was hoped) the creation of a democratically disposed middle class, while providing Myanmar's neighbors with access to raw materials and new markets. "Constructive engagement" stood in marked contrast to the outright disapprobation, threats, and sanctions employed by the United States and the European Union.[74] Underpinning the policy was ASEAN's uncertainty about China's growing power and regional ambitions and the imperative of bringing Myanmar within ASEAN's sphere of influence rather than leaving her to China.[75]

From the perspective of Myanmar's ruling elite, "constructive engagement" was perfectly suited to achieving the goals of increasing regional investment in the country while deflecting criticism from its internal politics. Myanmar saw the benefits of broadening its economic relationships, rather than limiting itself to an uneven dependence on China. Myanmar's military rulers did not accept that the goal of constructive engagement was to change Myanmar. According to Myanmar's foreign minister Ohn Gyaw, constructive engagement meant that "ASEAN would see Myanmar as an equal."[76]

ASEAN faced strong pressure from the United States and the European Union to refuse Myanmar's admission to the association until the regime had fulfilled certain conditions toward the restoration of democracy.[77] Outwardly, ASEAN's existing members strongly rejected external attempts to steer the course of ASEAN policy,[78] and it is possible that these attempts, and the desire of Southeast Asian leaders to be seen to resist them, in fact encouraged ASEAN's admission of Myanmar.[79] In his opening keynote address to the Annual Ministerial Meeting in 1997, welcoming new ASEAN members Myanmar and Laos, Malaysian prime minister Mahathir referred directly to the pressure that had been put on ASEAN by the United States and the European Union to "pass judgement, deny membership and apply pressure on a potential candidate so as to force that country to remain poor and therefore unstable." He said: "ASEAN must resist and reject such attempts at coercion" that are "not a part of the ASEAN way" and that "no one, but no one, should assume that only they know the solutions to all problems. They have failed far too often for us to be convinced that only they know what is right and what is wrong."[80]

Responding to Mahathir's speech, Myanmar's minister for foreign affairs, H. E. U. Ohn Gyaw, emphasized Myanmar's commitment to "the principles and objectives of the Association" and Myanmar's national goal of achieving a "peaceful, prosperous, modern and developed Myanmar" via "harmony in political development, social cohesiveness and economic growth."[81] Not all ASEAN members were as supportive of Myanmar's admission as Malaysia, which together with Singapore had pushed domestic firms to invest in Myanmar in the hope that "ASEAN capital would lift the country up."[82] In October

1996, for example, Thailand's foreign minister suggested that there should be democracy in Myanmar before it was admitted as a member of ASEAN.[83]

Nonetheless, in July 1997, Myanmar became a member of ASEAN. On balance, most of ASEAN's original members held the view that constructive engagement would be enhanced if Myanmar were a member. Malaysian prime minister Mahathir Mohamad was a particularly strong proponent of Myanmar's inclusion in ASEAN, which he viewed as a way of "hav[ing] a very positive effect on them," exposing them to "how Malaysia manages its free market and its system of democracy," which would make them less "afraid of the democratic process" and "over time, they will tend to give more voice to the people. . . . They become a member first, then put their house in order."[84] Mahathir argued that foreign investment and economic development would change the generals' "attitude and perception" regarding democratic transformation.[85] Indonesia, under President Suharto, largely shared Malaysia's view in this regard.

The dividends of "constructive engagement," in terms of reform within Myanmar, were difficult to discern. In 1998, in the wake of the Asian financial crisis, Thailand (under a new liberal government) moved to reorient ASEAN policy toward Myanmar. This occurred against a backdrop of recurrent clashes along the Thai-Myanmar border, growing numbers of political and ethnic minority refugees, the unchecked flow of drugs from Myanmar into Thailand,[86] and the fact that, from 1988 onward, Thailand became the theater of choice for Myanmar's dissidents attempting to draw the world's attention to their plight.[87] In this context, Thailand called for a policy of "flexible engagement," by which it meant the liberty to publicly comment on and collectively discuss fellow ASEAN members' domestic policies where these have either regional implications or the potential to adversely affect other ASEAN members.[88] The Philippines supported the Thai proposal, but the perception of other ASEAN members was that the policy was ambiguous and lacked criteria for its application and would in all likelihood lead only to mistrust and resentment. To most members, it seemed a policy that would have precisely the opposite effect of an adherence to the "ASEAN way," to which some ASEAN leaders attributed three decades of peace and stability in Southeast Asia.[89] Thus the policy of constructive engagement was maintained with an additional element: "enhanced interaction." "Enhanced interaction" meant that individual member states could comment on the domestic policies of other members but not under the auspices of ASEAN.[90]

The Depayin incident of 2003 showed the limits of "enhanced interaction."[91]

In May 2003, Aung San Suu Kyi's motorcade was ambushed by members of the pro-military Union Solidarity and Development Association. At least four people were killed and Aung San Suu Kyi was arrested, together with her entourage. For ASEAN, the incident was deeply embarrassing. Singapore's foreign minister, S. Jayakumar, informed the ASEAN Ministerial Retreat in 2003 that Depayin was a setback not only for Myanmar but also for ASEAN because ASEAN had admitted Myanmar and the other Indochinese countries in the face of strong opposition from some Western countries.[92]

In response, Myanmar's Foreign Ministry director of political affairs, Thaung Tun, asked for "breathing space" in order to "create democracy and stability."[93] At the 2005 Annual Ministers Meeting, Myanmar's representative accepted an Indonesian proposal to send a delegation to Myanmar to encourage the junta to hasten democratic reforms, using the experience of the other ASEAN countries that had gone through a similar struggle. Philippine foreign secretary Blas Ople stated that "the goal is not merely the release of Madame Suu Kyi, but the release of the entire people of Burma from a regime of oppression and repression."[94] Despite these efforts, Lee Jones marks the Depayin incident as the beginning of ASEAN's drift toward "critical disengagement" with Myanmar.[95] The clearest example of the change in attitude was the Philippines' support for a resolution against Myanmar in the UN Security Council in 2006. When Burma asked for ASEAN's support in voting against the resolution, at the December 2005 summit, ASEAN's secretary-general, Ong KengYong, was told that ASEAN had lost the ability to defend Myanmar.[96] When the issue of Myanmar was put to a vote in the UN General Assembly in November 2006, the Indochinese states voted against the EU draft resolution, but the other ASEAN states merely abstained.[97]

In 2006, ASEAN's envoy to Myanmar, Syed Hamid, returned from a visit to Myanmar and publicly vented ASEAN's frustration with Myanmar's government. In a *Wall Street Journal* editorial titled "It Is Not Possible to Defend Myanmar," Hamid outlined the conditional nature of ASEAN's support for Myanmar and the practice of noninterference, explaining that ASEAN had only "stood together with Myanmar to endure international criticism because we were assured that a 'step-by-step' transition process was in place." Hamid explained that "the majority of ASEAN members" now felt that Burma's intransigence was "putting into question ASEAN's credibility and image," denying it the "maximum benefits" of cooperation with partners by holding external relations "hostage." Hamid concluded that "Myanmar does not want us to stand with them . . . it is best that it is handled by the UN." He said that ASEAN expected Burma to "be more responsive to the damage done to ASEAN by the Myanmar issue" rather than "digging in and maintaining that they should not be subjected to pressure from ASEAN or anybody else."[98]

Myanmar had been scheduled to take the 2006–7 chairmanship of ASEAN, but ASEAN states faced intense pressure to prevent this from happening, from two quarters. The first was the ASEAN Inter-Parliamentary Caucus on Myanmar, formed in 2004 and based in Malaysia, which lobbied to prevent Myanmar from assuming the chairmanship. The second was the European Union and the United States, who made clear that they would boycott a Burma-chaired ASEAN. Although Laos and Cambodia provided some muted support for Myanmar, all ASEAN states were largely in agreement that irrevocable damage would be done to the prestige and credibility of the association if Myanmar took the chair. These views were made clear to Myanmar in the lead-up to and at the 2005 ASEAN foreign ministers meeting in Vientiane. The official statement issued at that meeting announced that Myanmar had decided to relinquish its turn to be the chair of ASEAN in 2006 because it wanted to focus on the ongoing national reconciliation and democratization process, in what was a critical year for the country. The statement expressed ASEAN's "sincere appreciation" to Myanmar's government "for not allowing its national preoccupation to affect ASEAN's solidarity and cohesiveness" and assured Myanmar that once "it is ready to take its turn to be the ASEAN Chair, it can do so."[99] In Myanmar, preparations and construction for assuming the chairmanship of ASEAN, and hosting the hundreds of ASEAN-related diplomatic meetings that were associated with the chairmanship, were already underway. The response of Myanmar's government to ASEAN's announcement was a weeklong news blackout of the decision.[100]

In August 2007, the junta suddenly and without warning raised fuel prices 500 percent, threatening the livelihoods of much of the country's population. Protests originating with city dwellers spread to the Buddhist sangha (monks), who joined civilians in demonstrations against the regime. Andrew Selth writes: "Such was the popular mood that some activists and foreign journalists even began to predict the downfall of the military government."[101] Myanmar's government responded to the "Saffron Revolution" with tear gas, baton charges, and, in Yangon, machine-gun fire.[102] Yangon's Buddhist monasteries were raided and thousands of monks were forcibly detained.[103] The number of political prisoners doubled in the wake of the riots and came to include not only members of opposition political parties but also monks, journalists, and community activists. Many were sentenced to lengthy prison terms in closed court proceedings. At the same time, fighting against non-Burman minorities along the country's eastern border intensified.[104]

In 2007, as ASEAN's foreign ministers gathered in New York for the UN General Assembly, news broke of the Saffron Revolution and its suppression. ASEAN's foreign ministers issued a statement expressing "revulsion" that the government of Myanmar had suppressed protests by violent force.[105] Singapore's foreign minister George Yeo said that ASEAN had no choice but to express its condemnation of events in Myanmar: "If here at the UN we had no common response, how could we face the Secretary-General? Or what do we say to the other countries? We would have lost all credibility."[106] Yeo explained that the situation was like "a family meeting where we had to confront one member who had behaved badly. It was unpleasant but unavoidable. Whatever others may say, it remains for us that Myanmar is a member of the ASEAN family and, good or bad, we can't avoid a certain association, a certain responsibility, a certain connection with the fate of that country. But we have very little leverage over the internal development there. What we have is moral influence as members of the ASEAN family."[107]

Yeo admitted that the turmoil in Myanmar had tested the group's cohesion and unity but that if ASEAN avoided the issue of Myanmar "it stood to lose all credibility and respect. . . . When we talked about ASEAN integration in the future, the international community would ignore us. We would feel ashamed when we looked ourselves in the mirror. So, the ministers were determined to look the challenge in the eyes and respond."[108]

The following year, Cyclone Nargis struck Myanmar, devastating the country's Irrawaddy region. When Myanmar's government prevaricated about accepting international humanitarian assistance, there were calls from the French foreign minister (and others) for the UN Security Council to invoke the "responsibility to protect" doctrine to authorize the delivery of aid without the consent of the Myanmar government.[109] The ASEAN secretary-general, Surin Pitsuwan, was able to convince Myanmar's government to accept aid and "to establish a space, a humanitarian space, however small to engage with the Myanmar authorities."[110] Surin told an audience in Washington that ASEAN was "trying to work around a very, very strict resistance and mentality and mindset that have been there for a long, long time."[111] A Tripartite Core Group initiated by ASEAN and composed of representatives from Myanmar, ASEAN, and the United Nations was formed to create a mechanism for channeling international assistance into Myanmar. ASEAN's engagement with Myanmar in the wake of Cyclone Nargis represented a high point in the relationship between Myanmar and the regional association.[112]

ASEAN and the Rohingya Crisis

In April 2015, ASEAN Parliamentarians for Human Rights (APHR) published a report that drew attention to the regional implications of abuse against the Rohingya, which included increasing human trafficking out of Myanmar and flows of irregular migration, putting strain on regional economies, and providing an environment where extremist ideologies could take hold. APHR argued that these risks were a regional concern not only because of potential cross-border spill-over effects but also because "ASEAN member states share a moral responsibility to take all possible measures to prevent the commission of atrocities within ASEAN."[113] The body called on ASEAN to address the Rohingya issue at ASEAN Summit meetings, conduct an independent investigation into the violence, expand the mandate of AICHR to include country visits and investigations, deploy monitors to observe and report on the crisis, and protect refugees. Although the AICHR has the power to obtain information from ASEAN member states on the promotion and protection of human rights, its only action in relation to the Rohingya had been to hold a closed-door meeting on the situation.[114]

In May 2015 the regional implications of the Rohingya crisis became acute when almost eight thousand Rohingya and Bangladeshi migrants, crowded onto rickety fishing boats, were abandoned by people smugglers and left to float for weeks, starving and desperate, on the Andaman Sea. The governments of Indonesia, Thailand, and Malaysia at first refused to allow the migrants to land and ordered their navies and coast guards to drag the boats back out to sea. As the crisis intensified, Myanmar refused to attend regional meetings on the issue because it objected to the use of the term "Rohingya." After receiving assurances that the term "irregular migrant" would be used instead of "Rohingya," Myanmar agreed to support regional efforts to resolve the crisis, including tightening its borders to prevent migrants from leaving.[115] Indonesia, Thailand, and Malaysia allowed the boats to land and provided temporary shelter for those onboard. The governments of Indonesia, Malaysia, and Thailand were motivated in part by pragmatic concerns about reputation, security, and border control. There was also, however, a strong degree of humanitarian concern for the Rohingya from APHR and regionally based civil society organizations.

Eighteen months later, when Rohingya refugees spilled out of Myanmar in the hundreds of thousands after the government's "clearance operation" got under way, ASEAN was once again called upon to offer a regional response to the issue. Drawing on the precedent set by ASEAN's response to Cyclone Nargis, two of ASEAN's powerful Muslim majority countries, Malaysia and Indonesia, called for ASEAN to coordinate humanitarian aid for the Rohingya and to investigate alleged atrocities. Malaysia's foreign minister said, "Although Myanmar may not recognize the Rohingya as its citizens, we must not forget that they too deserve basic human rights."[116] In December 2016, Aung San Suu Kyi addressed a meeting of ASEAN's foreign ministers and attempted to explain what was happening in Rakhine State. The meeting ended without firm commitments for regional action, other than an offer of humanitarian assistance. The APHR chairperson called the meeting political theater and urged member governments to comply with their obligations in the ASEAN Charter to protect human rights. Myanmar's government emphasized the need for time and space to resolve the situation. It did, however, express its readiness to grant necessary humanitarian access.

The ASEAN Summit met in April 2017, two months after the Office of the High Commissioner for Human Rights published the "Flash Report," which showed in spare forensic detail how Myanmar's army used grenades, machine guns, and helicopters to fire on civilians, burned families alive, gang-raped girls and women, and tortured men and boys.[117] The report concluded that the attacks against the Rohingya population in the area seem to have been widespread and systematic, indicating the very likely commission of crimes against humanity.[118] Yet even as the Rohingya were fleeing Myanmar in the biggest movement of people in Asia since World War II, the issue failed to materialize on the ASEAN Summit agenda. The chairman's final statement on "regional issues and developments" identified only four issues: the South China Sea; maritime security and cooperation; the situation on the Korean peninsula; and terrorism and extremism. The statement also "noted with satisfaction the ASEAN Intergovernmental Commission on Human Rights' progress on the promotion of human rights" and reaffirmed the vision of a "people-oriented and people-centered ASEAN."[119]

ASEAN and Human Rights in Myanmar

Myanmar's engagement with ASEAN constitutes its most important and sustained multilateral engagement. Bilateral relations with neighbors such as China, India, and Bangladesh, though of consequence economically and for Myanmar's security, do not generate the web of institutional and diplomatic linkages spawned by Myanmar's ASEAN membership. Myanmar participates in almost all activities required by ASEAN from the summits to ministerial meetings to lower-level officials' meetings. This includes "first track" diplomacy (between government officials) and "second-track" engagement (between "think tanks" such as the Myanmar Institute of Strategic and International Studies and its regional counterparts). In relation to first-track engagement, within each of Myanmar's ministries there is an "ASEAN Unit" to coordinate ASEAN-related activities and to liaise with other ministries on ASEAN matters.[120] "Second-track" engagement, between the region's analysts, policy advisors, civil servants, academics, and military officials, leads to participation in workshops, conferences, and meetings between ASEAN state representatives.[121]

Yet in the decades following Myanmar's admission to ASEAN, the regional body played no significant role in encouraging human rights in Myanmar. The reasons are as follows.

First, human rights compliance is not a condition of membership in ASEAN. Myanmar became a member in 1997, while under the rule of the State Peace and Development Council, a military regime that carried out grave violations of fundamental rights. Once Myanmar was a member of ASEAN, it was not subject to the threat of suspension and the consequent economic and political costs of rights-violating behavior. Myanmar's rulers had no incentive to adopt and maintain human rights–compliant practices.[122] Second, regional organizations comprised of states that see themselves as liberal, democratic, rights-respecting nations, belonging to a community of similar nations, sometimes possess the ability to "shame" recalcitrant states into altering their behavior.[123] But ASEAN is not a community of states that self-identify as liberal, democratic, and rights respecting, where behavior that is inconsistent with this identity can result in shaming and loss of reputation. Until the mid-2000s, ASEAN was known as a "club of dictators," where the suppression of dissent, state violence, the absence of a free press, the arrest and imprisonment of political opponents, torture, and the death penalty were commonplace in most states. The signing of the ASEAN Charter in 2008, and the formal commitment to good governance, the principles of democracy, and constitutional government, did not reflect a fundamental change in the political character of most ASEAN states. Third, ASEAN possesses little ability to influence and "co-opt" elites along a path of liberal reform because the interdependencies and informal ties that characterize transnational relations within ASEAN do not support and reinforce the maintenance of human rights norms.[124] Communication between governmental elites and bureaucrats in different ASEAN states do not produce formal and informal ties that contribute to a "transnational society" that socializes members to liberal democracy.[125] Indeed the opposite is true. ASEAN is united by norms that run contra to the protection of human rights, such as the principle of noninterference.

It is unsurprising that ASEAN had little influence on Myanmar's human rights behavior during the years of dictatorship and that its influence postdictatorship, during Myanmar's period of transition to democracy, is constrained by adherence to norms of sovereignty and noninterference in the affairs of other states. All ASEAN countries have at different times struggled to resolve issues of authoritarianism, the role of the military within the state, the reconciliation of restless ethnic minorities, and the management of development and democracy.[126] The lesson learned by ASEAN states is that the source of liberalization is indigenous and that external pressure is at best irrelevant and at worst counterproductive. Although individual ASEAN members cajoled and encouraged Myanmar to become less overtly authoritarian, as a regional organization ASEAN lacked (and lacks) the military or economic power to bribe, or the moral stature to persuade, members such as Myanmar.

Conclusion

Regional human rights governance has the potential to serve as a via media between the particularistic nature of rights violations in their local contexts and the ideal of universalism, and it can be a practical way to monitor human rights when a court with global jurisdiction is problematic. But Southeast Asia's democratic deficit augurs strongly against the creation of a robust regional human rights system, and low levels of democracy substantially undercut the potential for the region's nascent human rights institutions to shape the behavior of the region's states. Democracy, in both a deliberative sense and in the sense of a system of government that represents the freely expressed will of the people, is essential to creating and maintaining legitimacy in regional human rights norms and institutions. Southeast Asia's democratic deficit undermines the authority of ASEAN's new institutions: the ASEAN Charter, Intergovernmental Commission on Human Rights, and Human Rights Declaration.

The primary difficulty is not that ASEAN's human rights body lacks powers of enforcement, or "teeth." The difficulty is that within most ASEAN states, the structural political conditions for human rights responsiveness—liberal democracy—do not exist. The region's colonial history left many within Southeast Asia ambivalent about human rights and democracy. Democratization played an insignificant role in Southeast Asia's experience of rapid economic development in the postwar period. The communist character of Laos and Vietnam, and the fact that Brunei is an Islamic sultanate, render it difficult for ASEAN to even define "democracy." There also remains the residue of the "Asian Values" debate, which advanced the idea that the peoples of Asia were of a different cultural, political, and social orientation than those in the West. In this context, a regional human rights institution will struggle to effect change.

Nor is it possible, in the absence of democratic conditions, for meaningful dialogue to occur on the scope and content of rights. A human rights declaration produced under nondemocratic conditions cannot hope to answer the needs of the people it is intended to protect. Key stakeholders largely dismissed the ASEAN Human Rights Declaration because of the undemocratic process that marked its creation and the fact that the declaration fails to meet international standards. This is particularly the case in relation to difficult questions around moral beliefs and cultural practices that influence the enjoyment of individual rights, as well as the question of what degree of deference should be shown to these beliefs and practices.

Examining how norms articulated at the regional level played out in relation to the rights of women and of trafficked persons let us explore the socializing mechanisms (coercion, rewards, persuasion and discourse, capacity building) at play in the contemporary international human rights regime and the interplay between these mechanisms at different stages of the socialization process, from repressive societies that initially deny human rights abuses and contest the validity of human rights norms to rule-consistent behavior by states that accept the prescriptive status of norms.

In relation to certain rights, but not others, regional rights regimes evidence a higher degree of legitimacy than norms articulated at the global level, in turn leading to greater commitment and greater compliance. In relation to human trafficking, it seems to be the case that regional approaches possess a legitimacy that global approaches do not. One reason for this concerns the actual geography of trafficking, which occurs not merely across borders but in the interstices between states in Southeast Asia and within states themselves. The global approach to trafficking, which is focused almost entirely on sovereignty and borders, is simply not fine-grained enough to capture the shifting movements of the human trafficking processes. Also, with human trafficking, there are strong geographic, economic, political, and security imperatives compelling state attention to the issue at the *regional* level. Another reason for the comparative legitimacy of regional approaches concerns the nature of the global anti-trafficking movement itself, which has been shaped by ideological concerns, many emanating from the United States, that do not sit easily with the actual experiences of Southeast Asian women or the reality of trafficking.

The issue of women's rights does *not* appear to be one in relation to which regional discourse and regional institutions possess a greater legitimacy than global ones. The reasons have to do with the nature of ASEAN states' commitment to women's rights, which in terms of the norm life cycle, remains largely at a stage of "tactical concessions" (in the form of ratification of CEDAW) rather than prescriptive status (for example, the transposition of commitments into domestic law). It seems that at the tactical concession stage of the spiral model, the invocation of *global* norms by civil society and rights advocates is more effective than appeal to regional norms: in Southeast Asia, at least, civil society activists find that an appeal to global norms about women's equality has greater legitimacy as a source of influence and engenders greater state responsiveness. Interestingly, while this line of argument holds in relation to women's equality rights (particularly when they are posited against religious norms), it does not appear to be the same across all aspects of women's rights. For example, in relation to the issue of violence against women, we see a move in Southeast Asia from tactical concession to prescriptive status: all ASEAN states have laws that criminalize violence against women, and the issue of violence against women has emerged as a regional issue, with regional dynamics reinforcing and supporting compliance. Unlike with trafficking, in the case of women's rights, there exists a strong global norm, which is only weakly mirrored in regional understandings about the meaning and scope of women's rights (*despite* regional-level commitment to the CEDAW). This has the effect of rendering the global norm the more powerful one as a dynamic in transnational legal processes.

Finally, the case study of Myanmar shows how the regional human rights effect does not apply to the case of Myanmar and ASEAN. The argument is simple: a regional association that represents a number of nondemocratic states, with a governing charter that does not set democracy as a condition of membership, does not possess the authority to shame a wayward state. In Southeast Asia, there is no regional effect operating to engender or sustain human rights reform in Myanmar or in any individual member state.

What do my conclusions suggest about the future evolution of human rights in Southeast Asia?

First, in relation to Southeast Asia, we should bear in mind that at the time of writing AICHR has released only one report, on corporate social responsibility as it relates to the promotion and protection of human rights in the ASEAN region.[1] We do not know how ASEAN states will respond to the report's recommendations. A positive and coordinated response, which results in domestic policy and legislative reform, would have immediate effects on AICHR's legitimacy. So too would a positive response from the judiciary or the legislature to efforts to implement the ASEAN Human Rights Declaration. Legitimacy is not static. In circumstances where states are prepared to respect the rulings and reports of institutions (in the way that, for the most part, the states of Europe implement the judgments of the European Court of Human Rights), legitimacy can accrue to an institution. This is the case, even if the circumstances of its birth are inauspicious.

Second, in assessing the power and legitimacy of ASEAN's human rights institutions, we should be alert not only to the behavior and responses of states but also to the rise and influence of informal institutions that coalesce around these institutions. Particularly important in this regard are networks of domestic and regional nongovernmental organizations, such as the Working Group for an ASEAN Human Rights Mechanism and Solidarity for Asian People's Advocacy. These groups lobbied states about the establishment and the original Terms of Reference of the ASEAN Intergovernmental Commission on Human Rights and later about the content of the ASEAN Human Rights Declaration. They are involved in the review of the Terms of Reference, which was scheduled to take place in 2014. The mere existence of ASEAN's human rights institutions has created new theaters for discourse between states and civil society.

Third, ASEAN's regional institutions have created new vectors for communication between the global and regional levels. I have pointed out that AICHR's commissioners are "accountable to their appointing governments" and that this is one of the factors that impugn the legitimacy of the institution. However, AICHR's commissioners might also find that they are subject to a new kind of accountability, which derives from their relations with peers in the world of international human rights. The standards of independence that AICHR commissioners are exposed to in the course of transnational interactions between judicial and quasi-judicial members around the world may have a significant effect on shaping their worldview and their ideas about the extent to which they can challenge their appointing states. It should be remembered that this kind of influence is not one-way. The ASEAN Intergovernmental Commission on Human Rights is now in a position to influence the international human rights agenda. For example, AICHR has decided that one of its next thematic reports will be on the right to peace, set out in Article 38 of the ASEAN Human Rights Declaration. As I discussed in Chapter 3, the scope of this right is unclear in international law. AICHR's study will be important beyond the borders of Southeast Asia.

Fourth, I have argued at several points that the legitimacy of regional human rights depends on the presence of shared concerns and commonalities. From this perspective, changes in the economic and security dynamic of

Southeast Asia have the potential to hasten (or impede) the formation of a regional human rights regime. ASEAN, as I have mentioned, is committed to establishing a common economic market. Critics point to the different levels of economic development of ASEAN states and the lack of intraregional trade. Nonetheless, even the existence of the goal may drive a greater degree of integration at government and societal levels, which might also (eventually) evolve into closer ties and interdependencies in the field of human rights. In relation to the security dynamic of Southeast Asia, this is highly uncertain. For example, at present, several ASEAN states have conflicting interests in the South China Sea. Disputes could splinter ASEAN cohesiveness and ultimately undermine stronger relationships in the field of human rights.

Is it possible to extend some of the conclusions about Southeast Asia's nascent human rights regime to other regions of the world? One should make this attempt very cautiously. The field of comparative regionalism is unsettled, largely because the particularities of each region are held to be unique and distinctive.[2] Nonetheless, there will be much that other regions (or subregions) where no formal human rights system currently exists (East Asia, South Asia, and the Pacific) can learn from the experience of Southeast Asia. We could predict that democracy in (at least) the political system of the dominant regional member (China, India, and Fiji, respectively) would be a minimum prerequisite for a regional human rights system to possess even minimal legitimacy. We would also predict that even with a democratic regional hegemon (for example, Indonesia in the case of ASEAN), the regional organization's ability to influence a "pariah state" (Myanmar in the case of ASEAN) would be limited.

Second, the experience of the Arab Human Rights Committee, and the projected Arab Court of Human Rights, is likely to be a difficult one. In this book, I suggest that in regions comprised of nondemocratic states, rights unrelated to civil and political freedoms may gain more traction, as there is likely to be a greater degree of state-level consensus around these issues. It is not clear whether this will indeed be the experience of the human rights institutions of the League of Arab States. Constraints placed on civil society in nondemocratic societies in the Middle East are likely to seriously constrain state responsiveness to the work of the Arab Human Rights Committee and the future court.

Finally, I have emphasized the primacy of democracy and the democratic deficit that exists in Southeast Asia. This, I argue, is what undergirds the lack of legitimacy that currently attaches to the region's human rights institutions.

Yet democracy in Southeast Asia is in flux. There are both positive and negative currents at play. Both may influence the future development of a regional human rights regime. Myanmar's elections in November 2015 brought the National League for Democracy to power (although they did not remove the presence of unelected military representatives in parliament) and altered the dynamics of regional relations. Until 2015, it had been possible to view the human rights goals and priorities of the CLMV states (Cambodia, Laos, Myanmar, and Vietnam) in sharp contradistinction to those of relatively more progressive states such as Indonesia, Thailand, and the Philippines. The picture is now more complicated. In 2016, Thai voters approved a constitution that entrenches the role of an unelected military in the political affairs of the nation. Regional shifts toward or away from democracy (and the way ASEAN responds to these shifts) have the potential to alter the democratic balance of power within the region. These shifts will certainly affect the relevance and potential of ASEAN's new human rights institutions.

The intuition that prompted this investigation into regionalism and human rights in the first place was a sense that the global human rights regime had perhaps overreached; that it lacked a necessary sense of accord about important beliefs and values; and that this accord might be more readily found at the more modest level of the region. Testing this intuition against the reality of Southeast Asia shows that a bifurcation along global/regional lines is too simplistic. The most we can say is that if there is potential for Southeast Asia's regional human rights system to positively shape the behavior of states, it lies in the fact that the new institutions emanate from the region itself. No Southeast Asian government will ever again be able to deflect criticism on the basis that human rights are a "Western imposition."

Introduction

1. ASEAN's current members are Brunei Darussalam, the Kingdom of Cambodia, the Republic of Indonesia, the Lao People's Democratic Republic, Malaysia, the Republic of the Union of Myanmar, the Republic of the Philippines, the Republic of Singapore, the Kingdom of Thailand, and the Socialist Republic of Vietnam. In 2011, Timor Leste applied to become a member.

2. Charter of the Association of Southeast Asian Nations (adopted November 20, 2007, entered into force December 15, 2008) (hereafter ASEAN Charter), Preamble.

3. Terms of Reference of the ASEAN Intergovernmental Commission on Human Rights (2009) (hereafter TOR AICHR) Articles 2.1(d) and 2.1(e) Other developments include the establishment, in 2010, of the ASEAN Commission on the Promotion and Protection of the Rights of Women and Children (ACWC) and in 2013 the adoption of the Declaration on the Elimination of Violence Against Women and Elimination of Violence Against Children in ASEAN, which provides a monitoring role for the ACWC (DEVWC).

4. ASEAN Human Rights Declaration, Phnom Penh, Cambodia, November 18, 2012, Articles 10, 26.

5. Ibid., Article 28(f).

6. Ibid., Articles 35–37.

7. Ibid., Article 38.

8. Damien Kingsbury, *Southeast Asia: A Political Profile*, 2nd ed. (Oxford: Oxford University Press, 2005).

9. European Convention for the Protection of Human Rights and Fundamental Freedoms (adopted November 4, 1950, 213 UNTS 2, entered into force September 3, 1953), as amended by Protocol 11 (1998) and Protocol 14 (2010) (hereafter European Convention), Preamble.

10. The major international conventions are: International Convention on the Elimination of All Forms of Racial Discrimination (adopted December 21, 1965, 660 UNTS 195, entered into force January 4, 1969) (ICERD); International Covenant on Civil and Political Rights (adopted December 16, 1966, 999 UNTS 171, entered into force March 23, 1976) (ICCPR); International Covenant on Economic, Social and Cultural Rights (adopted December 16, 1966, 993 UNTS 3, entered into force January 3, 1976) (ICESCR); Convention on the Elimination of All Forms of Discrimination Against Women (adopted December 18, 1979, 1249 UNTS 13, entered into force September 3, 1981) (CEDAW); Convention Against Torture and Other Cruel, Inhuman or Degrading Treatment or Punishment (adopted December 10, 1984, 1465 UNTS 85, entered

into force June 26, 1987); Convention on the Rights of the Child (adopted November 20, 1989, 1577 UNTS 3, entered into force September 2, 1990) (CRC); International Convention on Protection of the Rights of All Migrant Workers and Members of Their Families (adopted December 18, 1990, 2220 UNTS 3, entered into force July 1, 2003); Convention on the Rights of Persons with Disabilities (adopted December 13, 2006, 2515 UNTS 3, entered into force May 3, 2008).

11. See the discussion in Chapter 2.

12. Malaysia, Singapore, Myanmar, and Brunei have signed neither ICESCR nor ICCPR.

13. Mark R. Thompson, "Dead Idea (Still) Walking: The Legacy of the 'Asian Democracy' and 'Asian Values' Debate," in *Routledge Handbook of Southeast Asian Democratisation*, ed. William Case (New York: Routledge, 2015).

14. Andrea Durbach, Andrew Byrnes, and Catherine Renshaw, "A Tongue but No Teeth: The Emergence of a Regional Human Rights Mechanism in the Asia Pacific Region," *Sydney Law Review* 31, no. 2 (2009); Yuval Ginbar, "Human Rights in ASEAN—Setting Sail or Treading Water?" *Human Rights Law Review* 10, no. 3 (2010); Tan Hsien-Li, "The ASEAN Human Rights Body: Incorporating Forgotten Promises for Policy Coherence and Efficacy," *Singapore Year Book of International Law* 12 (2008); "ASEAN's Toothless Council," *Wall Street Journal*, July 22, 2009, available at http://online.wsj.com/news/articles/SB10001424052970203517304574303592053848748; K. Percy, Australian Broadcasting Corporation interview with Rafendi Djamin, "Critics Dismiss ASEAN Human Rights Charter," July 21, 2009, available at http://www.radioaustralia.net.au /international/radio/onairhighlights/critics-dismiss-asean-human-rights-charter; Tim Johnston, "Criticism of Asian Rights Body Rebuffed," *Financial Times*, July 20, 2009.

15. The European Court of Human Rights, established in 1959 pursuant to Article 19 of the European Convention on Human Rights, has jurisdiction over Council of Europe member states.

16. Ninth International Conference of American States, American Declaration on the Rights and Duties of Man, Bogota, Colombia, May 2, 1948. In 1959, the Inter-American Commission on Human Rights was created under the auspices of the Organization of American States (OAS), and in 1969, the American Convention on Human Rights was adopted by the OAS. The American Convention entered into force in 1978. Supervision of its implementation is by the Commission and the Inter-American Court of Human Rights. American Convention on Human Rights (adopted November 22, 1969, 1144 UNTS 143, entered into force July 18, 1978) (hereafter American Convention).

17. The African Charter, which came into force in 1986, provided for the establishment of the African Commission on Human and Peoples' Rights. In 1998, the OAU Assembly of Heads of State and Government approved the establishment of an African Court on Human and Peoples' Rights. African Charter on Human and Peoples' Rights (Banjul Charter) (adopted June 27, 1981, 1520 UNTS 217, entered into force October 21, 1986) (hereafter Banjul Charter). At the 24th African Union Summit, held in Addis Ababa in January 2015, member countries discussed the creation of an African Court of Justice and Human Rights to replace the existing African Court on Human and Peoples' Rights.

18. The Arab League agreed to establish a Permanent Commission of Human Rights in 1968. In 1994, the Arab League adopted the Arab Charter of Human Rights (hereafter Arab Charter), which failed to secure ratification by any of the League member states. A revised Arab Charter, reflecting greater compliance with international human rights principles and standards, was adopted in 2004. The revised charter, which took effect from March 2008, establishes, in Articles 45 and 48, an expert Arab Human Rights Committee to consider reports submitted by member

states on their progress in implementing Arab Charter provisions. Arab Charter on Human Rights (adopted September 15, 1994, entered into force March 15, 2008).

19. Louise Fawcett, "Exploring Regional Domains: A Comparative History of Regionalism," *International Affairs* 80, no. 3 (2004): 429–31; Andrew Hurrell, "One World? Many Worlds? The Place of Regions in the Study of International Society," *International Affairs* 83, no. 1 (2007): 131; Jon C. Pevehouse, *Democracy from Above: Regional Organisations and Democratisation* (Cambridge: Cambridge University Press, 2005), 19–28; Harry Estill Moore, "Regionalism and Permanent Peace," *Social Forces* 23, no. 1 (1944): 19; Burns Weston, Robin Lukes, and Kelly Hnatt, "Regional Human Rights Regimes: A Comparison and Appraisal," *Vanderbilt Journal of Transnational Law* 20 (1987): 590.

20. Report of the Commission to Study the Organization of Peace, "Regional Promotion and Protection of Human Rights," 28th Report (New York: Commission to Study the Organization of Peace, 1980), 15.

21. A. H. Robertson, *Human Rights in the World*, 2nd ed. (Manchester: Manchester University Press, 1982), 164–65.

22. Kai Alderson, "Making Sense of State Socialization," *Review of International Studies* 27, no. 3 (2001):417; Kong Qingjiang, "Construction of the Discourse on Legitimacy of International Institutions," in *Legitimacy in International Law*, ed. Rudiger Wolfrum and Volker Roben (Berlin: Springer, 2008), 378–79.

23. Report of the Commission to Study the Organization of Peace, "Regional Promotion and Protection of Human Rights."

24. Jean-Flavien Lalive, "The Protection of Human Rights Within the Framework of Existing Regional Organisations," in *Human Rights in National and International Law: The Proceedings of the Second International Conference on the European Convention on Human Rights Held in Vienna Under the Auspices of the Council of Europe and the University of Vienna*, ed. A. H. Robertson (Manchester: Manchester University Press, 1965), 330. In 1967, the UN Commission on Human Rights decided to study the possibility of setting up regional commissions in areas where they did not already exist. Recommendation 6 (XXIII) of March 23, 1967, United Nations General Assembly (UNGA), World Conference on Human Rights, Vienna Declaration and Programme of Action, A/CONF.157/23, June 25, 1993, para. 37.

25. Manfred Nowak, "The Need for a World Court of Human Rights," *Human Rights Law Review* 7, no. 1 (2007).

26. Dr. Herbert V. Evatt, first delegate of the Australian delegation, argued that an international human rights court would serve to deter would-be perpetrators of abuse and to protect individuals from the arbitrary will of majorities. See Dr. Herbert V. Evatt, statement, Australian Amendments and Proposed Additions to Draft Treaties, "War—Paris Peace Conference 1945–1946," August 21, 1946, Folder, Evatt Collection, Flinders University, Australia.

27. Hersch Lauterpacht, *An International Bill of the Rights of Man* (Oxford: Oxford University Press, 2013), 174–78.

28. Annemarie Devereux, *Australia and the Birth of the International Bill of Human Rights, 1946–1966* (Sydney: Federation Press, 2005), 180–89.

29. Ed Bates, *The Evolution of the European Convention on Human Rights: From Its Inception to a Permanent Court of Human Rights* (Oxford: Oxford University Press, 2010), 7.

30. Polys Modinos, "Effects and Repercussions of the European Convention on Human Rights," *International and Comparative Law Quarterly* 11, no. 4 (1962).

31. Lalive, "The Protection of Human Rights," 332.

32. Dinah Shelton, *Regional Protection of Human Rights* (Oxford: Oxford University Press, 2008), 68–71.

33. Lalive, "The Protection of Human Rights," 336–38.

34. Makau Mutua, "The African Human Rights Court: A Two-Legged Stool?" *Human Rights Quarterly* 21, no. 2 (1999).

35. U. O. Umozurike, "The African Charter on Human and Peoples' Rights," *American Journal of International Law* 77 (1983).

36. Robertson, *Human Rights in the World*, 200.

37. W. Allam, "The Arab Charter on Human Rights: Main Features," *Arab Law Quarterly* 28, no. 1 (2014): 40.

38. Salem Alshehri, "An Arab Court of Human Rights: The Dream Desired," *Arab Law Quarterly* 30, no. 1 (2016).

39. In 1965, the International Commission of Jurists sponsored the drafting of an Asian Convention on Human Rights, under the auspices of the Congress of Southeast Asian and Pacific Jurists. In 1982, at a UN seminar held in Colombo titled "National, Local and Regional Arrangements for the Promotion and Protection of Human Rights in the Asia-Pacific Region," a proposal emerged for a human rights mechanism for the Pacific. The idea was further explored at a LAWASIA meeting in 1985 in Fiji, at which a Pacific Charter of Human Rights was drafted. In 2007, at a meeting in Auckland, a Pacific-based nongovernmental organization, the Regional Rights Resource Team, was urged to "take a lead role in setting up or exploring the possibility of setting up a Pacific Island Regional Human Rights Commission." See Pacific Regional Rights Resource Team, Submission to the Parliament of Australia Joint Standing Committee on Foreign Affairs, Defence and Trade, "Inquiry into Human Rights Mechanisms and the Asia Pacific" (2008), file:///C:/Users/Cat/Downloads/http_www.aphref.aph.gov.au_house_committee_jfadt_asia _pacific_hr_subs_sub%2013%20(2).pdf.

40. Lalive, "The Protection of Human Rights," 340, 362; J. A. Cabranes, "The Protection of Human Rights by the Organization of American States," *American Journal of International Law* 62, no. 4 (1968): 890; Edwin D. Dickinson, *Law and Peace* (Philadelphia: University of Pennsylvania Press, 1951), 121; R. Vincent, *Human Rights in International Relations* (Cambridge: Cambridge University Press, 1986), 50.

41. UNGA, World Conference on Human Rights, Vienna Declaration and Programme of Action, A/CONF.157/23, June 25, 1993, para. 37.

42. Andrew Hurrell, "Power, Principles and Prudence: Protecting Human Rights in a Deeply Divided World," in *Human Rights in Global Politics*, ed. Tim Dunne and Nicholas J. Wheeler (Cambridge: Cambridge University Press, 1999), 294–97.

43. Virginia Brodine and Mark Selden, eds., *Open Secret: The Kissinger-Nixon Doctrine in Asia* (New York: Harper and Row, 1972). On U.S. perceptions of ASEAN as a component of the Nixon Doctrine, see *United States Foreign Policy for the 1970's: Building for Peace—A Report by President Nixon to the Congress* (Washington, D.C.: U.S. GPO, February 25, 1971), 79–80.

44. Jürgen Haacke, "Myanmar and ASEAN," *Adelphi Papers* 46, no. 381 (2006): 42.

45. R. S. Milne, Diane K. Mauzy, and Institute of Southeast Asian Studies, *Politics and Government in Malaysia* (Singapore: Federal Publications, 1978).

46. Quoted in Yuen Foon Khong, "ASEAN and the Southeast Asian Security Complex," in *Building Security in a New World*, ed. David A. Lake and Patrick M. Morgan (University Park: Pennsylvania State University Press, 1997), 327.

47. The ASEAN Declaration (hereafter Bangkok Declaration), First ASEAN Ministerial Meeting, Bangkok, Thailand, August 8, 1967.

48. Chin Kin Wah, "ASEAN: The Long Road to 'One Southeast Asia,'" *Asian Journal of Political Science* 5, no. 1 (1997): 3.

49. Hans Indorf, "The Kuala Lumpur Summit (A Second for ASEAN)," *Southeast Asian Affairs* 5 (1978): 44.

50. Amitav Acharya, *Constructing a Security Community in Southeast Asia* (London: Routledge, 2001), 59; Shaun Narine, *Explaining ASEAN: Regionalism in Southeast Asia* (Boulder, Colo.: Lynne Rienner Publishers, 2002), 23.

51. Michael Leifer, *ASEAN and the Security of South East Asia* (London: Routledge, 1989), 7.

52. Zone of Peace, Freedom and Neutrality (ZOPFAN) Declaration, Special ASEAN Foreign Ministers Meeting, Kuala Lumpur, Malaysia, November 27, 1971.

53. Declaration of ASEAN Concord, First ASEAN Summit, Bali, Indonesia, Association of Southeast Asian Nations, February 24, 1976.

54. Treaty of Amity and Cooperation in Southeast Asia, First ASEAN Summit, Bali, Indonesia, February 24, 1976.

55. Kay Moller, "Cambodia and Burma: The ASEAN Way Ends Here," *Asian Survey* 38, no. 12 (1988) 1087-1104, 1087.

56. M. R. Sukhumbhand Paribatra, "Burma, ASEAN, Democracy, Dreams and Realities," *Nation* (Bangkok), July 16, 1999, quoted in John Funston, *ASEAN and the Principle of Non-intervention: Practice and Prospects* (Singapore: Institute of Southeast Asian Studies, 2000), 12. See also Termsak Chalermpalanupap, "ASEAN-10: Meeting the Challenges" (Paper presented at the Asia-Pacific Roundtable held in Kuala Lumpur, June 1, 1999, available at http://asean.org/asean-10-meeting-the-challenges-by-termsak-chalermpalanupap/).

57. The Bangkok Declaration of August 8, 1967, states that ASEAN is "open for participation to all States in the South-East Asian Region subscribing to the [association's] aims, principles and purposes." The origins of this idea, however, are unclear—the desire is not expressed anywhere in ASEAN's founding documents. See Hermann Kraft, "ASEAN and Intra-ASEAN Relations: Weathering the Storm?" *Pacific Review* 13, no. 3 (2000).

58. Wah, "ASEAN."

59. James Cotton, *East Timor, Australia and Regional Order: Intervention and Its Aftermath in Southeast Asia* (London: Routledge, 2004), 81.

60. Indeed, when Malaysian TV screened a CNN report showing graphic scenes of the Dili massacre, Malaysian prime minister Mahathir Mohammad sent his information minister to Jakarta as a personal envoy to extend his apology to Indonesia's president Suharto. Funston, *ASEAN and the Principle of Non-intervention*, 3.

61. Geoffrey Robinson, "Human Rights in Southeast Asia: Rhetoric and Reality," in *Southeast Asia in the New World Order: The Political Economy of a Dynamic Region*, ed. David Wurfel and Bruce Burton (New York: Macmillan, 1996), 76.

62. Amitav Acharya, *The Making of Southeast Asia: International Relations of a Region* (Ithaca, N.Y.: Cornell University Press, 2013), 216.

63. See "Human Rights Watch Concerns on Laos," *Human Rights Watch*, November 5, 2015; "Vietnam: Crackdown on Peaceful Environmental Protestors," *Human Rights Watch*, May 18, 2016.

64. See Rudy Guyon, "Violent Repression in Burma: Human Rights and the Global Response," *Pacific Basin Law Journal* 10, no. 2 (1992).

65. See, for example, UN Office of the High Commissioner of Human Rights, "Report of the Special Rapporteur on the Situation of Human Rights in Myanmar," UN Doc. A/53/654, ¶ 59, September 10, 1998; Statement by Special Rapporteur Paulo Sérgio Pinheiro on the Situation of Human Rights in Myanmar to the 61st Session of the Commission of Human Rights, Item 9, March 29, 2009; UN Office of the High Commissioner for Human Rights, "Report of the Special Rapporteur on the Situation of Human Rights in Myanmar, Tomás Ojea Quintana," UN Doc. A/HRC/10/19, ¶ 15, March 11, 2009.

66. Paul Chambers, "Thailand on the Brink: Resurgent Military, Eroded Democracy," *Asian Survey* 50, no. 5 (2010): 843.

67. Peter Bouckaert, "Descent into Chaos: Thailand's 2010 Red Shirt Protests and the Government Crackdown," *Human Rights Watch*, May 3, 2011; "Thailand: UN Review Highlights Junta's Hypocrisy: End Downward Rights Spiral, Restore Civilian Rule," *Human Rights Watch*, May 11, 2016; Kim McQuay, "Two Years After Thailand's Coup, Draft Constitution Stirs Controversy," *Asia Foundation*, May 18, 2016.

68. In 2013, ASEAN issued a statement in relation to Thailand that called "on all parties concerned to resolve the current situation through dialogue and consultations in a peaceful and democratic manner." ASEAN, "Statement of ASEAN Heads of State December 14, 2013," http://www.asean.org/storage/images/2013/resources/40thASEAN-Japan/statement%20on%20current%20developments%20in%20thailand%20-%20final.pdf.

69. Muhammad Arief Iskandar, "ASEAN Must Address Coup in Thailand: Yudhoyono," *Antara News*, May 24, 2014. The joint statement issued after the 20th EU-ASEAN Joint Ministerial Meeting in Brussels on July 23, 2014, which was attended by the Thai acting minister for foreign affairs, notes that the EU ministers expressed concern about recent political developments in Thailand. No mention is made of the response of ASEAN ministers. *Co-Chair's Statement of the 20th EU-ASEAN Ministerial Meeting*, European Union External Action Service, July 23, 2014. See Walter Woon, *The ASEAN Charter: A Commentary* (Singapore: Institute of Southeast Asian Studies, 2016), 65.

70. "Malaysia PM Urges World to Act Against 'Genocide' of Myanmar's Rohingya," *Guardian Australia*, December 4, 2016.

71. Anita Jetschke, "Linking the Unlinkable: International Norms and Nationalism in Indonesia and the Philippines," in *The Power of Human Rights: International Norms and Domestic Change*, ed. Thomas Risse, Stephen C. Ropp, and Kathryn Sikkink (Cambridge: Cambridge University Press, 1999), 139–40.

72. William Branigin, "Manila Denounces Rights Report; Amnesty International Sees 'No Substantial Change' Since Marcos Era," *Washington Post*, February 27, 1992; R. Weissman, "Development and the Denial of Human Rights in Ramos's Philippines," *Harvard Human Rights Journal* 7 (1994).

73. Funcinpec is the United National Front for an Independent, Neutral, Peaceful, and Cooperative Cambodia.

74. Amitav Acharya, "Democratising Southeast Asia: Economic Crisis and Political Change," Working Paper 87 (Perth: Asia Research Centre, Murdoch University, August 1998).

75. The thematic study report on corporate social responsibility and human rights was submitted to ASEAN foreign ministers on August 8, 2014. Thomas Thomas and Alexander Chandra, *AICHR's Thematic Study on CSR and Human Rights in ASEAN* (2014), available at http://aichr.org/?dl_name=AICHRs_Thematic_Study_on_CSR_and_Human_Rights_in_ASEAN.pdf.

76. AICHR, "Five-Year Work Plan of the ASEAN Intergovernmental Commission on

Human Rights (2010–2015)" (2012), available at http://aichr.org/?dl_name=AICHR_Five-Year_Work_Plan_2012-2015.pdf.

77. Solidarity for Asian People's Advocacy Task Force on ASEAN and Human Rights, *The Future of Human Rights in ASEAN: Public Call for Independence and Protection Mandates* (Bangkok: Asian Forum for Human Rights and Development, 2014), 67.

78. Thomas Risse, Stephen C. Ropp, and Kathryn Sikkink, *The Power of Human Rights: International Norms and Domestic Change* (New York: Cambridge University Press, 1999).

79. Ibid., 11–16.

80. Ibid., 33.

81. Ibid., 31–36.

82. Ibid., 30.

83. Beth Simmons, *Mobilizing for Human Rights* (Cambridge: Cambridge University Press, 2009); Jutta Brunee and Stephen J. Toope, *Legitimacy and Legality in International Law* (Cambridge: Cambridge University Press, 2010); Risse, Ropp, and Sikkink, *The Power of Human Rights*; Thomas Risse, Stephen C. Ropp, and Kathryn Sikkink, eds., *The Persistent Power of Human Rights: From Commitment to Compliance* (Cambridge: Cambridge University Press, 2013); Harold Koh, "How Is International Human Rights Law Enforced?" *Indiana Law Journal* 74, no. 4 (1999): 1397–98.

84. Emilie Hafner-Burton and Kiyoteru Tsutsui, "Human Rights in a Globalizing World: The Paradox of Empty Promises," *American Journal of Sociology* 110, no. 5 (2005); Emilie Hafner-Burton and K. Tsutsui, "Justice Lost! The Failure of International Human Rights Law to Matter Where Needed Most," *Journal of Peace Research* 44, no. 4 (2007).

85. Joseph Nye, *Peace in Parts: Integration and Conflict in Regional Organization* (Boston: Little, Brown, 1971); Nico Krisch, "International Law in Times of Hegemony: Unequal Power and the Shaping of the International Legal Order," *European Journal of International Law* 16, no. 3 (2005).

86. See Ian Hurd, "Legitimacy and Authority in International Politics," *International Organization* 53, no. 2 (Spring 1999); Jean-Marc Coicaud and Veijo Heiskanen, eds., *The Legitimacy of International Organizations* (Tokyo: United Nations University Press, 2001); Jens Steffek, "The Legitimation of International Governance: A Discourse Approach," *European Journal of International Relations* 9, no. 2 (2003).

Part I

1. Rhoda Howard and Jack Donnelly, "Human Dignity, Human Rights, and Political Regimes," *American Political Science Review* 80, no. 3 (1996): 802.

2. Thomas Carothers, "Democracy and Human Rights: Policy Allies or Rivals?" *Washington Quarterly* 17, no. 3 (1994): 109.

3. Gregory Fox and Brad R. Roth, eds., *Democratic Governance in International Law* (Cambridge: Cambridge University Press, 2000), 5.

4. Jack Donnelly, "Human Rights, Democracy, and Development," *Human Rights Quarterly* 21, no. 3 (1999).

5. See also *Sahin v. Turkey*, Application No. 44774/98, European Court of Human Rights, November 10, 2005; Jürgen Habermas, *The Postnational Constellation* (Cambridge, Mass.: Massachusetts Institute of Technology Press, 2001), 118. But see Makau Mutua, "The Ideology of Human Rights," *Virginia Journal of International Law* 36 (1996): 601–7, particularly section I: "Liberalism, Democracy and Human Rights: A Holy Trinity?"

6. E/CN.4/2003/59, Section VII, Geneva, November 25 and 26, 2002, Resolution 2003/36; E/CN.4/2005/58E/CN.4/2005/58E/CN.4/2005/58E/CN.4/2005/58 Geneva, February 28–March 2, 2005.

7. E/CN.4/2005/58E/CN.4/2005/58E/CN.4/2005/58E/CN.4/2005/58 Geneva, February 28–March 2, 2005, Paragraph 34. The seminar also noted that periodic elections are essential to ensure the accountability of representatives for the exercise of the legislative or executive powers vested in them. The seminar noted that freedom of expression, assembly, and association were essential conditions for democracy and for a democratic election process.

8. On shaming, see Thomas Risse, Stephen C. Ropp, and Kathryn Sikkink, "The Socialization of International Human Rights Norms into Domestic Practices: Introduction," in *The Power of Human Rights: International Norms and Domestic Change* (Cambridge: Cambridge University Press, 1999).

Chapter 1

1. Constitution of the United Nations Educational, Scientific, and Cultural Organization (adopted November 16, 1945, 4 UNTS 275, entered into force November 4, 1946) and amended by the General Conference at its second, third, fourth, fifth, sixth, seventh, eighth, ninth, tenth, twelfth, fifteenth, seventeenth, nineteenth, twentieth, twenty-first, twenty-fourth, and twenty-fifth sessions, available at http://unesdoc.unesco.org/images/0022/002269/226924e.pdf#page=6.

2. European Convention for the Protection of Human Rights and Fundamental Freedoms (adopted November 4, 1950, 213 UNTS 2, entered into force September 3, 1953), as amended by Protocol 11 (1998) and Protocol 14 (2010).

3. Organization of American States (OAS), *Charter of the Organisation of American States*, April 30, 1948, available at http://www.refworld.org/docid/3ae6b3624.html.

4. Ezetah writes, "The meaning of 'democracy', especially as expounded in scholarly writing and state practice, remains a riddle of immense proportions." Reginald Ezetah, "The Right to Democracy: A Qualitative Inquiry," *Brooklyn Journal of International Law* 22, no. 3 (1996): 495.

5. Immanuel Kant, "Perpetual Peace: A Philosophical Sketch," in *Kant's Principles of Politics, Including His Essay on Perpetual Peace: A Contribution to Political Science*, trans. W. Hastie, Online Library of Liberty (1891) http://lf-oll.s3.amazonaws.com/titles/357/0075_Bk.pdf; Bruce Russett, "The Fact of Democratic Peace," in *Debating the Democratic Peace*, ed. Sean Lynn-Jones, Michael Brown, and Steven Miller (Cambridge, Mass.: Massachusetts Institute of Technology Press, 1996); David Lake, "Powerful Pacifists: Democratic States and War," *American Political Science Review* 86, no. 1 (1992).

6. Michael Doyle, "Kant, Liberal Legacies, and Foreign Affairs," in *Debating the Democratic Peace*, ed. Sean Lynn-Jones, Michael Brown, and Steven Miller (Cambridge, Mass.: Massachusetts Institute of Technology Press, 1996); Russett, "The Fact of Democratic Peace."

7. Erik Kuhonta, "Towards Responsible Sovereignty," in *Hard Choices: Security, Democracy, and Regionalism in Southeast Asia*, ed. Donald K. Emmerson (Baltimore: Walter H. Shorenstein Asia-Pacific Research Center/Freeman Spogli Institute for International Studies, Stanford University, 2008).

8. Counting from the year of the first democratic elections after authoritarian rule, democracy began in the Philippines in 1986, in Thailand in 1992 (with a short interruption in 2006–7), and in Indonesia in 1999. In his influential study of the origins of the human rights regime in postwar Europe, Andrew Moravcsik categorizes European political systems at the end of World War II as either "established democracies" (systems that had been continuously under demo-

cratic rule since before 1920 and remained so thereafter), "new democracies" (systems established between 1920 and 1950), or "semi-democracies and dictatorships," governments that were not fully democratic by 1950 because of civil war or internal repression. Adopting Moravcsik's taxonomy, at the time of the inauguration of AICHR, only the Philippines and Indonesia were established democracies (not counting the "soft authoritarian democracies"); all others are "semi-democracies." Andrew Moravcsik, "The Origins of Human Rights Regimes: Democratic Delegation in Postwar Europe," *International Organization* 54 (2000). See also Andrew Moravcsik, "Explaining International Human Rights Regimes: Liberal Theory and Western Europe," *European Journal of International Relations* 1, no. 2 (1995).

9. Quoted in *Bangkok Post*, July 31, 1966.

10. Harvey Stockwin, "Tricky Negotiations," *Far Eastern Economic Review* (August 24, 1967) 379.

11. Kay Moller, "Cambodia and Burma: The ASEAN Way Ends Here," *Asian Survey* 38, no. 12 (1988).

12. The ASEAN Declaration (Bangkok Declaration), Bangkok, Thailand, August 8, 1967.

13. Zone of Peace, Freedom and Neutrality (ZOPFAN) Declaration, Special ASEAN Foreign Ministers Meeting, Kuala Lumpur, Malaysia, November 27, 1971.

14. Declaration of ASEAN Concord, First ASEAN Summit, Bali, Indonesia, Association of Southeast Asian Nations, February 24, 1976.

15. Treaty of Amity and Cooperation, Association of Southeast Asian Nations (1976) http://asean.org/treaty-amity-cooperation-southeast-asia-indonesia-24-february-1976/.

16. Charles R. Larson, "Implications of US Withdrawal from Clark and Subic Bases," Statement to Congress, Committee on Foreign Affairs, March 5, 1992.

17. Declaration of ASEAN Concord II (Bali Concord II), Ninth ASEAN Summit, Bali, Indonesia, October 7, 2003.

18. ASEAN, "ASEAN Vision 2020," December 15, 1997, available at http://asean.org/?static_post=asean-vision-2020.

19. Amitav Acharya, *Constructing a Security Community in Southeast Asia* (New York: Routledge, 2001), 148–91.

20. Tivo Kivimäki, "The Long Peace of ASEAN," *Journal of Peace Research* 38, no. 1 (2001): 11.

21. Ibid., 12.

22. "ASEAN Trade Too Low," *Bangkok Post*, December 1, 2010, available at http://www.pressreader.com/thailand/bangkok-post/20101201/282119222946355/.

23. Mark Thompson, "Pacific Asia After 'Asian Values': Authoritarianism, Democracy, and 'Good Governance,'" *Third World Quarterly* 25, no. 6 (2004): 1080.

24. Amitav Acharya, *Constructing a Security Community in Southeast Asia: ASEAN and the Problem of Regional Order* (New York: Routledge, 2001), 169.

25. Amartya Sen, "Public Action to Remedy Hunger," *Interdisciplinary Science Reviews* 16, no. 4 (1991); Amartya Sen, *Poverty and Famines: An Essay on Entitlement and Deprivation* (Oxford: Clarendon Press, 1981); Amartya Sen, "Democracy as a Universal Value," *Journal of Democracy* 10, no. 3 (1999).

26. David P. Chandler, *The Tragedy of Cambodian History: Politics, War, and Revolution Since 1945* (New Haven, Conn.: Yale University Press, 1991).

27. Melanie Chew, "Human Rights in Singapore: Perceptions and Problems," *Asian Survey* 34, no. 11 (1994).

28. Juliet Johnson, "In Pursuit of a Prosperous International System," in *Exporting Democracy: Rhetoric vs. Reality*, ed. Peter Schraeder (Boulder, Colo.: Lynne Rienner, 2002).

29. Kishore Mahbubani, "Dangers of Decadence: What the Rest Can Teach the West," *Foreign Affairs* 72, no. 4 (1993); Kishore Mahbubani, "An Asian Perspective on Human Rights and Freedom of the Press" (Paper delivered at the Asian and American Perspectives on Capitalism and Democracy conference, jointly organized by the Asia Society of New York and Singapore's Institute of Southeast Asian Studies, International Foundation, and Institute of Policy Studies, Singapore, January 1993).

30. Quoted in Michael Vatikiotis, *Political Change in Southeast Asia: Trimming the Banyan Tree* (London: Routledge, 1996), 103.

31. Rudolf Severino, *Southeast Asia in Search of an ASEAN Community* (Singapore: Institute of Southeast Asian Studies, 2006), 151. See also Thompson, "Pacific Asia After 'Asian Values,'" 1079.

32. Donald K. Emmerson, ed., *Hard Choices: Security, Democracy, and Regionalism in Southeast Asia* (Baltimore: Walter H. Shorenstein Asia-Pacific Research Centre, Freeman Spogli Institute for International Studies, Stanford University, 2008), 18.

33. Amitav Acharya, "Southeast Asia's Democratic Moment," *Asian Survey* 39, no. 3 (1999).

34. Thompson, "Pacific Asia After 'Asian Values.'"

35. Surain Subramaniam, "The Dual Narrative of Good Governance: Lessons for Understanding Political and Cultural Change in Malaysia and Singapore," *Contemporary Southeast Asia* 23, no. 1 (2001).

36. Acharya, "Southeast Asia's Democratic Moment," 422.

37. "Riots Not a Call for Democracy," interview with Lee Kuan Yew, *Straits Times*, June 16, 1998, 33, quoted in ibid., 422.

38. Mahbubani, "Dangers of Decadence"; Mahbubani, "An Asian Perspective on Human Rights and Freedom of the Press."

39. Thomas Franck, "The Emerging Right to Democratic Governance," *American Journal of International Law* 86, no. 1 (1992): 49.

40. Joshua Cohen, "Is There a Human Right to Democracy?" in *The Egalitarian Conscience: Essays in Honour of G. A. Cohen*, ed. Christine Syprowich (Oxford: Oxford University Press, 2006), 241.

41. Article 29 of the UDHR is also relevant, as it invokes "the general welfare of a democratic society" as the basis on which individual rights can legitimately be limited (together with morality and public order).

42. Article 25 of the International Covenant on Civil and Political Rights (adopted December 16, 1966, 999 UNTS 171, entered into force March 23, 1976) (ICCPR).

43. As of October 2017, the following states have not ratified the ICCPR: Malaysia, Myanmar, Brunei, and Singapore.

44. Henry Steiner, "Political Participation as a Human Right," *Harvard Human Rights Year Book* 1 (1988): 77.

45. UNGA Res. 45/150, February 21, 1991.

46. A/RES/46/137, "Enhancing the Effectiveness of the Principle of Periodic and Genuine Elections." In 1993, the Vienna World Conference on Human Rights adopted the Vienna Declaration and Programme of Action. Paragraph 8 of Section I of the Vienna Declaration asserts, "Democracy, development and respect for human rights and fundamental freedoms are interdependent and mutually reinforcing. . . . The international community should support the strength-

ening and promoting of democracy, development and respect for human rights and fundamental freedoms in the entire world." See UNGA, World Conference on Human Rights, Vienna Declaration and Programme of Action, A/CONF.157/23, June 25, 1993. Three years later, UN secretary-general Boutros-Boutros Ghali submitted "An Agenda for Democratization" to the United Nations General Assembly: B. Boutros-Ghali, "An Agenda for Democratization, Supplement to the Reports A/50/332 and A/51/512 on Democratization," December 17, 1996.

47. General Comment No. 25, "The Right to Participate in Public Affairs, Voting Rights and the Right of Equal Access to Public Service (Art. 25)," CCPR/C/21/Rev.1/Add.7, July 12, 1996, available at http://www.refworld.org/docid/453883fc22.html. See Same Varayudej, "Right to Democracy in International Law: Its Implications for Asia," *Annual Survey of International and Comparative Law* 12, no. 1 (2006). General Comment 25 has been applied in the Human Rights Committee's review of state reports submitted under Article 40 of the ICCPR and in its decisions on applications under the Optional Protocol.

48. UN Commission on Human Rights, "Promotion of the Right to Democracy," Res. 1999/57, available at http://www.refworld.org/docid/3b00f02e8.html.

49. UN Commission on Human Rights, Res. 2000/47, "Promoting and Consolidating Democracy," E/CN.4/RES/2000/47, April 25, 2000, available at http://www.unhchr.ch/huridocda /huridoca.nsf/(Symbol)/E.CN.4.RES.2000.47.En?Opendocument. Bhutan, China, Congo, Cuba, Pakistan, Qatar, Rwanda, and Sudan abstained on the final vote. Cuba, China, and Pakistan were particularly vocal critics of the resolution, arguing that it imposed a single model of democracy upon member states. Nonetheless, the General Assembly reviewed and approved this document with only minor modifications. UNGA Resolution 55/96, "Promoting and Consolidating Democracy," December 4, 2000. See Michael Dennis, "The Fifty-Sixth Session of the UN Commission on Human Rights," *American Journal of International Law* 95, no. 1 (2001). Christian Tomuschat draws attention to the political character of the countries who abstained from voting: Bahrain, Bhutan, Brunei Darussalam, China, Cuba, Democratic Republic of the Congo, Honduras, Laos, Libya, Maldives, Myanmar, Oman, Qatar, Saudi Arabia, Swaziland, and Vietnam. Christian Tomuschat, *Human Rights: Between Idealism and Realism* (Oxford: Oxford University Press, 2008), 61.

50. Marco Bunte and Andreas Ufen, *Democratization in Post-Suharto Indonesia* (New York: Routledge, 2008).

51. Mark Askew, ed., *Legitimacy Crisis in Thailand* (Chiang Mai: Silkworm Books, 2010).

52. Surin Maisrikrod, "Learning from the 19 September Coup: Advancing Thai-Style Democracy?" in *Southeast Asian Affairs*, ed. Lorraine Carlos Salazar (Singapore: Institute of Southeast Asian Studies, 2007), 340–59. See also Kevin Hewison, "Constitutions, Regimes and Power in Thailand," *Democratization* 14, no. 5 (2009).

53. Institute for Democracy and Electoral Assistance, Draft Constitution of the Kingdom of Thailand International 2016 http://www.un.or.th/wp-content/uploads/2016/06/2016_Thailand-Draft -Constitution_EnglishTranslation_Full_Formatted_vFina....pdf (unofficial English translation).

54. Catherine Renshaw, Andrew Byrnes, and Andrea Durbach, "Testing the Mettle of National Human Rights Institutions: A Case Study of the Human Rights Commission of Malaysia," *Asian Journal of International Law* 1, no. 1 (2011). On September 15, 2011, Malaysian prime minister Datuk Seri Najib Razak announced the repeal of the Internal Security Act 1960 (ISA) and Malaysia's three Emergency Declarations. See http://eng.518.org/ease/board.es?mid=a5050 1000000&bid=0028&act=view&list_no=686/.

55. Larry Diamond, "Thinking About Hybrid Regimes," *Journal of Democracy* 13, no. 2 (2002).

56. Duncan McCargo, "Cambodia: Getting Away with Authoritarianism?" *Journal of Democracy* 16, no. 4 (2005): 106.

57. Ronald St. John, *Revolution, Reform and Regionalism in Southeast Asia: Cambodia, Laos and Vietnam* (Montreal: Routledge, 2005).

58. See Chapter 6.

59. See Xue Hanqi, "Meaningful Dialogue Through a Common Discourse: Law and Values in a Multi-Polar World," *Asian Journal of International Law* 1 (2010).

60. Sienho Yee, "The Role of Law in the Formation of Regional Perspectives in Human Rights and Regional Systems for the Protection of Human Rights: The European and Asian Models as Illustrations," *Singapore Year Book of International Law* 8 (2004): 163; Mahathir Bin Mohamad, "Rethinking Human Rights" (keynote address, JUST International Conference, Kuala Lumpur, 1994), 9.

61. Joanne Bauer and Daniel Bell, eds., *The East Asian Challenge for Human Rights* (Cambridge: Cambridge University Press, 1999), 9. Bauer and Bell quote Onuma Yasuaki, professor of international law at the University of Tokyo. Yasuaki, writes, "For those who have experienced colonial rule and interventions under such beautiful slogans as 'humanity' and 'civilization,' the term 'human rights' looks like nothing more than another beautiful slogan by which great powers rationalize their interventionist policies."

62. Adamantia Pollis and Peter Schwab, "Human Rights: A Western Construct with Limited Applicability," in *Human Rights: Cultural and Ideological Perspectives*, ed. Adamantia Pollis and Peter Schwab (New York: Praeger, 1979), 2–4.

63. Mohammad Hatta, "Indonesia's Foreign Policy," *Foreign Affairs* 31, no. 3 (1953): 451–52.

64. H. E. U. Khin Maung Win, "Myanmar Roadmap to Democracy: The Way Forward" (Paper presented at the Seminar on Understanding Myanmar, Yangon, Myanmar Institute of Strategic and International Studies, January 27–28, 2004).

65. See Damien Kingsbury, *Southeast Asia: A Political Profile* (Oxford: Oxford University Press, 2001).

66. T. H. Pham, "What Remains: Vietnam in My Heart," *Open Democracy*, April 28, 2005, available at http://www.opendemocracy.net/node/2464.

67. Amado Guerrero, *Philippine Society and Revolution* (originally published in mimeograph by the Revolutionary School of Mao Tsetung Thought, 1970), 12, available at http://www.geocities.ws/kabataangmakabayan64/psr.pdf, 12.

68. See the 2008 Constitution of the Republic of the Union of Myanmar, chapter 7, "Defence Services," available online at http://www.burmalibrary.org/docs5/Myanmar_Constitution-2008-en.pdf.

69. George notes that the attitudes of the north and south had been "poisoned by the fears and hatreds planted in their mind by colonial masters." T. J. S. George, *Revolt in Mindanao: The Rise of Islam in Philippine Politics* (Kuala Lumpur: Oxford University Press, 1980), 119.

70. Anek Laothamatas, ed., *Democratisation in Southeast and East Asia* (Singapore: Institute of Southeast Asian Studies, 1997).

71. Win, "Myanmar Roadmap to Democracy."

72. Yee, "The Role of Law in the Formation of Regional Perspectives in Human Rights and Regional Systems for the Protection of Human Rights," 163.

73. Severino, *Southeast Asia in Search of an ASEAN Community*, 93.

74. Article 17, Bangkok Declaration. The ministers and representatives of Asian States met at Bangkok from March 29 to April 2, 1993, pursuant to General Assembly Resolution 46/116 of

December 17, 1991, in the context of preparations for the World Conference on Human Rights, and adopted the declaration, "Final Declaration of the Regional Meeting for Asia of the World Conference on Human Rights," Report of the Regional Meeting for Asia of the World Conference on Human Rights, A/Conf.1 57/ASRM/ 8 - A/Conf.157/PC/59, April 7, 1993.

75. Article 18, Bangkok Declaration.

76. Article 19, Bangkok Declaration.

77. Liu Huaqiu, "Proposals for Human Rights Protection and Promotion" (Speech by vice foreign minister given at World Conference on Human Rights, Vienna, 1993), published in *Beijing Review* (June 28–July 4, 1993): 9, quoted in Joseph Chan, "The Asian Challenge to Universal Human Rights," in *Human Rights and International Relations in the Asia Pacific*, ed. James Tang (London: Pinter, 1995), 38.

78. Ali Alatas, "Indonesia Against Dictates on Rights and Wants Better Mechanism for Rights" (Speech by minister of foreign affairs of the Republic of Indonesia given at the World Conference on Human Rights, Vienna, 1993), quoted in Chan, "The Asian Challenge to Universal Human Rights," 17.

79. E. Benvenisti, "Margin of Appreciation, Consensus, and Universal Standards," *New York University Journal of International Law and Policy* 31 (1988): 843.

80. John Tasioulas, "The Moral Reality of Human Rights," in *Freedom from Poverty as a Human Right: Who Owes What to the Very Poor?* ed. Thomas Pogge (Oxford: Oxford University Press, 2007), 76–77.

81. Chan, "The Asian Challenge to Universal Human Rights," 31.

82. Mely Caballero-Anthony, "Human Rights, Economic Change and Political Development: A Southeast Asian Perspective," in *Human Rights and International Relations in the Asia Pacific*, ed. James Tang (London: Pinter, 1995). See also Yash Ghai, "Human Rights and Governance: The Asia Debate," *Asia-Pacific Journal of Human Rights and the Law* 1, no. 1 (2000): 42.

83. Won Kang Sen, "The Real World of Human Rights" (Speech by the minister for foreign affairs of Singapore at the Second World Conference on Human Rights, Vienna, June 16, 1993, reported in the *Straits Times*, June 17, 1993), quoted in Caballero-Anthony, "Human Rights," 43.

84. Michael Vatikiotis and Robert Delfs, "Cultural Divide: East Asia Claims the Right to Make Its Own Rules," *Far Eastern Economic Review*, June 17, 1993.

85. Ibid. See also *Jakarta Post*, June 16 and 17, 1993, and *Straits Times*, June 17, 1993.

86. Ali Alatas, *A Voice for a Just Peace* (Singapore: Institute of Southeast Asian Studies, 2001), 474.

87. Some Western intellectuals are sympathetic to the idea that economic development must precede democracy. See H. P. Schmitz, "Domestic and Transnational Perspectives on Democratization," *International Studies Review* 6, no. 3 (2004). Samuel Huntington and Joan M. Nelson write, "Political development must be held down, at least temporarily, in order to promote economic development." Samuel Huntington and Joan M. Nelson, *No Easy Choice: Political Participation in Developing Countries* (Cambridge, Mass.: Harvard University Press, 1976), 23.

88. Tu Wei-Ming, ed., *Confucian Traditions in East Asian Modernity: Moral Education and Economic Culture in Japan and the Four Mini-Dragons* (Cambridge, Mass.: Harvard University Press, 1996), 347.

89. Tommy Koh, "10 Asian Values That Help East Asia's Economic Prosperity," *Straits Times*, December 14, 1993.

90. Quoted in Subramaniam, "The Dual Narrative of Good Governance," 65. See also, by former Singaporean prime minister Lee Kuan Yew, *From Third World to First: The Singapore Story, 1965–2000, Memoirs of Lee Kuan Yew* (Singapore: Singapore Press Holdings, 2000), 542.

91. Ranjoo Seodu Herr, "Democracy in Decent Non-Liberal Nations: A Defense," *Philosophical Forum, Inc.* (2009): 332; C. D. Neher, "Asian Style Democracy," *Asian Survey* 34, no. 11 (1994): 949.

92. Khin, "Myanmar Roadmap to Democracy."

93. Ghai, "Human Rights and Governance," 62.

94. Yash Ghai, "Asian Perspectives on Human Rights," in *Human Rights and International Relations in the Asia Pacific*, ed. James Tang (London: Pinter, 1995), 61.

95. Christopher G. Weeramantry, *Universalising International Law* (Leiden: Martinus Nijhoff, 2004), 2.

96. Amartya Sen, "Human Rights and Asian Values" (paper presented at Sixteenth Morgenthau Memorial Lecture on Ethics & Foreign Policy, May 1997), available at http://www.nyu.edu/classes/gmoran/SEN.pdf. See also Stephanie Lawson, "Democracy and the Problem of Cultural Relativism: Normative Issues for International Politics," *Global Society* 12, no. 2 (1998).

97. Joshua Cohen, "Minimalism About Human Rights: The Most We Can Hope For?" *Journal of Political Philosophy* 12, no. 2 (2004): 190.

98. Ghai, "Asian Perspectives on Human Rights."

99. Randall Peerenboom, "Beyond Universalism and Relativism: The Evolving Debates About 'Values in Asia,'" *Indiana International and Comparative Law Review* 14, no. 1 (2003): 6.

100. Constitution of the Socialist Republic of Vietnam 1992, Article 4.

101. Constitution of the Lao People's Democratic Republic, 2003, No. 25/NA, May 6, 2003.

102. Kyaw Yin Hlaing, "ASEAN's Pariah: Insecurity and Autocracy in Myanmar (Burma)," in *Hard Choices: Security, Democracy, and Regionalism in Southeast Asia*, ed. Donald K. Emmerson (Baltimore: Walter H. Shorenstein Asia-Pacific Research Centre, Freeman Spogli Institute for International Studies, Stanford University, 2008), 187.

103. Laos and Vietnam take similarly narrow approaches to contestation. The Lao People's Revolutionary Party (LPRP), for example, is the only vehicle permitted to organize politically. In 2010, of the National Assembly's 115 seats, the LPRP holds 113, leaving but two for independents. William Case, "Laos in 2010," *Asian Survey* 51, no. 1 (2011).

104. Lin Chun, "Human Rights and Democracy: The Case for Decoupling," *International Journal of Human Rights* 5, no. 3 (2001): 23.

105. Bertrand Russell, *In Praise of Idleness* (Oxford: Routledge, 1935), 73.

106. Rhoda Howard and Jack Donnelly, "Human Dignity, Human Rights, and Political Regimes," *American Political Science Review* 80, no. 3 (1986): 810.

107. Ibid., 811.

108. Karl Marx and Friedrich Engels, *The Communist Manifesto* (1848; London: Penguin, 2002), chap. 2.

109. Interview of Mr. Vo Van Ai, speech on receipt of Special Prize for Freedom by the Società Libera in Italy, June 2011, available at http://www.fidh.org/Conversation-with-Vo-Van-Ai.

110. Aung Bwa, "The Jewel in My Crown," in *The Making of the ASEAN Charter*, ed. Tommy Koh, Rosario G. Manolo, and Walter Woon (Singapore: World Scientific Publishing, 2009), 33.

Chapter 2

1. Yi-hung Chiou, "Unravelling the Logic of ASEAN's Decision-Making: Theoretical Analysis and Case Examination," *Asia Politics and Policy* 3, no. 2 (2008): 371; Maria-Gabriela Manea, "How and Why Interaction Matters: ASEAN's Regional Identity and Human Rights," *Nordic International Studies Association Online Publications* (2009), available at http://cac.sagepub.com

/cgi/content/abstract/44/1/27; Hiro Katsumata, "ASEAN and Human Rights: Resisting Western Pressure or Emulating the West?" *Pacific Review* 22 (2009): 628.

2. Charter of the Association of Southeast Asian Nations (adopted November 20, 2007, entered into force December 15, 2008) (hereafter ASEAN Charter), Article 1(7).

3. Ibid., Article 2(2)(h). The Preamble to the ASEAN Charter also refers to "the principles of democracy, the rule of law and good governance, respect for and protection of human rights and fundamental freedoms."

4. Chiou, "Unravelling the Logic," 371; Katsumata, "ASEAN and Human Rights," 628.

5. Steven Greer, *The European Convention on Human Rights: Achievements, Problems and Prospects* (Cambridge: Cambridge University Press, 2006), 199.

6. Ibid., 18–19.

7. Organisation of American States, Inter-American Democratic Charter, Lima, September 11, 2001, http://www.oas.org/charter/docs/resolution1_en_p4.htm.

8. The International Congress on the Human Right to Peace, held in Santiago on December 9 and 10, 2010, concluded with the adoption of the Santiago Declaration.

9. Organization of African States, Constitutive Act of the African Union (OAU), Lome, Togo, July 11, 2000.

10. African Charter on Human and Peoples' Rights (hereafter Banjul Charter) (adopted June 27, 1981, 1520 UNTS 217, entered into force October 21, 1986), Article 13.

11. Akwasi Aidoo, "Africa: Democracy Without Human Rights?" *Human Rights Quarterly* 15, no. 4 (1993): 703–15.

12. Katsumata, "ASEAN and Human Rights," 628. Cf. Manea, "How and Why Interaction Matters."

13. Jörn Dosch, "ASEAN's Reluctant Liberal Turn and the Thorny Road to Democracy Promotion," *Pacific Review* 21, no. 4 (2008).

14. Abdul Khalik, "Indonesia Holds Ground on ASEAN Charter," *Jakarta Post* (June 14, 2007), available at http://pseudonymity.wordpress.com/2007/06/16/expert-says-spore-opposes-inclusion-of-human-rights-and-democratic-principles-in-asean-charter/.

15. Ibid.

16. Ibid.

17. Rizal Sukma, "Political Development: A Democracy Agenda for ASEAN?" in *Hard Choices: Security, Democracy, and Regionalism in Southeast Asia*, ed. Donald K. Emmerson (Baltimore: Walter H. Shorenstein Asia-Pacific Research Center/Freeman Spogli Institute for International Studies, Stanford University, 2008).

18. Ibid. The conception of democracy presented by Indonesia closely matched that found in Article 21 of the Universal Declaration of Human Rights. UNGA Res. 217 A (III), Universal Declaration of Human Rights, A/810, December 10, 1948: "the will of the people shall be the basis of the authority of government: this will shall be expressed in periodic and genuine elections which shall be by universal and equal suffrage and shall be held by secret vote or by equivalent voting procedures." The 1993 Vienna World Conference on Human Rights describes democracy, development, and respect for human rights and fundamental freedoms as interdependent and mutually reinforcing. Article 8, UNGA, World Conference on Human Rights, Vienna Declaration and Programme of Action, A/CONF.157/23, June 25, 1993.

19. When the ASEAN Summit met in the Philippines in January 2007, however, four months after a military junta seized power from an elected government in Thailand, the junta representatives were welcomed and the ASEAN chair's statement did not mention the recent coup d'état in

Bangkok. See the discussion in Termsak Chalermpalanupap, "Institutional Reform: One Charter, Three Communities, Many Challenges," in *Hard Choices: Security, Democracy, and Regionalism in Southeast Asia*, ed. Donald K. Emmerson (Baltimore: Walter H. Shorenstein Asia-Pacific Research Center/Freeman Spogli Institute for International Studies, Stanford University, 2008), 112.

20. See Mathew Davies, *Realising Rights: How Regional Organisations Socialise Human Rights* (London: Routledge, 2014), 53–54.

21. The EPG Report was transmitted to the HLTF in January 2007, which then submitted the final text of the ASEAN Charter to ASEAN leaders in November that year. Jörn Dosch notes that a comparison of the recommendations in the EPG Report and the submissions made by the most active of civil society organizations, Solidarity for Asian People's Advocacy (SAPA) Working Group on ASEAN, shows "a striking convergence of core concepts." Dosch, "ASEAN's Reluctant Liberal Turn," 78.

22. EPG Report, para. 3(1).

23. Pavin Chachavalpongpun, ed., *The Road to Ratification and Implementation of the ASEAN Charter* (Singapore: Institute of Southeast Asian Studies, 2009), 64–66, 9.

24. ASEAN Charter, Article 2(2)(h).

25. Detailed in ASEAN Charter, Article 2(a).

26. Outlined in ASEAN Charter, Article 2(e).

27. Described in ASEAN Charter, Article 2(f).

28. ASEAN Charter, Article 2(k).

29. Walter Woon, *The ASEAN Charter: A Commentary* (Singapore: NUS Press, 2016), 64–66. As Woon points out, in the end the charter was actually signed on behalf of Thailand by General Surayud Chulanot, who had been installed after the coup.

30. Djoko Susilo, "The Ratification of the ASEAN Charter: A View from a Parliamentarian," in *The Road to Ratification and Implementation of the ASEAN Charter*, ed. Pavin Chachavalpongpun (Singapore: Institute of Southeast Asian Studies, 2009), 64–66.

31. Dewi Fortuna Anwar, "The ASEAN Charter: The Case for Ratification," in *The Road to Ratification and Implementation of the ASEAN Charter*, ed. Pavin Chachavalpongpun (Singapore: Institute of Southeast Asian Studies, 2009), 32–41.

32. Susilo, "The Ratification of the ASEAN Charter."

33. Abdul Khalik, "House Divided over ASEAN Charter," *Jakarta Post*, June 2, 2008.

34. Anwar, "The ASEAN Charter."

35. Ibid., 33.

36. Ernesto Simanungkalit, "Judicial Review of the ASEAN Charter?" *Jakarta Post*, May 13, 2011, available at http://www.thejakartapost.com/news/2011/05/13/judicial-review-asean-charter .html.

37. Juwana Hikmahanto, "The Constitution and Treaty," *Jakarta Post*, May 23, 2011.

38. Siyuan Chen, "The Relationship Between International Law and Domestic Law: Yong Vui Kong v PP," *Singapore Academy of Law Journal* 23, no. 1 (2011): 350–66.

39. Emmerson, *Hard Choices*. In Thailand, Parliament approved the ASEAN Charter in three readings on September 16, 2008. The legislation to enable the Thai government to implement and comply with the ASEAN Charter was endorsed by the Thai Senate and submitted to His Majesty the King of Thailand for his royal signature before proclamation into law. The Philippine Senate approved ratification of the charter on October 8, 2008, by a vote of 16–1, before submitting it to the president of the Republic of the Philippines.

40. Emmerson, *Hard Choices*, 35.

41. Pengiran Dato Paduka Osman Patra, "Heart Labour," in *The Making of the ASEAN Charter*, ed. Tommy Koh, Rosario G. Manolo, and Walter Woon (Singapore: World Scientific Publishing, 2009), 7.

42. Ibid., 13.

43. Aung Bwa, "The Jewel in My Crown," in *The Making of the ASEAN Charter*, ed. Tommy Koh, Rosario G. Manolo, and Walter Woon (Singapore: World Scientific Publishing, 2009), 33.

44. Ngyuyen Trung Thanh, "The Making of the ASEAN Charter in My Fresh Memories," in *The Making of the ASEAN Charter*, ed. Tommy Koh, Rosario G. Manolo, and Walter Woon (Singapore: World Scientific Publishing, 2009), 103.

45. Bwa, "The Jewel in My Crown," 31.

46. "Report of the Eminent Persons Group on the ASEAN Charter," December 2006, Article 23, available at http://www.asean.org/storage/images/archive/19247.pdf.

47. Ibid., para. 47.

48. Pengiran Dato Paduka Osman Patra, "Heart Labour," 3.

49. Bwa, "The Jewel in My Crown," 33.

50. Termsak Chalermpalanupap, "In Defence of the ASEAN Charter," in *The Making of the ASEAN Charter*, ed. Tommy Koh, Rosario G. Manolo, and Walter Woon (Singapore: World Scientific Publishing, 2009), 129.

51. Pengiran Dato Paduka Osman Patra, "Heart Labour," 13.

52. ASEAN Charter, Articles 14(1), 14(2).

53. Association of Southeast Asian Nations (ASEAN), "Terms of Reference of the ASEAN Intergovernmental Commission on Human Rights" (hereafter TOR AICHR), July 2009, Article 3, available at http://www.refworld.org/docid/4a6d87f22.html.

54. TOR AICHR, Article 1.1.

55. Ibid., Article 1.3.

56. Ibid., Article 1.4.

57. Ibid., Article 2.1(b).

58. Ibid., Article 2.3.

59. Ibid., Article 6.1.

60. Ibid., Articles 2.4, 2.5.

61. Ibid., Article 5.6.

62. Ibid., Article 9.6.

63. ASEAN, "The AICHR Annual Report 2016," August 1, 2016, available at http://aichr.org/report/the-aichr-annual-report-2016/.

64. Shalia Koshy, "Asean Panel Makes Report Public for First Time," *Star Online*, August 6, 2016, available at http://www.thestar.com.my/news/nation/2016/08/06/asean-panel-makes-report-public-for-first-time/.

65. ASEAN, "AICHR Annual Report 2016."

66. Thomas Thomas and Alexander Chandra, "AICHR's Thematic Study on CSR & Human Rights in ASEAN—Summary and Recommendations," October 2014, available at https://business-humanrights.org/en/business-human-rights-in-asean.

67. Pravit Rojanaphruk, "ASEAN Commission Fails Miserably in Promoting, Protecting Human Rights," *Nation*, August 8, 2011.

68. Beth Simmons, *Mobilizing for Human Rights* (Cambridge: Cambridge University Press, 2009).

69. Tom J. Farer, "The Rise of the Inter-American Human Rights Regime: No Longer a Unicorn, Not Yet an Ox," *Human Rights Quarterly* 19, no. 3 (1997): 510.

70. Joint Statement NGOs, "NGOs Call for the Drafting of the ASEAN Human Rights Declaration to Be Transparent and Subject to Meaningful Consultations with Civil Society," May 2, 2012, available at http://www.fidh.org/The-ASEAN-Human-Rights-Declaration.

71. TOR AICHR, Article 4.2: "To develop an ASEAN Human Rights Declaration with a view to establishing a framework for human rights cooperation through various ASEAN conventions and other instruments dealing with human rights."

72. Yuyun Wahyuningrum, senior advisor, Human Rights Working Group, Jakarta,, interview by the author, Canberra, Australia, December 12, 2012, copy on file with author.

73. Burns Weston, Robin Lukes, and Kelly Hnatt, "Regional Human Rights Regimes: A Comparison and Appraisal," *Vanderbilt Journal of Transnational Law* 20 (1987).

74. TOR AICHR, Article 5.2.

75. Ibid., Article 6.1.

76. At its simplest level, this argument took the form of observations such as this: How could a right to "rest and leisure, including reasonable limitation of working hours and periodic holidays with pay," which is guaranteed by Article 24 of the UDHR, be a "universal" right held (for example) by preindustrial agrarian communities, such as those that still exist in many parts of Southeast Asia?

77. Wahyuningrum, interview.

78. John Dryzek, "Transnational Democracy," *Journal of Political Philosophy* 7, no. 1 (1999).

79. United Nations Office of the High Commissioner for Human Rights, "Pillay Urges ASEAN to Set the Bar High with Its Regional Human Rights Declaration," press statement, May 11, 2012, available at http://www.ohchr.org/en/NewsEvents/Pages/DisplayNews.aspx?NewsID=12142&LangID=E.

80. A. W. B. Simpson, "Britain and the European Convention," *Cornell International Law Journal* 34 (2001).

81. Chhay Channyda, "NGOs Don't Need to See Rights Doc Draft: Official," *Phnom Penh Post*, June 14, 2012, available at http://www.phnompenhpost.com/national/ngos-don%E2%80%99t-need-see-rights-doc-draft-official.

82. International Covenant on Civil and Political Rights (adopted December 16, 1966, 999 UNTS 171, entered into force March 23, 1976); International Covenant on Economic, Social and Cultural Rights (adopted December 16, 1966, 993 UNTS 3, entered into force January 3, 1976).

83. Cha-am Hua Hin Declaration on the Intergovernmental Commission on Human Rights 2009, Fifteenth ASEAN Summit, Cha-am Hua Hin, Thailand, October 23, 2009, Article 7.

84. Copy on file with author. This document was leaked to the public mid-2011. At 4.2, the work plan discusses the drafting of the ASEAN declaration and lists as items to be completed: "1. Set up an ad hoc task force on drafting an ASEAN Human Rights Declaration (AHRD) with the TOR to be prepared by AICHR. 2. Take stock of and assess status of existing human rights mechanisms and instruments in ASEAN. 3. Work towards the ASEAN Convention on Human Rights upon the adoption of the ASEAN Human Rights Declaration. 4. Support the development of other ASEAN legal instruments on human rights undertaken by other ASEAN sectorial bodies. Support and strengthen the framework of legal cooperation on ASEAN Human Rights."

85. TOR AICHR, Article 1.6.

86. Ibid., Article 2.1(f).

87. Ibid., Article 6.1.

88. Ibid., Article 5.2.

89. Joint Statement NGOs, "NGOs Call for the Drafting of the ASEAN Human Rights Declaration."

90. See LBH Apik et al., "AHRD Is Hijacked by Narrow-Minded National Interests," *Burma Partnership*, September 13, 2012, available at http://www.burmapartnership.org/2012/09/ahrd-is -hijacked-by-narrow-minded-national-interests.

91. In April 2011, prior to the fourth meeting of AICHR, 136 CSOs released a joint statement calling for the immediate release of the draft declaration and for AICHR to engage in full and meaningful consultations with civil society. These calls continued throughout 2011 until AICHR finally announced that it would hold the June 22 consultation with civil society on the ASEAN Human Rights Declaration. The region's national human rights institutions were not invited to participate in the consultation.

92. The declaration was due to be submitted to ASEAN's foreign ministers on July 9, 2012.

93. The modalities for the second regional consultation were discussed during the 6th AICHR Meeting on the Declaration, held in Yangon, Myanmar, June 3–6, 2012. It was during this meeting that it was decided that each representative could select which four NGOs were to be invited. Each NGO was permitted to bring two persons to the consultation. AICHR also discussed regional and international NGOs that could be invited.

94. Amnesty International, International Commission of Jurists, Human Rights Watch, International Federation for Human Rights, Dignity International, and ARTICLE 19, "Less than Adequate: AICHR Consultation on ASEAN Human Rights Declaration," June 21, 2012, available at http://www.article19.org/resources.php/resource/3338/en/less-than-adequate:-aichr-consultation -on-asean-human-rights-declaration; "ASEAN Human Rights Declaration: ASEAN Intergovernmental Commission on Human Rights Urged to Hold Meaningful Consultations with CSOs," *Asia Pacific Update* 9 (June 2012): 4.

95. Lim Chee Wee, "ASEAN Human Rights Declaration: Hear the Voices of the Peoples of ASEAN," press release, April 12, 2012, available at http://www.malaysianbar.org.my/press _statements/press_release_asean_human_rights_declaration_hear_the_voices_of_the_peoples _of_asean.html.

96. ASEAN, "The Seventh Meeting of the ASEAN Intergovernmental Commission on Human Rights (AICHR) on an ASEAN Human Rights Declaration (AHRD) and the Second Regional Consultation of AICHR on the AHRD, Kuala Lumpur," press release, June 25, 2012, available at http://asean.org/the-seventh-meeting-of-the-asean-intergovernmental-commission -on-human-rights-aichr-on-an-asean-human-rights-declaration-ahrd-and-the-second-regional -consultation-of-aichr-on-the-ahrd/. In this release, AICHR reaffirmed that the draft AHRD would be submitted to the ASEAN Foreign Ministers' Meeting in July 2012 and adopted by the ASEAN leaders in November 2012 in Cambodia.

97. Human Rights Working Group, "CSOs Indonesia Highlight 8 Priority Issues on Improving AHRD," September 9, 2012, available at http://www.hrwg.org/en/hrwg/press-release/item /3917-csos-indonesia-highlight-8-priority-issues-on-improving-ahrd.

98. Email distribution briefing letter from Yuyun Wahyuningrum, senior advisor to the HRWG, September 7, 2012, copy on file with author.

99. These recommendations were prepared at the national level by Indonesian CSOs and finalized by the HRWG, AMAN, Jakarta Legal Aid, and Kalyanamitra.

100. See LBH Apik et al., "AHRD Is Hijacked by Narrow-Minded National Interests."

101. Ibid.

102. Ibid.

103. See Working Group for an ASEAN Human Rights Mechanism, "News and Updates," undated, available at http://www.aseanhrmech.org/news/phil-aichr-rep-dialogues-with-cso-of-aseanhrd.htm.

104. The SAPA Task Force on ASEAN and Human Rights, *Civil Society's Position Paper on ASEAN Human Rights Declaration*, June 21, 2011, available at http://forum-asia.org/documents/ SAPA TFAHR Position Paper AHRD final.pdf. In May 2012, the American Bar Association Rule of Law Initiative produced a seventy-page "Experts Note on the ASEAN Human Rights Declaration (AHRD)." Written by a group of international legal experts, the note was published as part of an effort "to share expertise and promote dialogue regarding the purpose and content of the AHRD."

105. Lim, "ASEAN Human Rights Declaration."

106. The Human Rights Working Group produced a detailed account of what transpired at the First Consultation: Human Rights Working Group, 2nd Regional Consultation on ASEAN Human Rights Declaration (AHRD), Ritz-Carlton Hotel, Kuala Lumpur, Malaysia, June 22, 2012, copy on file with author.

107. AICHR did not release to the public the TOR that it had supplied to the drafting team. According to a press release issued by AICHR, the drafting group was instructed to prepare a working copy of the ASEAN Human Rights Declaration and "in particular take into account the values and principles in the ASEAN Charter, the TOR of AICHR as well as international human rights instruments including the Universal Declaration of Human Rights." See ASEAN Secretariat, "Press Release of the Fifth ASEAN Intergovernmental Commission on Human Rights," April 25, 2015, available at http://aichr.org/press-release/press-release-of-the-fifth-asean-intergovernmental -commission-on-human-rights-asean-secretariat/.

108. Nonbracketed clauses included nondiscrimination and recognition before the law, most of the major civil and political rights found in the ICCPR, and the full range of economic and social rights set out in ICESCR. The draft also contained a section on the "right to development" and a section on the duties and responsibilities of corporations.

109. "Draft of the ASEAN Human Rights Declaration," January 9, 2012, Article 56, copy on file with author.

110. Laos also recommended a clause relating to freedom of religion, which included the following provision: "No one shall use religion as the pretext to violate the law and order of the State. Advocacy or dissemination of religions or beliefs shall be in compliance with national law of each ASEAN Member State." Several of the potential limitations clauses contained in the draft permitted derogations from rights on grounds such as national security and respect for the reputations of others, as well as (the commonly accepted grounds of) public order, public health, public morality, and the general welfare of the peoples in a democratic society. In light of this, Amnesty International, the International Commission of Jurists, and a joint submission by the Mekong Lawyers Network, Earthrights International, and the Sydney Centre for International Law all recommended that reference be made to the international law principle of non-derogability of fundamental human rights. They hoped that, if adopted, this reference would be sufficient to displace the usual presumption that the rules of international law did not apply to "soft law" such as declarations.

111. International Commission of Jurists, "The ICJ Urges BroadBased Civil Society Consul-tations and Respect for the Principle of Universality in Elaboration of the ASEAN Human Rights Declaration," March 13, 2012, available at http://www.enable.org.tw/iss/pdf/20120821-3.pdf.

112. Ibid.

113. LBH Apik et al., "AHRD Is Hijacked by Narrow-Minded National Interests."

114. "Final Declaration of the Regional Meeting for Asia of the World Conference on Human Rights," Report of the Regional Meeting for Asia of the World Conference on Human Rights, A/Conf.1 57/ASRM/ 8 A/Conf.157/PC/59, April 7, 1993. The declaration states: "Reaffirming their commitment to principles contained in the Charter of the United Nations and the Universal Declaration on Human Rights."

115. Ibid., Article 6.

116. Quoted in Simon S. C. Tay, "Human Rights, Culture, and the Singapore Example," *McGill Law Journal* 41 (1995): 743–80, 768.

Chapter 3

1. Thomas Risse, Stephen C. Ropp, and Kathryn Sikkink, eds., *The Power of Human Rights: International Norms and Domestic Change* (Cambridge: Cambridge University Press, 1999).

2. Tassia Sipahutar and Yohanna Ririhena, "ASEAN Declaration Should Be 'Equally Powerful' to UN's," *Jakarta Post*, June 28, 2012, available at http://www.thejakartapost.com/news/2012/06/28asean-declaration-shoild-be-equally-powerful-un-s.html.

3. AHRD, Articles 10, 26.

4. It is notable that the declaration does not contain, among the specific rights listed, Article 24 in the UDHR, which provides a right to "rest and leisure, including reasonable limitation of working hours and periodic holidays with pay."

5. Article 3 of the declaration states: "Every person is equal before the law. Every person is entitled without discrimination to equal protection of the law."

6. Article 5 of the declaration states: "Every person has the right to an effective and enforceable remedy, to be determined by a court or other competent authorities, for acts violating the rights granted to that person by the constitution or by law." The equivalent provision in the UDHR, Article 8, states: "Everyone has the right to an effective remedy by the competent national tribunals for acts violating the fundamental rights granted him by the constitution or by law."

7. Article 14 of the declaration states: "No person shall be subject to torture or to cruel, inhuman or degrading treatment or punishment." Article 5 of the UDHR states: "No one shall be subjected to torture or to cruel, inhuman or degrading treatment or punishment." There is no significance to the deletion of the "ed" in "subjected" in the declaration formulation of this Article.

8. AHRD, Article 13. The UDHR, Article 4, merely refers to slavery and servitude and the prohibition of the slave trade.

9. AHRD, Article 15; UDHR, Article 13.

10. AHRD, Article 16.

11. Ibid., Article 22.

12. UDHR, Article 18.

13. Tad Stahnke, "Proselytism and the Freedom to Change Religion in International Human Rights Law," *Brigham Young University Law Review* (1999).

14. UDHR, Article 20.

15. AHRD, Article 24. According to Yuyun Wahyuningrum, senior legal advisor to the Working Group for an ASEAN Human Rights Mechanism, reference to freedom of association was removed at the insistence of Vietnam. Yuyun Wahyuningrum, senior advisor, Human Rights

Working Group, Jakarta, interview by author, Canberra, Australia, December 12, 2012, copy on file with author.

16. UDHR, Article 16.

17. AHRD, Article 19.

18. UDHR, Article 23.

19. AHRD, Article 27. Both the AHRD and the UDHR provide that everyone has the right to form trade unions and join the trade union of his or her choice for the protection of his or her interests; but the AHRD adds the phrase "in accordance with national laws and regulations." AHRD, Article 27(2); UDHR, Article 23(4).

20. AHRD, Article 26(3).

21. Ibid., Article 29(2).

22. Ibid., Article 29(1).

23. Ibid., Articles 35–37.

24. European Convention for the Protection of Human Rights and Fundamental Freedoms (adopted November 4, 1950, 213 UNTS 2, entered into force September 3, 1953), as amended by Protocol 11 (1998) and Protocol 14 (2010); American Convention on Human Rights (adopted November 22, 1969, 1144 UNTS 143, entered into force July 18, 1978). Article 20 of the African Charter on Human and Peoples' Rights (hereafter Banjul Charter) (adopted June 27, 1981, 1520 UNTS 217, entered into force October 21, 1986) contains a right to self-determination of peoples.

25. Charter of the United Nations (adopted June 26, 1945, 1 UNTS XVI, entered into force October 24, 1945).

26. UNGA Res. 61/295, Declaration on the Rights of Indigenous Peoples, A/RES/61/295, September 13, 2007.

27. Ibid., Article 3.

28. Declaration on Principles of International Law Concerning Friendly Relations and Co-operation Among States in Accordance with the Charter of the United Nations, UNGA Res. 2625 (XXV), October 24, 1970; Martii Koskenniemi, "National Self Determination Today: Problems of Legal Theory and Practice," *International and Comparative Law Quarterly* 43 (1994): 245.

29. Jan Klabbers, "The Right to Be Taken Seriously: Self-Determination in International Law," *Human Rights Quarterly* 28, no. 1 (2006).

30. The Shan peoples have an added degree of autonomy, in a "self-administered zone." Constitution of the Union of the Republic of Myanmar, Article 56.

31. *Philippine Muslim News (Manila)*, July 2, 1968, 7–12: "We do not want to be included in the Philippines for once an independent Philippines is launched, there would be trouble between us and the Filipinos because from time immemorial these two peoples have not lived harmoniously together. Our public land must not be given to people other than the Moros."

32. Andreo Calonzo, "Govt, MILF Agree to Create 'Bangsamoro' to Replace ARMM," *GMA News Online*, October 7, 2012, available at www.gmanetwork.com/news/story/277218/news /nation/govt-milf-agree-to-create-bangsamoro-to-replace-armm.

33. Comprehensive Agreement on Bangsamoro, signed March 27, 2014, available at http:// www.gov.ph/downloads/2014/03mar/20140327-Comprehensive-Agreement-on-the-Bangsamoro .pdf; Ted Regencia, "Philippines Prepares for Historic Peace Deal," *Al Jazeera*, March 25, 2014, available at www.aljazeera.com/indepth/features/2014/03/philippines-prepares-historic-peace -deal-milf-201432411220461644.html.

34. Over the years, the Muslim National Liberation Front (MNLF) has splintered into several factions, including the Moro Islamic Liberation Front (MILF), which currently constitutes

the largest and strongest separatist group. Stanford University, "Mapping Militant Organizations: Moro Islamic Liberation Front" (2015), available at web.stanford.edu/group/mappingmilitants /cgi-bin/groups/view/309. From MILF splintered Bangsamaro Islamic Freedom Fighters (BIFF), which prefers an independent Islamic state rather than an autonomous region and armed struggle rather than peace talks. Stanford University, "Mapping Militant Organizations: Bangsamoro Islamic Freedom Fighters" (2015), available at web.stanford.edu/group/mappingmilitants/cgi -bin/groups/view/601.

35. Regencia, "Philippines Prepares for Historic Peace Deal."

36. Trisha Macas and Analyn Perez, "Infographic: The Proposed Bangsamoro Entity and Its Powers," *GMA News Online*, February 18, 2015, available at http://www.gmanetwork.com/news /story/439259/news/nation/infographic-the-proposed-bangsamoro-entity-and-its-powers.

37. The clashes resulted in the deaths of forty-four police, eighteen MILF soldiers, and three civilians. Simone Orendain, "Philippines, Muslim Rebels Try to Salvage Peace Pact," *VOA News*, March 28, 2015, available at www.voanews.com/a/philippines-muslim-rebels-try-to-salvage -peace-pact/2698026.html. Macas and Perez, "Infographic."

38. Christina Mendez, "Senate Sets New Timeline for BBL Approval," *Philippine Star*, August 4, 2015, available at www.philstar.com/headlines/2015/08/04/148 4327/senate-sets-new-timeline -bbl-approval; Jess Diaz, "Bangsamoro Basic Law Relegated to Backburner," *Philippine Star*, November 21, 2015, available at www.philstar.com/headlines/2015/11/21/1524243/bangsamoro -basic-law-relegated-backburner; Jose Rodel Clapano, "Congress Buries Bangsamoro Bill," *Philippine Star*, February 4, 2016, available at www.philstar.com/headlines/2016/02/04/1549507 /congress-buries-bangsamoro-bill.

39. Jonathan de Santos, "Duterte: Correct Historical Injustice, Pass Bangsamoro Law," *Philippine Star*, July 25, 2016, available at www.philstar.com/headlines/2016/07/25/1606520/duterte -correct-historical-injustice-pass-BBL; Ferdinandh B. Cabrera, "Duterte: Pass BBL and Make Bangsamoro an 'Example' for the Rest to Follow," *Minda News*, February 28, 2016, available at www.mindanews.com/peace-process/2016/02/duterte-pass-bbl-and-make-bangsamoro-an -example-for-the-rest-to-follow/.

40. Joan Carling, "The Cordillera Peoples and the Movement for Regional Autonomy," in *Reclaiming Balance*, ed. Victoria Tauli-Corpuz and Joji Carino (Baguio City, Philippines: Indigenous People's International Centre for Policy Research and Information Tebtebba Foundation, 2004).

41. Vincent Cabreza, "Cordillerans Ponder on Autonomy," *Philippine Daily Inquirer*, July 17, 2012, available at newsinfo.inquirer.net/230458/cordillerans-ponder-on-autonomy.

42. Ibid.

43. Marc Jayson Cayabyab, "Cordillera Lawmakers Revive Autonomy Bid," *Inquirer.net*, September 22, 2014, available at newsinfo.inquirer.net/639893/cordillera-lawmakers-revive -autonomy-bid; Jojo Lamaria, "Act Establishing Cordillera Autonomous Region Filed," *Philippines News Agency*, June 18, 2014, available at www.canadianinquirer.net/2014/06/18/act-establishing -cordillera-autonomous-region-filed/.

44. Thom F. Picaña, "Alliance Finds Cordillera Bill 'Totally Unacceptable,'" *Manila Times*, September 4, 2016, available at www.manilatimes.net/alliance-finds-cordillera-bill-totally -unacceptable/283946/.

45. Carlito C. Dar, "Cordillera as Autonomous Region Within Federal State Possible, Says Pimentel," *Philippine Information Agency*, August 25, 2016, available at http://news.pia.gov.ph /article/view/61471935635/cordillera-as-autonomous-region-within-federal-state-possible-says -pimentel.

46. Aceh was never part of Indonesia. In 1949, when the United Nations brokered an agreement to transfer all the former colonial territory of the Dutch East Indies to the sovereign state of the Federal Republic of Indonesia, Aceh was included in the new republic.

47. On April 25, 1950, the South Moluccas declared independence from Indonesia, a move violently ended by Indonesian troops four months later.

48. UNGA Res. 2504 (XXIV), Agreement Concerning West New Guinea (West Irian), A/RES/2504, December 19, 1969 (Indonesia and the Netherlands).

49. See LBH Apik et al., "AHRD Is Hijacked by Narrow-Minded National Interests," *Burma Partnership*, September 13, 2012, available at http://www.burmapartnership.org/2012/09/ahrd-is -hijacked-by-narrow-minded-national-interests.

50. Singapore is perhaps the exception.

51. Gerard Clarke, "From Ethnocide to Ethnodevelopment? Ethnic Minorities and Indigenous Peoples in Southeast Asia," *Third World Quarterly* 22, no. 3 (2001).

52. For example, in the January 2012 draft, the Preamble stated:

viii. STRESSING the indivisibility of human rights and that civil and political rights, economic, social and cultural rights and right to development should be treated on equal footing with a view to creating conducive environment to achieve the betterment of human rights in the region, and ASEAN's commitment to progressively narrow the development gap among ASEAN Member States through relevant mechanisms; and:

ix. EMPHASIZING the interrelatedness of rights, duties and responsibilities of the human person and the ASEAN common values in the spirit of unity in diversity in the promotion and protection of human rights, while ensuring the balance between such rights, duties and responsibilities, and the primary responsibility to promote and protect human rights and fundamental freedoms, which rests with each Member State.

53. Working draft of the ASEAN Human Rights Declaration, January 8, 2012, clause vii.

54. AHRD, Preamble.

55. AHRD, Articles 1–9 are "General Principles."

56. In the AHRD, "humanity" replaces the word "brotherhood," which is contained in the UDHR.

57. Mary Ann Glendon, "The Forgotten Crucible: The Latin American Influence on the Universal Human Rights Idea," *Harvard Human Rights Journal* 16 (2003).

58. S. P. Sinha, "The Axiology of the International Bill of Human Rights," *Pace International Law Review* 1 (1989): 53.

59. ASEAN Inter-Parliamentary Organisation, Kuala Lumpur Declaration on Human Rights, Kuala Lumpur, September 1993.

60. The Kuala Lumpur Declaration on Human Rights (1993) refers to "everyone."

61. UDHR, Article 1.

62. Article 6 of the ICCPR, referring to the right to life, begins with a reference to "every human being." Article 6 of ICESCR refers to "everyone": for example, "the States Parties to the present Covenant recognize the right to work, which includes the right of everyone to the opportunity to gain his living by work which he freely chooses or accepts, and will take appropriate steps to safeguard this right."

63. For example, the Working Group for an ASEAN Human Rights Mechanism.

64. Jacques Maritain, introduction to *Human Rights Comments and Interpretations: A Symposium*, ed. United Nations Educational, Social and Cultural Organization (New York: Columbia University Press, 1949), 17.

65. The Confucian view of the human person is one where moral duties and rights arise solely from social relationships (father-son, husband-wife, elder brother–younger brother, ruler-ruled, friend-friend). See Joseph Chan, "A Confucian Perspective on Human Rights," in *The East Asian Challenge for Human Rights*, ed. Joanne E. Bauer and Daniel A. Bell (Cambridge: Cambridge University Press, 1999), 217. Peerenboom writes that because human rights are rights to which humans are entitled *from birth*, human beings must be thought of as beings "qua members of a biological species" and not "qua social beings," which is a view deeply incompatible with the Confucian one. R. P. Peerenboom, "What Is Wrong with Chinese Rights? Towards a Theory of Rights with Chinese Characteristics," *Harvard Human Rights Journal* 6 (1993): 40.

66. Saneh Chamarik, *Buddhism and Human Rights* (Bangkok: Thai Khadi Research Institute, 1982); Damien V. Keown, Charles S. Prebish, and Wayne R. Husted, eds., *Buddhism and Human Rights* (Surrey: Curzon Press, 1997); Henry Rosemont, "Why Take Rights Seriously? A Confucian Critique," in *Human Rights and the World's Religions*, ed. Leroy Rounner (Notre Dame, Ind.: University of Notre Dame Press, 1988).

67. Andreas Follesdal, "Human Rights and Relativism," in *Real World Justice: Grounds, Principles, Human Rights Standards and Institutions*, ed. Andreas Follesdal and Thomas Pogge (The Netherlands: Springer, 2005).

68. Abdullahi A. An-Na'im, *Towards an Islamic Reformation: Civil Liberties, Human Rights and International Law* (Syracuse, N.Y.: Syracuse University Press, 1990), 171.

69. Yuyun Wahyuningrum, correspondence with the author, December 19, 2013, copy on file with author.

70. Maritain, introduction, 13.

71. Charles R. Beitz, *The Idea of Human Rights* (Oxford: Oxford University Press, 2009).

72. Richard Rorty, "Human Rights, Rationality and Sentimentality," in *On Human Rights: The Oxford Amnesty Lectures*, ed. S. Shute and S. Hurley (New York: Basic Books, 1993).

73. Thomas Nagel, "Personal Rights and Public Space," in *Deliberative Democracy and Human Rights*, ed. Harold Hongju Koh and Ronald C. Slye (New Haven, Conn.: Yale University Press, 1999), 34.

74. Julia Ching, "Human Rights: A Valid Chinese Concept?" in *Confucianism and Human Rights*, ed. W. M. Theodore de Bary and Tu Weiming (New York: Columbia University Press, 1998), 70–71; Irene Bloom, "Fundamental Intuitions and Consensus Statements: Mencian Confucianism and Human Rights," in *Confucianism and Human Rights*, ed. W. M. Theodore de Bary and Tu Weiming (New York: Columbia University Press, 1998).

75. Joseph Chan, "An Alternative View," *Journal of Democracy* 8, no. 2 (1997). See also J. Cohen, "Minimalism About Human Rights: The Most We Can Hope For?" *Journal of Political Philosophy* 12, no. 2 (2004).

76. Sulak Sivaraksa, *Seeds of Peace: A Buddhist Vision for Renewing Society* (Berkeley, Calif.: Parallax Press, 1992), ch. 9.

77. R. Pannikar, "Is the Notion of Human Rights a Western Concept?" *Diogenes* 30, no. 120 (1982): 75.

78. Simon Jones, "Human Rights in Diverse Cultures," in *Human Rights and Global Diversity*, ed. Simon Caney and Peter Jones (Illford, Essex: Frank Cass Publishers, 2001), 34.

79. Onuma Yasuaki, "Towards an Intercivilizational Approach to Human Rights," in *The East*

Asian Challenge for Human Rights, ed. Joanne E. Bauer and Daniel A. Bell (Cambridge: Cambridge University Press, 1999), 109.

80. Alison Dundes Renteln, "The Unanswered Challenge of Relativism and the Consequences for Human Rights," *Human Rights Quarterly* 7, no. 4 (1985).

81. Charles Taylor, "Conditions of an Unforced Consensus on Human Rights," in *The East Asian Challenge for Human Rights*, ed. Joanne E. Bauer and Daniel A. Bell (Cambridge: Cambridge University Press, 1999), 126.

82. Jack Donnelly, *Universal Human Rights in Theory and Practice* (Ithaca, N.Y.: Cornell University Press, 2003).

83. Bernard Williams, "In the Beginning Was the Deed," in *Deliberative Democracy and Human Rights*, ed. Harold Hongju Koh and Ronald C. Slye (New Haven, Conn.: Yale University Press, 1999), 57.

84. Nagel identifies as some of these things "the maintenance of power by the torture and execution of public dissidents or religious minorities, denial of civil rights to women, [and] total censorship." Nagel, "Personal Rights and Public Space," 83–84.

85. Examples commonly given of the contested scope of core rights are abortion and infanticide, in the context of the right to life. Abortion is at present legal in most Western countries. Centre for Reproductive Rights, "The World's Abortion Laws," available at http://worldabortionlaws.com/map/. In ancient Greece, Plato and Aristotle supported infanticide in cases of weak or deformed infants who might be a burden on the state. B. R. Sharma, "Historical and Medico-Legal Aspects of Infanticide: An Overview," *Medicine, Science and the Law* 46, no. 2 (2006).

86. Jeremy Waldron, "Dignity, Rights, and Responsibilities," *Arizona State Law Journal* 43 (2011).

87. International Gay and Lesbian Human Rights Commission, *Report from the Peoples' Forum in Phnom Penh Cambodia*, April 30, 2012, available at http://iglhrc.wordpress.com/2012/04/30/lgbt-report-from-the-peoples-forum-in-phnom-pehn-cambodia/.

88. International Gay and Lesbian Human Rights Commission, "Inclusion of SOGI Issues and Rights in the ACSC/APF and in the ASEAN Human Rights Declaration," March 29, 2012, available at http://www.iglhrc.org/cgi-bin/iowa/article/takeaction/resourcecenter/1510.html.

89. Azril Mohd Amin, "LGBTIQ Rights Should Be Excluded," letter, September 10, 2012, available at http://www.malaysiakini.com/letters/208463.

90. Alex Au, "Singapore Choosing to be Anti–Human Rights," *Yawning Bread* (blog), September 14, 2012, available at http://yawningbread.wordpress.com/2012/09/14/at-asean-singapore-choosing-to-be-anti-human-rights/#more-8006.

91. Ibid.

92. Wahyuningrum, interview.

93. Nagel, "Personal Rights and Public Space," 42.

94. Draft ASEAN Human Rights Declaration, January 9, 2012, Article 12.

95. Ibid., Article ix.

96. Human Rights Working Group, "Submission on the ASEAN Human Rights Declaration," September 12, 2012.

97. High Commissioner for Human Rights, Statement at the Bali Democracy Forum, November 7, 2012, available at http://www.ohchr.org/en/NewsEvents/Pages/DisplayNews.aspx?NewsID=12752&LangID=E.

98. Mary Ann Glendon, "Knowing the Universal Declaration of Human Rights," *Notre Dame Law Review* 73 (1997): 1162.

99. Ibid.

100. Ninth International Conference of American States, American Declaration of the Rights and Duties of Man, Bogota, Colombia (hereafter American Declaration), May 2, 1948, Preamble. There is also a special section in the American Declaration that emphasizes specific duties: to society; toward children and parents; to vote; to acquire an elementary education; to obey the law; to cooperate with the state and the community with respect to social security and welfare; to pay taxes; and to work. Ch. 2, Articles XXIX–XXXVIII.

101. American Convention on Human Rights, Article 32(1). The Preamble to the International Covenant on Civil and Political Rights also recognizes duties: "the individual having duties to other individuals and to the community to which he belongs, is under a responsibility to strive for the promotion and observance of the rights recognised in the present Covenant." International Covenant on Civil and Political Rights (adopted December 16, 1966, 999 UNTS 171, entered into force March 23, 1976).

102. Banjul Charter. The Preamble recognizes "that the enjoyment of rights and freedoms also implies the performance of duties on the part of everyone," and Articles 27–29 of the charter contain specific duties of individuals.

103. J. J. Paust, "The Other Side of Right: Private Duties Under Human Rights Law," *Harvard Human Rights Journal* 5 (1992): 62.

104. Michael Freeman, "Human Rights, Democracy and 'Asian Values,'" *Pacific Review* 9, no. 3 (1996).

105. Joseph Raz, *The Morality of Freedom* (Oxford: Clarendon, 1986), 166.

106. Amartya Sen, "Elements of a Theory of Human Rights," *Philosophy & Public Affairs* 32, no. 4 (2004).

107. Thomas Pogge, "Cosmopolitanism and Sovereignty," *Ethics* 103, no. 1 (1992).

108. UNESCO, *Human Rights Comments and Interpretations: A Symposium*, 18. The Kuala Lumpur declaration includes a provision on duties, providing that "the peoples of ASEAN recognize that human rights have two mutually balancing aspects: those with respect to rights and freedom of the individual, and those which stipulate obligations of the individuals to society and state; all human beings, individually and collectively, have a responsibility to participate in their total development, taking in account the need for full respect of their human rights as well as their duties to the community. Freedom, progress and national stability are promoted by balance between the rights of the individual and those of the community."

109. Ben Saul, "In the Shadow of Human Rights: Human Duties, Obligations and Responsibilities," *Columbia Human Rights Law Review* 32 (2000).

110. Singapore Parliament, *Shared Values*, White Paper (Singapore: Singapore National Printers, 1991), 3. See N. Balakrishnan, "Esprit de Core: Values Offer Shares in Confucian Society," *Far Eastern Economic Review* 7 (1991): 27.

111. Singapore Parliament, *Shared Values*.

112. Ibid.

113. See Charlene Tan, "Creating 'Good Citizens' and Maintaining Religious Harmony in Singapore," *British Journal of Religious Education* 30, no. 2 (2008); Charlene Tan and Yew Leong Wong, "Moral Education for Young People in Singapore: Philosophy, Policy and Prospects," *Journal of Youth Studies* 13, no. 2 (2010); Beng-Huat Chua, *Communitarian Ideology and Democracy in Singapore* (London: Routledge, 1995); Beng-Huat Chua, "The Cost of Membership in Ascribed Community," in *Multiculturalism in Asia*, ed. Will Kymlicka and Baogang He (Oxford: Oxford University Press, 2005).

114. Mahathir Mohamad, "Speech to World Youth Foundation," in *Human Rights: Views of Dr. Mahathir Mohamad* (Kuala Lumpur, Melaka: World Youth Foundation, 1999).

115. Yash Ghai, "Human Rights and Governance: The Asia Debate," *Asia-Pacific Journal of Human Rights and the Law* 1, no. 1 (2000).

116. Neil Englehart, "Rights and Culture in the Asian Values Argument: The Rise and Fall of Confucian Ethics in Singapore," *Human Rights Quarterly* 22, no. 2 (2000).

117. Ronald Dworkin, *Taking Rights Seriously* (London: Duckworth, 1977), xi.

118. Jeremy Waldron, "Rights in Conflict," *Ethics* 99, no. 3 (1989): 508.

119. Rhoda Howard and Jack Donnelly, "Human Dignity, Human Rights, and Political Regimes," *American Political Science Review* 80, no. 3 (1986).

120. Ibid.

121. Human Rights Working Group, "Submission on the ASEAN Human Rights Declaration," September 12, 2012, Article 29: "Every person shall have duties towards his/her family, community, State and the international community."

122. CSOs viewed as particularly problematic Malaysia's statement in the draft ASEAN Declaration of January 9, 2012, which proposed an article stating: "The parameters of the enjoyment and exercise of human rights and fundamental freedoms [are] dependent on the fulfilment of duties and responsibilities towards other individuals, societies, future generations and the State." Vietnam put forward a proposal that stated: "The rights of persons are inseparable from their duties. The State protects these rights and the persons fulfil their duties towards the State and society." Draft declaration, January 9, 2012, Article 27.

123. Glendon, "Knowing the Universal Declaration of Human Rights."

124. UNGA, World Conference on Human Rights, Vienna Declaration and Programme of Action, A/CONF.157/23, June 25, 1993, Article 5.

125. James W. Nickel, "Rethinking Indivisibility: Towards a Theory of Supporting Relations Between Human Rights," *Human Rights Quarterly* 30, no. 4 (2008); L. J. Laplante, "On the Indivisibility of Rights: Truth Commissions, Reparations, and the Right to Develop," *Yale Human Rights and Development Law Journal* 10 (2007).

126. International Conference on Human Rights, Final Act of the International Conference on Human Rights: Proclamation of Teheran, A/CONF. 32/41, April 22–May 13, 1968.

127. Amartya Sen, *The Idea of Justice* (Cambridge, Mass.: Harvard University Press, 2009).

128. Ibid.

129. Heraldo Muñoz, "The Right to Democracy in the Americas," *Journal of Inter-American Studies and World Affairs* 40, no. 1 (1998).

130. Nickel, "Rethinking Indivisibility."

131. Even social and economic rights have minimum core elements that are immediately enforceable. Philip Alston and Gerard Quinn, "The Nature and Scope of States Parties' Obligations Under the International Covenant on Economic, Social and Cultural Rights," *Human Rights Quarterly* 9, no. 2 (1987): 156.

132. Sunai Phasuk, senior researcher at Human Rights Watch Thailand, quoted in Sok Khemara, "Mixed Reviews of ASEAN Human Rights Declaration," *VOA Khmer*, December 19, 2012, available at http://www.voacambodia.com/content/mixed-reviews-of-asean-rights-declaration/1567319.html.

133. The 1993 Kuala Lumpur Declaration contains a slightly different phrase, referring in its preamble to "changing economic, social, political and cultural realities."

134. Kuala Lumpur Declaration (1993), Preamble.

135. AHRD, Article 29(1).

136. Ibid., Article 8.

137. I do not consider the addition of "public health" and "public security" to be substantive additions, given that the ICCPR permits limitations on grounds of public security and public health (as well as public order and morals), in relation to certain rights (one of which is *not* freedom of thought, conscience, and religion).

138. UDHR, Article 29(2): "In the exercise of his rights and freedoms, everyone shall be subject only to such limitations as are determined by law solely for the purpose of securing due recognition and respect for the rights and freedoms of others and of meeting the just requirements of morality, public order and the general welfare in a democratic society."

139. European Convention for the Protection of Human Rights and Fundamental Freedoms (adopted November 4, 1950, 213 UNTS 2, entered into force September 3, 1953), as amended by Protocol 11 (1998) and Protocol 14 (2010).

140. Arab Charter on Human Rights (adopted September 15, 1994, entered into force March 15, 2008), Articles 24 and 31.

141. For example, Article 41 of the 1993 constitution of Cambodia provides in relation to freedom of expression that Khmer citizens have freedom of expression, press, publication, and assembly. No one may exercise this right to infringe upon the rights of others, to affect the good traditions of the society, or to violate public law and order and national security; Article 28J of the 2002 constitution of the Republic of Indonesia permits the limitation of some rights on the basis of "morality, religious values, security and public order in a democratic society"; Article 44 of the Amended Constitution of the Lao's People's Democratic Republic provides that Lao citizens have the right and freedom of speech, have the right to press and assembly, and have the right to set up associations and to stage demonstrations, which are not contrary to the laws. The constitution of Malaysia (1957), Article 10(2), permits restrictions on the rights of expression, assembly, and association on the grounds of morality (among other things).

142. The Southeast Asia Women's Caucus on ASEAN, "Submission on the ASEAN Human Rights Declaration," October 21, 2011, available at http://womenscaucusonasean.wordpress.com /2011/10/25/full-text-womens-caucus-submission-on-ahrd-on-aichr/.

143. Asia Pacific Forum on Women, Law and Development, "Adding Value: Removing Morality from the ASEAN Human Rights Declaration" (2011). See APWLD Annual Report 2012, available at apwld.org/wp-content/uploads/2013/09/ANNUAL_REPORT_2012.pdf.

144. Ibid. In their submission, the Asia Pacific Forum on Women's Law and Development drew attention to the comments of the Human Rights Committee, which had stated that "the concept of morals derives from many social, philosophical, and religious traditions; consequently, limitations on the freedom to manifest a religion or belief for the purpose of protecting morals must be based on principles not deriving exclusively from a single tradition." UN Human Rights Committee, General Comment No. 22: Article 18 (Freedom of Thought, Conscience or Religion), CCPR/C/21/Rev.1/Add.4, July 30, 1993, available at http://www.refworld.org/docid /453883fb22.html.

145. *Toonen v. Australia*, Communication No. 488/1992, CCPR/C/50/D/488/1992 (1994).

146. Julia Suryakusuma, "Gays Are Us: LGBT Rights Are Human Rights," *Jakarta Post*, October 31, 2012, available at http://www.thejakartapost.com/news/2012/10/31/viewpoint-gays-are -us-lgbt-rights-are-human-rights.html.

147. Lao People's Democratic Republic Penal Law (1990), Articles 117 and 119, available at http://www.asianlii.org/la/legis/laws/pl199076.pdf.

148. Ibid., Article 121: "Any monk or novice who commits a sexual act with a female or male person shall be punished by 6 months to 3 years' imprisonment and shall be fined 500,000–3,000,000 kip."

149. Ibid., Article 127: "Dissemination of Pornographic objects and objects contrary to fine tradition: any person engaging in the widespread production, distribution or dissemination of pornographic items, magazines or pictures, video cassettes, or other materials contrary to fine traditions, shall be punishable by 3 months to one year imprisonment and 300,000 to 5,000,000 kip."

150. Section 6.

151. Nonetheless, in 2010, the Supreme Court of the Philippines reversed a decision of the electoral commission, which refused to accredit an LGBT organization called Ang Ladlad as a political party on the grounds of its "immoral doctrines." *Ladlad LGBT Party v. Commission on Elections* (Rep. of the Philippines S.C.), G.R. No. 190582, April 8, 2010, 4–5. The commission had based its decision on moral grounds. According to the commission, Ang Ladlad advocated "immoral doctrines," and if the commission accredited it as a political party, it would be failing in its constitutional duty "to protect our youth from moral and spiritual degradation." The Supreme Court reversed the decision on grounds of equal protection and freedom of expression.

152. Constitution of the Socialist Republic of Vietnam, 1992, Article 64.

153. Penal Code of Singapore, Section 377A.

154. Ibid., Section 294.

155. Ibid., Section 298.

156. Ibid., Section 377.

157. International Lesbian, Gay, Bisexual, Trans and Intersex Association, "LGBT Groups Call for Burma's Penal Code to Be Amended," December 8, 2013, available at http://ilga.org/ilga/en/article/opoqnVe1uh.

158. Article 3 of the Malaysian constitution also provides that other religions may be practiced in peace and harmony.

159. Penal Code of Malaysia, Section 377A. This section provides that "any person who has sexual connection with another person by the introduction of the penis into the anus or mouth of the other person is said to commit carnal intercourse against the order of nature."

160. Sylvia Tan, "Gay Sex Acts Should Not Be Criminalised: Malaysian Bar Council Human Rights Committee," *Fridae*, August 13, 2009, available at http://www.fridae.asia/newsfeatures/2009/08/13/8773.gay-sex-acts-should-not-be-criminalised-malaysian-bar-council-human-rights-committee?n=sec.

161. The Southeast Asian Women's Caucus on ASEAN, "ASEAN Human Rights Declaration Limited by 'Morality' Say Women's Organisations," statement, Chiang Mai, Thailand, November 19, 2012.

162. In 2000, *Time* magazine published an interview with Abdul Kadir Che Kob, a government official in Malaysia's Islamic Affairs Department. Kadir was quoted as saying: "Homosexuals are shameless people." The interviewer asked Abdul Kadir if people should not have the right to choose whom they want to be with. He replied: "What right are you talking about? This is sin, end of story. How can men have sex with men? God did not make them this way. This is all Western influence." "Homosexuality Is a Crime Worse than Murder," *Time*, September 26, 2000, available at http://www.time.com/time/world/article/0,8599,2040451,00.html.

163. Tan, "Gay Sex Acts Should Not Be Criminalised." Tan reports that there have been seven charges under Section 377 of the penal code since 1938. Of the seven, four were connected to Anwar Ibrahim. Anwar Ibrahim, former deputy prime minister, was convicted of sodomy and corruption in 1998. The sodomy conviction was overturned in 2004.

164. Hafidz Baharom Najib, "LGBTs, Liberalism, Pluralism Are Enemies of Islam," *Malaysian Insider*, July 19, 2012, available at http://www.themalaysianinsider.com/malaysia/article/najib-lgbts-liberalism-pluralism-are-enemies-of-islam.

165. "Malaysia's Anwar Ibrahim Denies Supporting Homosexuality," *Hindustan Times*, July 19, 2012, available at http://www.hindustantimes.com/world-news/RestOfAsia/Malaysia-s-Anwar-Ibrahim-denies-supporting-homosexuality/Article1-891801.aspx.

166. Samar Habib, ed., *Islam and Homosexuality* (Santa Barbara, Calif.: Praeger, 2010), 11.

167. An-Na'im, *Towards an Islamic Reformation*.

168. This is according to the official 2000 census data on religious preference. U.S. Department of State, Bureau of Democracy, Human Rights and Labor, Philippines: International Religious Freedom Report 2004, available at http://www.state.gov/j/drl/rls/irf/2004/35425.htm.

169. "Excommunication for Philippines President 'a Possibility,' Bishop States," *Catholic News Agency*, October 6, 2010, available at http://www.catholicnewsagency.com/news/excommunication-for-philippines-president-a-possibility-in-contraception-dispute-bishop-states/.

170. Julius Bautista, "Church and State in the Philippines: Tackling Life Issues in a 'Culture of Death,'" *SOJOURN: Journal of Social Issues in Southeast Asia* 25, no. 1 (2010): 29.

171. Ibid.

172. Ibid.

173. Sylvia Estrada-Claudio, "Voices and Choices in Reproductive Rights: Scholarship and Activism," in *The Social Sciences in the Asian Century*, ed. Carol Johnson, Vera Mackie, and Tessa Morris-Suzuki (Canberra: Australian National University Press, 2015).

174. World Conference on Human Rights, Report of the Regional Meeting for Asia of the World Conference on Human Rights, A/Conf.1 57/ASRM/ 8A/Conf.157/PC/59, April 7, 1993 (Bangkok Declaration), Article 3: "Stress the urgent need to democratize the United Nations system, eliminate selectivity and improve procedures and mechanisms in order to strengthen international cooperation, based on principles of equality and mutual respect, and ensure a positive, balanced and non-confrontational approach in addressing and realizing all aspects of human rights"; Article 7: "Stress the universality, objectivity and non-selectivity of all human rights and the need to avoid the application of double standards in the implementation of human rights and its politicization, and that no violation of human rights can be justified."

175. These consultations took place September 10–11, 2012.

176. AHRD, Article 28(f).

177. Ibid., Article 35.

178. Ibid., Article 38.

179. For example, the Preamble to the 1967 Bangkok Declaration includes the following, along with several other references to peace: "DESIRING to establish a firm foundation for common action to promote regional cooperation in South-East Asia in the spirit of equality and partnership and thereby contribute towards peace, progress and prosperity in the region."

180. Charter of the Association of Southeast Asian Nations (adopted November 20, 2007, entered into force December 15, 2008), Article 1.

181. It is notable that the Banjul Charter mentions the right to peace only as a right of

peoples. The Banjul Charter does, however, specifically name the right to national (domestic) peace as well as international peace.

182. International Federation for Human Rights, "Civil Society Rejects Flawed ASEAN Human Rights Declaration," press release, November 15, 2012, available at http://www.fidh.org /Civil-society-rejects-flawed-ASEAN-12429.

183. "ASEAN Declaration Falls Short on Human Rights: UN," *Australian Broadcasting Corporation News*, November 9, 2012, available at http://www.abc.net.au/news/2012-11-09/an-un -hr-high-commissioner-warns-on-asean-declaration/4364384.

184. AHRD, Preamble.

Part II

1. In 1989, the government of Burma changed the English-language name of the country from "Burma" to "Myanmar." Throughout this chapter, I use "Burma" when referring to events before 1988 and "Myanmar" for the post-1989 period. According to Nardi, this usage reflects accepted academic practice in Burmese studies. Dominic Nardi, "Discipline-Flourishing Constitutional Review: A Legal and Political Analysis of Myanmar's New Constitutional Tribunal," *Australian Journal of Asian Law* 12, no. 1 (2010): 27.

Chapter 4

1. UN General Assembly, Convention on the Elimination of All Forms of Discrimination Against Women, 1249 UNTS 13, December 18, 1979, available at http://www.refworld.org/docid /3ae6b3970.html (hereafter the Convention). There were ten abstentions; the Convention entered into force in 1981.

2. Ibid., Preamble.

3. Beth Simmons, *Mobilizing for Human Rights: International Law in Domestic Politics* (New York: Cambridge University Press, 2011), 205–6.

4. Equality between men and women is, of course, mentioned in other postwar human rights instruments, such as the Preamble to the United Nations Charter.

5. The Convention, Article 2(f).

6. CEDAW, Report of the Committee on the Elimination of All Forms of Discrimination Against Women, Eighteenth and Nineteenth Sessions, A/53/38/Rev. 1, May 14, 1998, 6.

7. United Nations Entity for Gender Equality and the Empowerment of Women (UN Women), Convention on the Elimination of All Forms of Discrimination Against Women: Reservations to CEDAW, available at http://www.un.org/womenwatch/daw/cedaw/reservations .htm.

8. The CEDAW Committee passed a resolution at its eighth session in Vienna in 1989 expressing concern that this issue be on its agenda and instructing states to include in their periodic reports information about statistics, legislation, and support services in this area. CEDAW Newsletter, 3rd issue, A/44/38, April 13, 1989, 2 (Summary of U.N. Report on the Eighth Session, UN Doc. A/44/38, April 14, 1989).

9. CEDAW, General Recommendations Nos. 9, 10, 11, 12, and 13, adopted at the Eighth Session, A/44/38 (1989), available at http://www.refworld.org/docid/453882aa10.html; CEDAW, General Recommendations Nos. 19 and 20, adopted at the Eleventh Session, A/47/38 (1992), available at http://www.refworld.org/docid/453882a422.html.

10. Optional Protocol to the Convention on the Elimination of All Forms of Discrimination Against Women (adopted October 6, 1999, 2131 UNTS 83, entered into force December 22, 2000).

11. UNGA, World Conference on Human Rights, Vienna Declaration and Programme of Action, A/CONF.157/23, June 25, 1993, Article 18.

12. UNGA Res. 48/104, Declaration on the Elimination of Violence Against Women, A/RES/48/104, December 20, 1993.

13. See Simmons, *Mobilizing for Human Rights*, 208.

14. Rome Statute of the International Criminal Court (adopted July 17, 1998, 2187 UNTS 3, entered into force July 1, 2002), Article 7(1)(g).

15. UN Security Council, Resolution 1820 on acts of sexual violence against civilians in armed conflicts, S/RES/1820, June 19, 2008, available at http://www.refworld.org/docid/3b00f4672e.html; UN Security Council, Security Council Resolution 1820 [on acts of sexual violence against civilians in armed conflicts], June 19, 2008, S/RES/1820 (2008), available at http://www.refworld.org/docid/485bbca72.html.

16. Doris Buss and Ambreena Manji, introduction to *International Law: Modern Feminist Approaches*, ed. Doris Buss and Ambreena Manji (Oxford: Hart Publishing, 2005).

17. UNGA Res. 48/104, Declaration on the Elimination of Violence Against Women, A/RES/48/104, December 20, 1993.

18. Cambodia, Indonesia, the Philippines, and Vietnam signed the Convention in 1980.

19. Optional Protocol to the Convention on the Elimination of All Forms of Discrimination Against Women. Indonesia has signed but not ratified the protocol.

20. See Singapore Parliament, *Shared Values*, White Paper (Singapore: Singapore National Printers, 1991).

21. See Maila Stivens, "'Family Values' and Islamic Revival: Gender, Rights and State Moral Projects in Malaysia," *Women's Studies International Forum* 29, no. 4 (2006): 354–67.

22. Ryan Goodman and Derek Jinks, "How to Influence States: Socialization and International Human Rights Law," *Duke Law Journal* 54, no. 3 (2004).

23. Martha Finnemore and Kathryn Sikkink, "International Norm Dynamics and Political Change," *International Organization* 52, no. 4 (1998).

24. Steffanie Scott and Truong Thi Kim Chuyen, "Gender Research in Vietnam: Traditional Approaches and Emerging Trajectories" (Paper presented at the Women's Studies International Forum, Canberra, Australia, 2003); Stephanie Fahey, "Vietnam's Women in the Renovation Era," in *Gender and Power in Affluent Asia*, ed. Krishna Sen and Maila Stivens (New York: Routledge, 1998).

25. William Turley, "Women in the Communist Revolution in Vietnam," *Asian Survey* 12, no. 9 (1972): 799.

26. Beth Simmons, "From Ratification to Compliance," in *The Persistent Power of Human Rights: International Norms and Domestic Change*, ed. Thomas Risse, Stephen C. Ropp, and Kathryn Sikkink (Cambridge: Cambridge University Press, 2013), 52.

27. On Thailand's withdrawal of reservations to Article 16, see Ministry of Foreign Affairs of the Kingdom of Thailand, "Thailand Withdraws Its Reservation to Article 16 of the Convention on the Elimination of Discrimination against Women," press release, July 26, 2012, available at http://www.mfa.go.th/main/en/media-center/14/25491-Thailand-withdraws-its-reservation-to-Article-16-o.html. On reservations generally, see Jennifer Riddle, "Making CEDAW Universal: A Critique of CEDAW's Reservation Regime Under Article 28 and the Effectiveness of the Reporting Process," *George Washington International Law Review* 34 (2002): 625–28; on ASEAN states' reservations specifically, see Susan Linton, "ASEAN States, Their Reservations to Human Rights Treaties and the Proposed ASEAN Commission on Women and Children," *Human Rights Quarterly* 30, no. 2 (2008).

28. SUHAKAM, *Annual Report 2005*, available at https://drive.google.com/file/d/0B6FQ 7SONa3PRMEw4dmtjSkY3cUU/edit.

29. Muzaffar Syah Mallow, "CEDAW in Malaysia," *Cherie Blair*, March 3, 2013, available at cherieblair.org/speeches/2013/03/cedaw-in-malaysia.html.

30. Laos submitted a combined initial, second, third, fourth, and fifth periodic report in 2003 (reviewed in the 32nd session of the CEDAW Committee, 2005). A combined sixth and seventh periodic report was submitted in 2008 (reviewed in the 44th session of the CEDAW Committee, 2009).

31. CEDAW Committee, "Consideration of Reports Submitted by States parties under Article 18 of the Convention—Initial and Second Periodic Reports of States Parties Due in 2011— Brunei Darussalam," CEDAW/C/BRN/1-2, November 1, 2013, available at http://tbinternet .ohchr.org/_layouts/treatybodyexternal/Download.aspx?symbolno=CEDAW%2fC%2fBRN%2f1 -2&Lang=en; CEDAW Committee, "Concluding Observations on the Combined Initial and Second Periodic Reports of Brunei Darussalam," CEDAW/C/BRN/CO/1-2, November 14, 2014, available at http://tbinternet.ohchr.org/_layouts/treatybodyexternal/Download.aspx?symbolno =CEDAW%2fC%2fBRN%2fCO%2f1-2&Lang=en.

32. In General Recommendation No. 11, the CEDAW Committee pointed out that as of March 3, 1989, 96 states had ratified CEDAW but that only 60 initial and 19 second periodic reports had been received and that 36 initial and 36 second periodic reports were due but had not yet been received. UN Women, Convention on the Elimination of All Forms of Discrimination Against Women General Recommendations, Eighth Session (1989), available at http://www .un.org/womenwatch/daw/cedaw/recommendations/recomm.htm#recom11.

33. See Thomas Risse, Stephen C. Ropp, and Kathryn Sikkink, eds., *The Power of Human Rights: International Norms and Domestic Change* (Cambridge: Cambridge University Press, 1999).

34. Simmons, "From Ratification to Compliance," 53.

35. See, in relation to Laos, CEDAW/C/LAO/CO/7 para. 9; see, in relation to the Philippines, CEDAW/C/PHI/CO/6.

36. This is so, even though in Cambodia, the constitution stipulates recognition of and respect for international human rights agreements. Article 45.1 of the constitution calls for the abolition of all forms of discrimination against women, and under the constitution the Convention takes precedence over domestic law. Yet there is no evidence in practice that the Convention is regarded as self-executing.

37. CEDAW Committee, Indonesia: Concluding Comments, A/53/38/Rev. 1 (1998), [276].

38. See, for example, *Marcos v. Commission on Elections* (Rep. of the Philippines S.C.), GR. No. 119976, September 18, 1995.

39. *Chayed bin Basirun & Ors v Noorfadilla bt Ahmad Saikin, Malayan Law Journal* 1 (2012): 832. See Christopher Leong, Malaysian Bar Council, "A Right Step in a Long and Unfinished Journey," press release, June 30, 2013, available at http://www.malaysianbar.org.my/press_statements /press_release_a_right_step_in_a_long_and_unfinished_journey.html.

40. Simmons, "From Ratification to Compliance," 53.

41. Simmons, *Mobilizing for Human Rights*.

42. The Article stipulates that the prohibition applies in relation to the holding or disposition of property or establishing or carrying on of any trade, business, profession, vocation, or employment.

43. Constitution of Malaysia (Amendment) Act 2001, Act A1130. See SUHAKAM, Report on the Status of Women's Rights in Malaysia (2010), available at http://www.suhakam.org.my/wp

-content/uploads/2013/11/SUHAKAM-Report-on-The-Status-of-Women-s-Rights-in-Malaysia -2010.pdf. In its initial report to CEDAW in 2004, Malaysia stated that as a consequence of this amendment, all existing laws were being reviewed in order to ensure gender equality, including the Domestic Violence Act 1994; the Penal Code; the Criminal Procedure Code; the Evidence Act; the Law Reform (Marriage and Divorce) Act 1976; and the Land (Group Settlement Areas) Act 1960. CEDAW, Consideration of Reports Submitted by States Parties under Article 18 of the Convention on the Elimination of All Forms of Discrimination Against Women Combined Initial and Second Periodic Reports of States Parties—Malaysia, CEDAW/C/MYS/1-2, April 14, 2004, available at http://daccess-dds-ny.un.org/doc/UNDOC/GEN/N04/309/80/PDF/N0430980 .pdf?OpenElement.

44. In the court hierarchy, the High Court of Malaysia sits below the Federal Court and the Court of Appeal.

45. The Court in *Noorfadilla* took note of recent correspondence between the Malaysian government and the United Nations, in which the government pledged its continued commitment to CEDAW.

46. Bangalore Principles of Judicial Conduct (2002), reported in UN Commission on Human Rights, Report of the Special Rapporteur on the independence of judges and lawyers, Annex E/CN.4/2003/65, January 10, 1993, Article 7. See Michael Kirby, "Implementing the Bangalore Principles on Human Rights Law," *South African Law Journal* 106 (1989).

47. *Minister for Immigration and Ethnic Affairs v. Teoh*, 128 ALR 353 (1995).

48. *Vishaka v. State of Rajasthan AIR*, SC 3011 (1997).

49. Isabelle Law, "Malaysian Bar Wants Specific Anti–Gender Discrimination Laws," *Nation*, June 30, 2013, available at http://www.thestar.com.my/News/Nation/2013/06/30/Malaysian-Bar -wants-specific-anti-gender-discrimination-laws.aspx.

50. *Beatrice Fernandez v. Sistem Penerbangan Malaysia & Anor*, Civil Appeal No. W-02-186-96, October 5, 2004. A clause in the flight attendant's employment contract required her to resign on becoming pregnant and gave the company the right to terminate her services if she refused to do so.

51. Malaysian Bar Council Report, "Gender Discrimination: Beatrice Fernandez v. Sistem Penerbangan Malaysia & Anor 2004 [CA]," October 5, 2004, available at http://www.malaysianbar.org .my/selected_judgements/gender_discrimination_beatrice_fernandez_v._sistem_penerbangan _malaysia_anor_2004_ca.html.

52. The Court in the *Fernandez* case was at this point quoting from Dr. (Justice) Durga Das Basu in his book *Comparative Constitutional Law*.

53. Anne-Marie Slaughter, *A New World Order* (Princeton, N.J.: Princeton University Press, 2004), 102.

54. In *Fernandez*, counsel for the appellant attempted to rely on the Indian Supreme Court case *Air India v. Nergesh Meerza*, 68 AIR 1829 (SC) (1981).

55. Polygamy is also practiced in Laos by ethnic groups. See Gender and Development Group, Statement to CEDAW session (2008), available at http://www2.ohchr.org/english/bodies /cedaw/docs/ngos/GDG_Laos_44.pdf. See also Ann Black, "The Re-positioning of Women in Brunei," in *Mixed Blessings: Laws, Religions and Women's Rights in the Asia-Pacific Region*, ed. Amanda Whiting and Carolyn Evans (Leiden: Martinus Nijhoff, 2006), 222 ; Rafiq A. Tschannen, "Malaysian State Mulls Reward for 'Good' Muslim Husbands in Polygamous Marriages," *Muslim Times*, October 1, 2013, available at http://www.themuslimtimes.org/2011/06/religion/islam /malaysian-state-mulls-reward-for-good-muslim-husbands-in-polygamous-marriages.

56. Sharifah Mahsinah Abdullah and Nik Nur Aisyah Nik Len, "Looking for the Ideal Polygamist," *New Straits Times*, July 30, 2013, available at http://www.nst.com.my/nation/general/looking-for-the-ideal-polygamist-1.329251#ixzz2izf6j9lx.

57. Sisters in Islam, "Focus on Effective Enforcement of Polygamy Laws," press statement, July 30, 2013, available at http://www.sistersinislam.org.my/news.php?item.1191.7.

58. CEDAW, Consideration of Reports Submitted by States Parties Under Article 18 of the Convention: Malaysia, CEDAW/C/SR.732, July 13, 2006, [43]. As part of the discussion about what constitutes justice and fairness, SIS referred to the results of a study carried out in 2009: "The Impact of Polygamy on the Family Institution in the Klang Valley (Malaysia)," in which the Malaysian-based Islamic women's organization Musawah interviewed 1,500 husbands, first wives, subsequent wives, and children on their experience of the impact of polygamy, from a financial, social, and emotional perspective. Musawah, "Impact of Polygamy on the Family Institution" (2009), available at http://www.musawah.org/sites/default/files/CEDAW%20%26%20Muslim%20Family%20Laws.pdf; Jo-Ann Ding, "The Impact of Polygamy in Malaysia," *Nut Graph*, July 21, 2010, available at http://www.thenutgraph.com/the-impact-of-polygamy-in-malaysia/.

59. In General Recommendation No. 21, the CEDAW Committee stated that "polygamous marriage contravenes a woman's right to equality with men, and can have such serious emotional and financial consequences for her and her dependents that such marriages ought to be discouraged and prohibited." UN Committee on the Elimination of Discrimination Against Women, CEDAW General Recommendation No. 21: Equality in Marriage and Family Relations (1994), available at http://www.refworld.org/docid/48abd52c0.html, para. 14.

60. Musawah, "Impact of Polygamy on the Family Institution."

61. The demand of feminist groups is that issues "are approached holistically, integrating human rights and Islamic principles in a dynamic and constantly evolving process." Ibid.

62. Ibid.

63. Rasidah Hab and Rachel Thien, "HM Questions Delay in Syariah Law Enforcement," *Brunei Times*, February 28, 2016, available at www.bt.com.bn/frontpage-news-national/2016/02/28/hm-questions-delay-syariah-law-enforcement. The initial phase introduces fines or jail terms for offenses including indecent behavior, failure to attend Friday prayers, disrespecting the month of Ramadan, propagating religions other than Islam, and out-of-wedlock pregnancies. This phase was introduced in May 2014. A second phase covering crimes such as theft and robbery was introduced in 2016, involving more stringent penalties such as severing limbs and flogging. The third phase of the legislation is the introduction of the death penalty (death by stoning) for offenses including sodomy and adultery. This phase was scheduled to be introduced in 2018. See Anti-Death Penalty Asia Network, "Brunei: Update on Shariah Penal Code and Death Penalty," June 9, 2016, available at https://adpan.org/2016/06/09/brunei-update-on-Shariah-penal-code-and-death-penalty/.

64. Women Living Under Muslim Laws, "Brunei Darussalam: Fundamental Rights and Freedoms Violated Under the New Shari'a Penal Code," October 29, 2013, available at http://www.wluml.org/action/brunei-darussalam-fundamental-rights-and-freedoms-violated-under-new-shari%E2%80%99-penal-code.

65. Ibid. At the time of writing, Brunei still has not signed or ratified the ICCPR. Brunei signed the United Nations Convention Against Torture on September 22, 2015, but has not ratified it.

66. "Sultan of Brunei Introduces Tough Islamic Laws," *Channel News Asia*, October 22, 2013, available at http://www.channelnewsasia.com/news/asiapacific/sultan-of-brunei/856914.html.

67. The International Gay and Lesbian Human Rights Commission, the Global Initiative to End All Corporal Punishment of Children, and the International Commission of Jurists presented pre-session reports. The global Islamic NGO Musawah presented an oral statement at the hearing.

68. Rabiatul Kamit and Bandars Eri Begawan, "Rights of Women Protected in Brunei," *Brunei Times*, November 2, 2014, available at http://www.bt.com.bn/news-national/2014/11/02 /rights-women-protected-brunei.

69. These restrictions include prohibiting women from riding straddle on motorcycles (Circular 2 of 2013, Government of Lhoksemauwe, Aceh) and from wearing tight clothing. See Answer Styannes, "Achieving Substantive Gender Equality in Indonesia," *Ethics in Action* 7, no. 1 (February 2013), available at http://www.ethicsinaction.asia/archive/2013-ethics-in-action /2013V7N1/2013V7N1P7.

70. Elisabeth Oktofani, Khabar Southeast Asia, "ACEH Women Say They Suffer Discrimination," June 18, 2013, available at https://oktofani.com/category/khabar-southeast-asia/.

71. See CEDAW/C/IDN/CO/6-7.

72. See Permanent Mission of the Republic of Indonesia, Communication from Permanent Mission of the Republic of Indonesia to the United Nations New York, 424/SOC-301/Viii/12, August 6, 2012.

73. Ibid., 32.

74. In relation to Laos, see Prime Ministers Decree No. 26/PM of February 6, 2006, on the Implementation of the Law and Development and Protection of Women. The CEDAW Committee has pointed out that there is in this document no definition of "discrimination" that encompasses both direct and indirect discrimination, in accordance with Article 1 of the Convention CEDAW/C/LAO/CO/7. In relation to Vietnam, see Law on Gender Equality 2006.

75. The Philippines, Republic Act 9710.

76. Gender Equality Act 2015, B.E. 2558 (Thailand).

77. Organizations opposed to the bill include the influential Indonesian Ulema Council, the Indonesian Consultative Council for Muslim Women Organizations, Aisyiah, Hizbut Tahrir Indonesia, and the Islamic Community Party. See "Indonesia Islamists Stall Gender Equality Bill," *Jakarta Globe*, May 9, 2012, http://www.thejakartaglobe.com/archive/indonesia-islamists-stall -gender-equality-bill/.

78. UNGA Res. 48/104, Declaration on the Elimination of Violence Against Women, A/RES/ 48/104, December 20, 1993.

79. See the Philippines Anti-Violence Against Women and Their Children Act of 2004; Law of the Republic of Indonesia Regarding Elimination of Violence in the Household 2004, No. 23/2004; the Thai Protection of Domestic Violence Victims Act, B.E. 2550 (2007); Vietnam's Law on Domestic Violence Prevention and Control 2007, 02/2007/QH12; Cambodia's 2005 Law on the Prevention of Domestic Violence and Protection of Victims; Laos Decree on the Promulgation of the Law on Development and Protection of Women 2004, No. 70/PO; Malaysia's Domestic Violence Act 1994; and Singapore's Women's Charter (Amendment) Bill 1996. In 2010, Brunei made amendments to the Married Women Act and the Islamic Family Law Order (1999) to provide new provisions relating to *dhararsyarie* (domestic violence). Some of these laws, like Indonesia's, do not refer to rape or marital rape; see CEDAW/C/IDN/CO/6-7 para. 25(d). In September 2013, Myanmar's Ministry of Social Welfare, Relief and Resettlement announced that it was drafting a domestic violence law, to be enacted in 2014. "Ministry Drafting Law on Domestic Violence," *Myanmar Times*, August 4, 2013, available at http://www.mmtimes.com/index.

php/national-news/7705-ministry-drafting-law-on-domestic-violence.html. The draft National Law on Protection and Prevention of Violence Against Women was still under review in July 2017. "New Bill to Seek More Protection for Women," *Myanmar Times*, September 25, 2017, available at https://www.mmtimes.com/news/new-bill-seek-more-protection-women.html.

80. Margaret E. Keck and Kathryn Sikkink, *Activists Beyond Borders: Advocacy Networks in International Politics* (Cambridge: Cambridge University Press, 1998).

81. UN Women, "Domestic Violence Legislation and Its Implementation: An Analysis for ASEAN Countries Based on International Standards and Good Practices" (2011), available at http://cedaw-seasia.org/docs/DomesticViolenceLegislation.pdf.

82. CEDAW Committee, Consideration of Reports Submitted by States Parties Under Article 18 of the Convention: Malaysia, CEDAW/C/SR.732, July 13, 2006, [54].

83. CEDAW Committee, "Indonesia: List of Issues and Questions," CEDAW/C/IDN/Q/5/Add.1 (2007), 25.

84. Lucinda Peach, "Sex or Sangha? Non-normative Gender Roles," in *Mixed Blessings: Law, Religion and Women's Rights in the Asia-Pacific Region*, ed. Amanda Whiting and Carolyn Evans Martinus (Leiden: Martin Nijhoff, 2006), 27–29.

85. Li-Ann Thio, "She's a Woman but She Acts Very Fast," in *Mixed Blessings: Law, Religion and Women's Rights in the Asia-Pacific Region*, ed. Amanda Whiting and Carolyn Evans Martinus (Leiden: Martin Nijhoff, 2006), 241–78.

86. CEDAW, Consideration of Reports Submitted by States Parties Under Article 18 of the Convention: Thailand, CEDAW/SR.708, February 9, 2006, [54].

87. Ronald Inglehart and Pippa Norris, *Rising Tide: Gender Equality and Cultural Change Around the World* (Cambridge: Cambridge University Press, 2003).

88. At that time, ASEAN had five members: Indonesia, Malaysia, the Philippines, Singapore, and Thailand.

89. Originally, the ASEAN Women's Leaders Conference had planned to create an "ASEAN Confederation of Women." The confederation did not eventuate, but the following year, the ASEAN Sub-Committee on Women (ASW) was established. In 1981, the ASW was renamed the ASEAN Women's Program. In 1999, the ASEAN Women's Program was given a new name, the ASEAN Committee on Women (ACW). See ASEAN Committee on Women, "Third Report on the Advancement of Women in ASEAN" (2007), available at http://www.asean.org/images/2012/Social_cultural/ACW/publications/Third%20Report%20on%20the%20Advancement%20of%20Women%20in%20ASEAN.pdf.

90. ASEAN, *Report of the ASEAN Women Leaders and International Women's Year Post Conference Meeting*, Jakarta, December 19–22, 1975, 161.

91. The point was reiterated by Professor Soenawar Soekawati, Indonesia's Special Minister for People's Welfare for the Republic of Indonesia. *Report of the ASEAN Women's Leaders and International Women's Year Post Conference Meeting*, Jakarta, December 19–22, 1975.

92. Ibid.

93. Carolyn I. Sobritchea, "Women's Movement in the Philippines and the Politics of Critical Collaboration with the State," in *Civil Society in Southeast Asia*, ed. Lee Hock Guan (Singapore: Institute of Southeast Asian Studies, 2004).

94. Aida F. Santos, "The Philippine Women's Movement: Problems of Perception" (Paper presented at the Seminar to Prepare the Alternative Philippine Report on the Impact of the Decade for Women, Quezon City, 1984), quoted in Sobritchea, "Women's Movement in the Philippines and the Politics of Critical Collaboration with the State," 103–4.

95. See A. Claire Cutler, "Artifice, Ideology and Paradox: The Public/Private Distinction in International Law," *Review of International Political Economy* 4, no. 2 (1997).

96. Ibid. Cf. Kathleen Barry, *Vietnam's Women in Transition* (New York: St. Martin's Press, 1996), 2.

97. Anne Orford, "Contesting Globalization: A Feminist Perspective on the Future of Human Rights," *Transnational Law & Contemporary Problems* 8 (1988).

98. Maila Stivens, "Introduction: Gender Politics and the Reimagining of Human Rights in the Asia Pacific," in *Human Rights and Gender Politics: Asia Pacific Perspectives*, ed. Martha Macintyre, Vera Mackie, and Maila Stivens (London: Routledge, 2000), 19.

99. Declaration of the Advancement of Women in the ASEAN Region, Bangkok, Thailand, July 5, 1988.

100. Ibid., Preamble.

101. Ibid., Article 2.

102. Ibid., Article 4.

103. Ibid., Article 5.

104. The third and most recent report, published in 2007, focuses on the impact of globalization on women, particularly the effect of market reforms and economic development.

105. Declaration on the Elimination of Violence Against Women in the ASEAN Region, Jakarta, Indonesia, June 30, 2004.

106. UNGA Res. 48/104, Declaration on the Elimination of Violence Against Women, A/RES/48/104, December 20, 1993.

107. Terms of Reference of the ASEAN Commission on the Promotion and Protection of the Rights of Women and Children (2010) (hereafter TOR ACWC), Article 2(1).

108. ACWC was inaugurated during the 16th ASEAN Summit in 2010.

109. ACWC has twenty representatives from ten ASEAN member states. Ten representatives deal with the rights of women, ten with the rights of children.

110. ACWC's TOR are similar to those of the ASEAN Intergovernmental Commission on Human Rights, in that they specify that the rights of women and children must be understood, "taking into consideration the different historical, political, sociocultural, religious and economic context in the region and the balances between rights and responsibilities." TOR ACWC, Article 2. Like the TOR of AICHR, ACWC's TOR also refer to respect for the principles embodied in Article 2 of the ASEAN Charter (which include respect for the independence, sovereignty, equality, territorial integrity, and national identity of all ASEAN member states and noninterference in the internal affairs of ASEAN member states). TOR ACWC, Article 2(1)(e). ASEAN Secretariat News, "Sixth Press Release of the ASEAN Commission on the Promotion and Protection of the Rights of Women and Children (ACWC)," April 3, 2013, available at http://www.asean.org/news/asean-secretariat-news/item/sixth-press-release-of-the-asean-commission-on-the-promotion-and-protection-of-the-rights-of-women-and-children-acwc.

111. ASEAN Declaration on the Elimination of Violence Against Women and Elimination of Violence Against Children in ASEAN, Twenty-Third ASEAN Summit, October 9, 2013.

112. UNGA Res. 48/104, Declaration on the Elimination of Violence Against Women, A/RES/48/104, December 20, 1993.

113. ASEAN Declaration on the Elimination of Violence Against Women and Elimination of Violence Against Children in ASEAN, Twenty-Third ASEAN Summit, October 9, 2013, Article 3.

114. Ibid., Preamble.

115. Ibid., Article 3. CSOs objected to the DEVWC, arguing that there had been no consultation on the contents of the declaration, despite the remit of the ACWC in its TOR to adopt a collaborative and consultative approach with civil society. They also objected to the inclusion of the phrases "taking into consideration the different historical, political, socio-cultural, religious and economic context in the region" and "balances between rights and responsibilities." In the end, the latter phrase was removed in the final draft of the DEVWC. Women's Caucus on ASEAN, "SAPA and Women Caucus Appeals ACWC to Share Finalized DEVAW/EVAC Draft," September 4, 2013, available at http://womenscaucusonasean.wordpress.com/; Amnesty International, Amnesty International's Briefing to the ASEAN Commission for the Promotion and Protection of the Rights of Women and Children on the Draft ASEAN Declaration on the Elimination of Violence Against Women and Children, May 2013, available at http://www.amnesty.org/es/library/asset /IOR64/001/2013/en/bb68d82a-eade-4cc6-a10f-f1d896e2e40d/ior640012013en.pdf.

116. Ha Noi Declaration on the Enhancement of Welfare and Development of ASEAN Women and Children, Ha Noi, Vietnam, October 28, 2010.

117. ASEAN Human Rights Declaration, Phnom Penh, Cambodia, November 18, 2012.

118. Charlotte Bunch, "Women's Rights as Human Rights: Toward a Re-vision of Human Rights," *Human Rights Quarterly* 12, no. 4 (1990): 492.

119. Ibid. Catharine MacKinnon has put the argument in perhaps its strongest terms: Catharine A. MacKinnon, "Rape, Genocide, and Women's Human Rights," *Harvard Women's Law Journal* 17, no. 5 (1994): 6.

120. Office of the Special Advisers on Gender Issues and Advancement of Women, *Gender Mainstreaming: An Overview* (2002), available at http://www.un.org/womenwatch/osagi/pdf /e65237.pdf; Office of the Special Adviser on Gender Issues and Advancement of Women, *Gender Mainstreaming: Strategy for Gender Equality* (2001), available at http://www.un.org/womenwatch /osagi/pdf/factsheet1.pdf.

121. The slogan was "women's rights are human rights" and the principle was that gender equality concerned men as much as it did women. Sari Kouvo, "The United Nations and Gender Mainstreaming: Limits and Possibilities," in *International Law: Modern Feminist Approaches*, ed. Doris Buss and Ambreena Manji (Oxford: Hart Publishing, 2005).

122. UN Commission on Human Rights, UN Doc CN4/1988/49, para. 8.

123. Bunch, "Women's Rights as Human Rights," 496.

124. See Therese Murphy, "Feminism Here and Feminism There: Law, Theory and Choice," in *International Law: Modern Feminist Approaches*, ed. Doris Buss and Ambreena Manji (Oxford: Hart Publishing, 2005), 67–86; Stivens, "'Family Values' and Islamic Revival." But see Avigail Eisenberg's work on precisely this endeavor in the Canadian context. Avigail Eisenberg, "Context, Cultural Difference, Sex and Social Justice," *Canadian Journal of Political Science* 35, no. 3 (2002); Avigail Eisenberg, "Diversity and Equality: Three Approaches to Cultural and Sexual Difference," *Journal of Political Philosophy* 11, no. 1 (2003); Avigail Eisenberg, *Diversity and Equality: The Changing Framework of Freedom in Canada* (Cambridge: Cambridge University Press, 2006).

125. Simmons, *Mobilizing for Human Rights*, 254.

126. Ibid., 255.

127. Gill Jagger and Caroline Wright, *Changing Family Values: Difference, Diversity and the Decline of Male Order* (New York: Routledge, 1999). The role of women was seen as essential to "moulding happy families." Stivens, "'Family Values' and Islamic Revival."

Chapter 5

1. Protocol to Prevent, Suppress and Punish Trafficking in Persons, Especially Women and Children, Supplementing the United Nations Convention against Transnational Organized Crime (adopted November 15, 2000, 2237 UNTS 319, entered into force December 25, 2003) (hereafter the Trafficking Protocol). See Anne T. Gallagher, *The International Law of Human Trafficking* (New York: Cambridge University Press, 2010), 36.

2. Ralf Emmers, Beth K. Greener, and Nicholas Thomas, "Securitising Human Trafficking in the Asia-Pacific," in *Security and Migration in Asia: The Dynamics of Securitisation*, ed. Siu-lun Wong and Melissa G. Curley (London: Routledge, 2008), 77.

3. ASEAN, "ASEAN Welcomes Entry into Force of ACTIP," press release, March 8, 2017, available at http://asean.org/asean-welcomes-entry-into-force-of-actip/.

4. A. Murray, "Debt-Bondage and Trafficking: Don't Believe the Hype," in *Feminist Post-Colonial Theory: A Reader*, ed. Reina Lewis and Sarah Mills (New York: Routledge, 1988).

5. Ibid.

6. United Nations Office on Drugs and Crime, Global Report on Trafficking in Persons, Vienna (2012).

7. Ruchira Gupta, "Human Trafficking in Asia: Trends and Responses," in *On the Move: Migration Challenges in the Indian Ocean Littoral*, ed. Ellen Laipson and Amit Pandya (Washington, D.C.: Henry L. Stimson Center, 2010), 69

8. Pierre Le Roux, "A Lethal Funnel: Prostitution and Trafficking for Women for Sexual Exploitation in Southeast Asia," in *Trade in Human Beings for Sex in Southeast Asia*, ed. Pierre Le Roux, Jean Baffie, and Gilles Beullier (Bangkok: White Lotus Company, 2010), 145.

9. United Nations Office on Drugs and Crime, Global Report on Trafficking in Persons, Vienna (2012); Cheah Wuiling, "Assessing Criminal Justice and Human Rights Models in the Fight Against Sex Trafficking: A Case Study of the ASEAN Region," *Essex Human Rights Review* 3, no. 1 (2006).

10. The Trafficking Protocol is one of three protocols attached to the Convention Against Transnational Organized Crime (adopted November 15, 2000, 2225 UNTS 209, entered into force September 29, 2003). Anne Gallagher, "Human Rights and the New UN Protocols on Trafficking and Migrant Smuggling: A Preliminary Analysis," *Human Rights Quarterly* 23 (2001): 976.

11. Trafficking Protocol, Article 4.

12. Convention Against Transnational Organised Crime, Article 2(b).

13. Trafficking Protocol, Articles 10(1)(a), 11(1)–(6), 12, 13.

14. Ibid., Article 3(a). See Phil Williams, "Trafficking in Women: The Role of Transnational Organised Crime," in *Trafficking in Humans: Social, Cultural and Political Dimensions*, ed. Sally Cameron and Edward Newman (New York: United Nations University Press, 2008), 133.

15. Trafficking Protocol, Article 3(b).

16. Ibid., Article 3(a), definition of trafficking in persons: "Exploitation shall include, at a minimum, the exploitation of the prostitution of others or other forms of sexual exploitation, forced labour or services, slavery or practices similar to slavery, servitude or the removal of organs." Gallagher, "Human Rights and the New UN Protocols on Trafficking and Migrant Smuggling," 984–85.

17. Victims of Trafficking and Violence Protection Act (TVPA) of 2000 [United States of America], Public Law 106-386 [H.R. 3244], October 18, 2000, available at http://www.refworld.org/docid/3ae6b6104.html.

18. TVPA, Sections 102(a) and (b).

19. Ibid., Section 108(a).

20. Ibid., Section 108(b).

21. United States Department of State, Trafficking in Persons Reports, available at http://www.state.gov/j/tip/rls/tiprpt/index.html.

22. Ibid. In 2008, the reauthorization of the TVPA established a two-year time limit for the Tier 2 watch list because previous practices allowed countries to remain indefinitely on this tier classification without incurring sanctions.

23. United Nations Convention against Transnational Organised Crime, Article 32(1); Conference of Parties to the United Nations Convention against Transnational Organised Crime, Decision 1/5, Protocol to Prevent, Suppress and Punish Trafficking in Persons, Especially Women and Children, Supplementing the United Nations Convention Against Transnational Organized Crime (adopted November 15, 2000, 2237 UNTS 319, entered into force December 25, 2003), reproduced in Conference of Parties to the United Nations Convention Against Transnational Organised Crime, "Report of the Conference of Parties to the United Nations Convention on Transnational Organised Crime on its first session, held in Vienna from June 28 to July 8, 2004," OTOC/COP/2004/6 (September 23, 2004), 5. The Organised Crime Convention establishes a Conference of Parties with the power to review implementation of the Convention, request and receive information on implementation of the Trafficking Protocol, and make recommendations to improve the protocol and its implementation. Gallagher, *The International Law of Human Trafficking*, 469.

24. TVPA, Section 110.

25. United States Department of State, "Trafficking in Persons Report 2003" (June 2003), available at http://www.state.gov/j/tip/rls/tiprpt/2003/index.html.

26. TVPA, Section 100 (b)(3).

27. Anne Gallagher, "A Shadow Report on Human Trafficking in Lao PDR: The U.S. Approach v. International Law," *Asian and Pacific Migration Journal* 16, no. 1 (2007): 531.

28. Ibid., 549.

29. Ibid., 550.

30. Janie Chuang, "The United States as Global Sheriff: Using Unilateral Sanctions to Combat Human Trafficking," *Michigan Journal of International Law* 27, no. 2 (2006).

31. Ashley Blackburn, Robert W. Taylor, and Jennifer Elaine Davis, "Understanding the Complexities of Human Trafficking and Child Sexual Exploitation: The Case of Southeast Asia," *Women & Criminal Justice* 20, no. 1–2 (2010).

32. United Nations Treaty Series (2237 UNTS 319, UN Doc A/55/383, 2000), available at https://treaties.un.org/doc/Publication/MTDSG/Volume%20II/Chapter%20XVIII/XVIII-12-a.en.pdf.

33. Ralf Emmers, "The Threat of Transnational Crime in Southeast Asia: Drug Trafficking, Human Smuggling and Trafficking, and Sea Piracy" (Research Unit on International Security and Cooperation [UNISCI] Discussion Paper, February 27, 2009), 5.

34. An example of this kind of work can be found in Michele Ford, Lenore Lyons, and Willem van Schendel, eds., *Labour Migration and Human Trafficking in Southeast Asia: Critical Perspectives* (Oxford: Routledge, 2012).

35. Sverre Molland, "The Inexorable Quest for Trafficking Hot-spots Along the Thai-Lao Border," in *Labour Migration and Human Trafficking in Southeast Asia: Critical Perspectives*, ed. Michele Ford, Lenore Lyons, and Willem van Schendel (Oxford: Routledge, 2012). See also R. Väyrynen, "Illegal Immigration, Human Trafficking, and Organised Crime Discussion Paper

No. 2003/72" (Helsinki: United Nations University, World Institute for Development Economics Research, 2003).

36. Sverre Molland, " 'The Perfect Business': Human Trafficking and Lao-Thai Cross-Border Migration," *Development and Change* 41, no. 5 (2010): 848; Sverre Molland, "The Value of Bodies: Deception, Helping and Profiteering in Human Trafficking Along the Thai-Lao Border," *Asian Studies Review* 34, no. 2 (2010): 222.

37. A. Derks, R. Henke, and L. Y. Vanna, *Review of a Decade of Research on Trafficking in Persons in Cambodia* (Phnom Penh: Centre for Advanced Study, 2006).

38. Thierry Bouhours, Roderic Broadhurst, Chenda Keo, and Brigitte Bouhours, "Human Trafficking and Moral Panic in Cambodia: The Unintended Consequences of Good Intentions," December 17, 2012, available at http://papers.ssrn.com/sol3/papers.cfm?abstract_id=2190704.

39. Trafficking Protocol, Article 3.

40. Blackburn, Taylor, and Davis, "Understanding the Complexities of Human Trafficking and Child Sexual Exploitation"; Larissa Sandy, "Sex Work in Cambodia: Beyond the Voluntary/ Forced Dichotomy," *Asian and Pacific Migration Journal* 15, no. 4 (2006); M. B. Mills, "Contesting the Margins of Modernity: Women, Migration and Consumption," *American Ethnologist* 24, no. 1 (1997).

41. Molland, "The Inexorable Quest for Trafficking Hot-spots Along the Thai-Lao Border"; Mely Caballero-Anthony, "Human Trafficking and Human Rights in Asia: Trends, Issues and Challenges," in *Cross Border Governance in Asia: Regional Issues and Mechanisms*, ed. G. Shabbir Cheema, Christopher McNally, and Vesselin Popovski (New York: United Nations University Press, 2011), 219; Ford, Lyons, and van Schendel, *Labour Migration and Human Trafficking in Southeast Asia*.

42. Didier Bertrand, "Migrations and Trafficking in the Lao PDR: Contextual Analysis of Sexual Exploitation and Victimisation," in *Trade in Human Beings for Sex in Southeast Asia*, ed. Pierre Le Roux, Jean Baffie, and Gilles Beullier (Bangkok: White Lotus Company, 2010), 159.

43. Blackburn, Taylor, and Davis, "Understanding the Complexities of Human Trafficking and Child Sexual Exploitation."

44. Susan Kneebone and Julie Debeljak, "Combating Transnational Crime in the Greater Mekong Subregion: The Cases of Laos and Cambodia," in *Trafficking and Human Rights: European and Asian Perspectives*, ed. Leslie Holmes (Cheltenham, UK: Edward Elgar Publishing Limited, 2010), 137.

45. Ibid., 140.

46. Thongchai Winichakul, *Siam Mapped: A History of the Geo-Body of a Nation* (Bangkok: Silkworm Books, 1994), 73; Pierre-Arnaud Chouvy, "Illegal Trades Across Mainland Borders of Southeast Asia," in *Trade in Human Beings for Sex in Southeast Asia*, ed. Pierre Le Roux, Jean Baffie, and Gilles Beullier (Bangkok: White Lotus Company, 2010), 312.

47. Kneebone and Debeljak, "Combating Transnational Crime in the Greater Mekong Subregion," 137.

48. Zhang Juan, "A Trafficking 'Not-Spot' in a China-Vietnam Border Town," in *Labour Migration and Human Trafficking in Southeast Asia: Critical Perspectives*, ed. Michele Ford, Lenore Lyons, and Willem van Schendel (Oxford: Routledge, 2012).

49. Bertrand, "Migrations and Trafficking in the Lao PDR"; José Edgardo Gomez Jr., Nittana Southiseng, John Walsh, and Samuel Sapuay, "Reaching Across the Mekong: Local Socioeconomic and Gender Effects of Lao-Thai Cross-Border Linkages," *Journal of Current Southeast Asian Affairs* 30, no. 3 (2011).

50. Laos prohibits trafficking under the penal code. Article 134 of the code prohibits all forms of human trafficking and prescribes penalties ranging from five years to life imprisonment, fines ranging from 10 to 100 million kip ($1,250 to $12,500), and confiscation of assets. In 2015, specific anti-trafficking legislation was drafted.

51. The Philippines, Republic Act 9208.

52. The Philippines, Republic Act 10364.

53. Michael Lim Ubac, "Aquino Signs Expanded Anti-trafficking Law," *Philippine Daily Inquirer*, February 14, 2013, available at http://globalnation.inquirer.net/64303/aquino-signs-expanded-anti-trafficking-law.

54. Trafficking and Smuggling of Persons Order, 2004 (No. S 82), Government Gazette, 2004–12–22, Part II, No. 43, 2651–62.

55. Trafficking Protocol refers at Article 3 to "the threat or use of force or other forms of coercion, of abduction, of fraud, of deception, of the abuse of power or of a position of vulnerability or of the giving or receiving of payments or benefits to achieve the consent of a person having control over another person, for the purpose of exploitation." Section 4 of the Brunei Trafficking and Smuggling of Persons Order refers to "(a) threat; (b) use of force or other forms of coercion; (c) abduction; (d) fraud; (e) deception; (f) abuse of power or of a position of vulnerability; (g) the giving or receiving of payments or benefits to achieve the consent of a person having control over another person."

56. The Anti-Trafficking in Persons Law (The State Peace and Development Council Law No. 5/2005) (The Waxing Day of Tawthalin, 1367, M.E.) (September 2005), Section 3(a).

57. Ibid., Section 3(a), "Explanation": "Exploitation includes receipt or agreement for receipt of money or benefit for the prostitution of one person by another, other forms of sexual exploitation, forced labour, forced service, slavery, servitude, debt-bondage or the removal and sale of organs from the body."

58. Anti-Trafficking in Persons Act 2007, Act 670 Part V, Section 13(a)–(h) (Malaysia).

59. Ibid., Section 2.

60. Ibid., Sections 16, 25–26.

61. The Anti-Trafficking in Persons Act 2008, B.E 2551.

62. Measures in Prevention and Suppression of Trafficking in Women and Children Act 1997, B.E 2540.

63. Anti-Trafficking in Persons Act, Section 4.

64. Cambodia, NS/RKM/0208/005.

65. Socialist Republic of Vietnam Law No. 66/2011/QH12 on Human Trafficking Prevention and Combat. See "New Law in Vietnam to Tackle Changing Face of Human Trafficking," *Voice of America*, November 28, 2011, available at http://www.voanews.com/content/new-law-in-vietnam-to-tackle-changing-face-of-human-trafficking-134671708/168246.html.

66. Prevention of Human Trafficking Act 2014, Singapore.

67. B. J. Murphy, "Anti-Trafficking Activities to Combat Human Trafficking Held in Champasak," *Lao People's Democratic Republic: The Rise of Socialist Laos* (blog), December 21, 2012, available at http://laospdrnews.wordpress.com/category/anti-trafficking/.

68. Memorandum on Cooperation in Preventing and Combating Trafficking in Persons and Protection of Victims of Trafficking, November 3, 2010 (Lao PDR and Vietnam).

69. Memorandum on Bilateral Cooperation in Eliminating Trafficking in Children and Women and Assisting Victims of Trafficking, May 31, 2003 (Cambodia and Thailand).

70. Memorandum of Understanding on Cooperation to Combat Trafficking in Persons, Especially Women and Children, July 13, 2005 (Thailand and Lao PDR).

71. Agreement on Bilateral Cooperation for Eliminating Trafficking in Women and Children and Assisting Victims of Trafficking, October 10, 2005 (Cambodia and Vietnam).

72. Memorandum of Understanding on Cooperation to Combat Trafficking in Persons, Especially Women and Children, April 24, 2009 (Myanmar and Thailand).

73. Agreement on Cooperation to Eliminate Trafficking in Persons, March 24, 2008 (Thailand and Vietnam).

74. Memorandum of Understanding on Strengthening the Cooperation on Combating Human Trafficking, November 11, 2009 (Myanmar and China).

75. Treaty on Extradition, Bangkok, May 6, 1998 (Thailand and Cambodia).

76. T. A. Borzel and T. Risse, "Human Rights in Areas of Limited Statehood," in *The Persistent Power of Human Rights: From Commitment to Compliance*, ed. Thomas Risse, Stephen C. Ropp, and Kathryn Sikkink (Cambridge: Cambridge University Press, 2013).

77. Jeffrey Checkel, "Why Comply? Social Learning and European Identity Change," *International Organization* 55, no. 3 (2001).

78. A similar argument underpins Simmons's work on compliance: Beth Simmons, *Mobilizing for Human Rights* (Cambridge: Cambridge University Press, 2009).

79. James G. March and Johan P. Olsen, "The Institutional Dynamics of International Political Orders," *International Organization* 52, no. 4 (1998).

80. Emanuel Adler and Michael Barnett, eds., *Security Communities* (Cambridge: Cambridge University Press, 1998).

81. Neha Misra, "The National Plan of Action," undated, available at http://www.solidarity center.org/files/IndoTraffickingPlan%20of%20Action.pdf.

82. Chuang, "The United States as Global Sheriff," 467.

83. United States Department of State, "Trafficking in Persons Report 2006," June 2006, available at http://www.state.gov/j/tip/rls/tiprpt/2006/index.html.

84. Yuyun Wahyuningrum, "Gender Politics in Trafficking Discourses in Indonesia" (Paper presented at the International Conference on Mainstreaming Human Security: Asia Contribution, Bangkok, October 4–5, 2007), copy on file with author.

85. ASEAN Trade Union Council, "ASEAN Convention on Human Trafficking Sought," press release, July 13, 2011, available at http://aseantuc.org/2011/07/asean-convention-on-human -trafficking-sought/.

86. Michael Lim Ubac, "Stricter Anti–Human Trafficking Law Signed," *Philippine Daily Inquirer*, February 13, 2013, available at http://www.philstar.com/headlines/2013/02/13/908396 /stricter-anti-human-trafficking-law-signed.

87. ASEAN Trade Union Council, press release.

88. Ubac, "Aquino Signs Expanded Anti-trafficking Law."

89. "Thailand Serious About Combating Human Trafficking and Protecting Victims," *Inside Thailand*, January 17, 2013, available at http://thailand.prd.go.th/view_news.php?id=6606 &a=2.

90. Gallagher, *The International Law of Human Trafficking*, 485. Gallagher writes: "Some of these responses have been highly problematic in human rights terms, a side effect that is not explored or even acknowledged by the U.S. Department of State's reports themselves."

91. "Singapore Urges U.S. to Adopt More Objective Methodology in Human Trafficking

Report," *Xinhua Singapore*, June 26, 2013, available at http://www.kpl.net.la/english/E-newspaper /2013/June/26.pdf.

92. United States Department of State, "United States–Myanmar Joint Plan on Trafficking in Persons," November 18, 2012, available at http://www.state.gov/r/pa/prs/ps/2012/11/200675.htm.

93. Chuang, "The United States as Global Sheriff."

94. Judy Hemming and Nicola Piper, "Trafficking and Human Security in Southeast Asia: A Sociological Perspective" (2004), available at http://www.idss-nts.org/theme_illegal3.htm; Alese Wooditch, "The Efficacy of the Trafficking in Persons Report: A Review of the Evidence," *Criminal Justice Policy Review* 22, no. 4 (2011).

95. United States Department of State, "Trafficking in Persons Report 2005," June 2005, available at http://www.state.gov/j/tip/rls/tiprpt/2005/index.html.

96. United States Department of State, "Trafficking in Persons Report 2006."

97. See United States Department of State, "Trafficking in Persons Report 2012," June 2012, available at http://www.state.gov/j/tip/rls/tiprpt/2012/index.html.

98. Gallagher, "A Shadow Report on Human Trafficking in Lao PDR."

99. Jose Alvarez, "Do States Socialize?" *Duke Law Journal* 54, no. 4 (2005): 969.

100. Ryan Goodman and Derek Jinks, "Social Mechanisms to Promote International Human Rights: Complementary or Contradictory?" in *The Persistent Power of Human Rights: From Commitment to Compliance*, ed. Thomas Risse, Stephen C. Ropp, and Kathryn Sikkink (Cambridge: Cambridge University Press, 2013), 106.

101. Ibid.

102. Ibid.

103. Ibid.

104. Ibid., 111.

105. Ibid., 114.

106. Ibid., 112.

107. Ibid., 114.

108. Declaration on the Elimination of Violence Against Women in the ASEAN Region, Jakarta, Indonesia, June 30, 2004.

109. Vientiane Action Program, Tenth ASEAN Summit, Vientiane, Lao PDR, November 29, 2004.

110. ASEAN Declaration Against Trafficking in Persons, Particularly Women and Children, Vientiane, Lao PDR, November 29, 2004.

111. Ibid., Preamble.

112. ASEAN Inter-Parliamentary Organization, Resolution on the Role of Parliament in Combating Trafficking in Women and Children in the ASEAN Region, 25th General Assembly, Phnom Penh, Cambodia, September 12–17, 2004.

113. AICHR, "Five-Year Work Plan of the ASEAN Intergovernmental Commission on Human Rights (2010–2015)" (2012), available at http://aichr.org/?dl_name=AICHR_Five-Year _Work_Plan_2012-2015.pdf; ASEAN Commission on the Promotion and Protection of the Rights of Women and Children (ACWC) Work Plan (2012–16) and Rule of Procedure (2012), available at http://srsg.violenceagainstchildren.org/sites/default/files/political_declarations/The -ASEAN-Commission-on-the-Promotion-and-Protection-of-the-Rights-of-Women-and -Children-ACWC-Work-Plan-2012-2016-and-Rules-of-Procedures-ROP.pdf. In 2016, the ACWC reported that it was conducting a "Regional Review of the Laws, Policies and Practices within ASEAN Member States Relating to the Identification and Treatment of Victims of Trafficking,

especially Women and Children," led by Lao PDR. See ASEAN Commission on Women and Children, press release, February 22, 2016, available at http://asean.org/press-release-of-the-asean-commission-on-the-promotion-and-protection-of-the-rights-of-women-and-children-acwc-2/.

114. ASEAN, Joint Communiqué of the Sixth ASEAN Ministerial Meeting on Transnational Crime (AMMTC) (2007), available at http://cil.nus.edu.sg/rp/pdf/2007%20Joint%20Communique%20of%20the%206th%20ASEAN%20MM%20on%20Transnational%20Crime-pdf.pdf.

115. ASEAN, "ASEAN Welcomes Entry into Force of ACTIP," press release.

116. In 1997, on the thirtieth anniversary of ASEAN, ASEAN leaders adopted "the ASEAN Vision 2020," foreshadowing the community: ten years later, the date for its birth was accelerated to 2015. Cebu Declaration on the Acceleration of the Establishment of an ASEAN Community by 2015, Cebu, Philippines, January 13, 2007. Each of the ASEAN pillars has its own blueprint, and together, these blueprints form the Roadmap for an ASEAN Community 2009–15.

117. ASEAN Economic Community, available at http://www.aseansec.org/18757.htm.

118. Charter of the Association of Southeast Asian Nations (adopted November 20, 2007, entered into force December 15, 2008), Article 1(6).

119. Phil Marshall, "Globalization, Migration and Trafficking: Some Thoughts from the Southeast Asian Region" (Paper presented to the Globalization Workshop, Kuala Lumpur, May 8–10, 2001), available at http://www.childtrafficking.com/Docs/marshall_uniap_mekong_2001_.pdf).

120. Jim Rolfe, "Pursuing Comprehensive Security: Linkages Between National and Regional Concepts, Some Applications," in *Conceptualizing Asia-Pacific Security*, ed. Mohamad Jawhar Hassan and Thangam Ramnath (Kuala Lumpur: Institute of Strategic and International Studies, 1996).

121. David Dewitt, "Common, Comprehensive, and Cooperative Security," *Pacific Review* 7, no. 1 (1994).

122. Mutthiah Alagappa, "Comprehensive Security: Interpretations in ASEAN Countries," in *Asian Security Issues: Regional and Global*, ed. Robert A. Scalapino et al. (Berkeley: University of California, Institute of East Asian Studies, 1988), 62.

123. Declaration of ASEAN Concord, First ASEAN Summit, Bali, Indonesia, Association of Southeast Asian Nations, February 24, 1976.

124. ASEAN, Treaty of Amity and Cooperation in Southeast Asia Indonesia, February 24, 1976, Article 11.

125. The Declaration of ASEAN Concord, First ASEAN Summit, February 24, 1976, called for "intensification of cooperation among member states as well as with the relevant international bodies in the prevention and eradication of the abuse of narcotics and the illegal trafficking of drugs." Subsequently, the ASEAN Declaration of Principles to Combat the Abuses of Narcotics Drugs (June 16, 1976) was adopted in Manila, and this led to some initial proposals in responding to the issue of narcotics.

126. Alagappa, "Comprehensive Security."

127. ASEAN, Joint Declaration for a Drug-Free ASEAN, Manila, July 25, 1998.

128. Ibid., [44].

129. Speech by His Excellency Fidel V. Ramos at the Meeting of ASEAN Ministers of Interior/Home Affairs (AMIHA) and First Conference to Address Transnational Crimes, Manila, Philippines, December 20, 1997.

130. ASEAN, Joint Communiqué of the 30th ASEAN Ministerial Meeting, Subang Jaya, Malaysia, July 15, 1997, available at http://www.asean.org/communities/asean-political-security -community/item/joint-comminuque-the-30th-asean-ministerial-meeting-amm-2.

131. ASEAN Declaration on Transnational Crime, Manila, Philippines, December 20, 1997.

132. ASEAN, "Plan of Action to Combat Transnational Crime" (1997), available at http:// cil.nus.edu.sg/rp/pdf/1999%20ASEAN%20Plan%20of%20Action%20to%20Combat%20 Transnational%20Crime-pdf.pdf.

133. In July 1996, the ASEAN Ministerial Meeting (AMM) declared that transnational crimes included drug trafficking and money laundering: ASEAN, Joint Communiqué of the 29th ASEAN Ministerial Meeting Jakarta, July 20–21, 1996, available at http://www.asean.org/communities /asean-political-security-community/item/joint-communique-of-the-29th-asean-ministerial -meeting-amm-jakarta-20-21-july-1996. Ralf Emmers, "Globalization and Non-Traditional Security Issues: A Study of Human and Drug Trafficking in East Asia," IDSS Working Papers, no. 62 (2004): 18; ASEAN, "Responses to Trafficking in Persons: Ending Impunity for Traffickers and Securing Justice for Victims" (2006): 81.

134. "Malaysia to Erect Wall Along Thai-Malaysian River Border," Thailand Construction News, September 28, 2013, available at http://www.thailand-construction.com/news/903 -construction-news/1642-malaysia-to-erect-wall-along-thai-malaysian-river-border-.html. See Emmers, "The Threat of Transnational Crime in Southeast Asia."

135. Quoted in Wahyuningrum, "Gender Politics in Trafficking Discourses in Indonesia," 16.

136. "Indonesia Belum Serius Antisipasi Perdagangan Manusia" [Indonesia Is Not Yet Serious in Anticipating Human Trafficking Problem], www.detiknews.com, August 26, 2006, quoted in Rizal Sukma, "Different Treatment: Women Trafficking in the Securitisation of Trans-National Crimes" (Paper presented at the 2nd NTS Convention, Beijing, November 9–11, 2008), available at http://www.rsis-ntsasia.org/activities/conventions/2008-beijing/rizal.pdf.

137. Surin Pitsuwan, "ASEAN Keynote Address Vision 20/20: Strengthening Human Security in the Aftermath of the Economic Crisis," in The Quest for Human Security: The Next Phase of ASEAN? ed. Pranee Thriparat (Bangkok: Institute of International and Security Studies, 2001); Amitav Acharya, "Human Security: East Versus West," International Journal 56, no. 3 (2001).

138. The 2008 ASEAN Charter establishes the ASEAN Political-Security Council to coordinate the work of the ASEAN foreign ministers meeting, the ASEAN Law Ministers Meeting, and the ASEAN Ministerial Meeting on Transnational Crime. ASEAN, "ASEAN Political-Security Community Blueprint" (2008), available at http://law.nus.edu.sg/sybil/downloads/articles/SYBIL -2008/SYBIL-2008-281.pdf.

139. The conference was organized by the government of Thailand in cooperation with the Office of the High Commissioner for Human Rights and the International Office for Migration and attended by ministers and government representatives from all ASEAN states and from other states within the broader Asia Pacific region.

140. See Joakim Palme and Kristof Tamas, eds., Globalizing Migration Regimes: New Challenges to Transnational Cooperation (Aldershot: Ashgate, 2006).

141. Mathew Davies, "Explaining the Vientiane Action Programme: ASEAN and the Institutionalisation of Human Rights," Pacific Review 26, no. 4 (2013); Hiro Katsumata, "ASEAN and Human Rights: Resisting Western Pressure or Emulating the West?" Pacific Review 22, no. 5 (2009).

142. Catherine Renshaw and Kieren Fitzpatrick, "National Human Rights Institutions in the Asia Pacific Region: Change Agents Under Conditions of Uncertainty," in Human Rights, State

Compliance and Social Change, ed. Ryan Goodman and Thomas Pegram (Cambridge: Cambridge University Press, 2012).

143. Mary Robinson, "Address to the International Coordinating Committee of National Institutions for the Promotion and Protection of Human Rights," Geneva (1999), published in "Background Paper: Consideration of the Issue of Trafficking" by Anne Gallagher, prepared for the Advisory Council of Jurists of the Asia Pacific Forum, November 2002, copy on file with author.

144. Anne Gallagher, "The Role of National Institutions in Advancing the Human Rights of Women: A Case Study on Trafficking in the Asia-Pacific Region," November 11–12, 2002, available at http://www.asiapacificforum.net/support/issues/acj/references/trafficking/downloads/reference-on-trafficking/background.pdf.

145. Southeast Asia National Human Rights Institutions Forum, Memorandum of Understanding Against Trafficking of Women and Children, Manila, the Philippines, March 30, 2010.

146. Ibid.

147. Human Rights Commission of Malaysia (SUHAKAM), "Trafficking in Women and Children: Report of the Human Rights Commission of Malaysia (SUHAKAM)," Kuala Lumpur (2004), available at http://www.suhakam.org.my/c/document_library/get_file?p_l_id=10127&folderId=26482&name=DLFE-2011.pdf.

148. The forum was held on April 13 and 14, 2004. Details are reported in SUHAKAM, "Trafficking in Women and Children."

149. Ibid.

150. The workshop was held in in Makati on November 27–28, 2013. See Philippines Human Rights Commission Report, "Trafficking in Persons," November 29, 2013, available at https://www.dfa.gov.ph/index.php/2013-06-27-21-50-36/dfa-releases/1501-philippines-promotes-human-rights-based-approach-to-combat-trafficking-in-persons-especially-women-and-children-in-asean.

151. Ibid.

152. See, for example, in relation to the Myanmar National Human Rights Commission, "Field and Investigation Trips," available at http://mnhrc.org.mm/en/field-and-investigation-trips/.

Chapter 6

1. United Nations High Commissioner for Human Rights on the Activities of His Office and Recent Human Rights Developments, Item 2: Annual Report and Oral Update to the 34th session of the Human Rights Council, March 8, 2017, http://www.ohchr.org/EN/NewsEvents/Pages/DisplayNews.aspx?NewsID=21316.

2. United Nations High Commissioner for Human Rights, opening statement by Zeid Ra'ad Al Hussein, Human Rights Council, 36th session, September 11, 2017.

3. "US Withdraws Assistance from Myanmar Military amid Rohingya Crisis," *Guardian*, October 24, 2017.

4. International Crisis Group, "Myanmar: A New Muslim Insurgency in Rakhine State," Asia Report No. 283, December 15, 2016.

5. Internal Displacement Monitoring Centre, "Myanmar (Burma): Worst Army Attacks in Years Displace Thousands: A Profile of the Internal Displacement Situation" (May 10, 2006), available at www.refworld.org/pdfid/3ae6a6120.pdf; Stella Naw, " 'Four Cuts' Strategy Deepens Myanmar's War Wounds," *Asia Times*, July 15, 2017, available at http://www.atimes.com/article/four-cuts-strategy-deepens-myanmars-war-wounds/; see also Martin Smith, *Burma: Insurgency and the Politics of Ethnicity* (London: Zed Books, 1999).

6. Mary Kate Long, "Dynamics of State, Sangha and Society in Myanmar: A Closer Look at the Rohingya Issue," *Asian Journal of Public Affairs* 6, no. 1 (2013).

7. "Burma Census Bans People Registering as Rohingya," BBC NEWSAsia, March 30, 2014.

8. Kofi A. Annan, "Towards a Peaceful, Fair and Prosperous Future for the People of Rakhine: Final Report of the Advisory Commission on Rakhine State" (August 24, 2017), http://www .rakhinecommission.org/.

9. Catherine Renshaw, "Human Trafficking in Southeast Asia: Uncovering the Dynamics of State Commitment and Compliance," *Michigan Journal of International Law* 37, no. 4 (2017).

10. The 2010 elections took place within the framework of the Constitution of the Republic of the Union of Myanmar (2008), available at http://www.ilo.org/dyn/natlex/natlex4.detail?p _lang=en&p_isn=79572&p_classification=01.01.

11. Chapter 8 of the constitution is called "Citizen, Fundamental Rights and Duties of the Citizens."

12. The Constitution of the Republic of the Union of Myanmar, Article 21(a).

13. Ibid., Article 37(c).

14. Ibid., Article 38(a).

15. Ibid., Article 34.

16. Ibid., Article 348.

17. Ibid., Article 354.

18. Ibid., Article 355.

19. Ibid., Articles 366 (a) and (b).

20. J. Szep and A. R. C. Marshall, "Myanmar Minister Backs Two-Child Policy for Rohingya Minority," Reuters, June 11, 2013.

21. Section 109(b) and Article 141(b).

22. Lawi Weng, "Burma Parliament Committee: Keep Main Points of Constitution," *Irrawaddy*, January 31, 2014.

23. Oliver Holmes, "US Commends 'Free and Fair' Myanmar Election as NLD Closes in on Majority," *Guardian*, November 12, 2015; UN News Centre, "In Call to Myanmar's President, Ban Urges Cooperation Following Opposition Election Win," November 19, 2015, http://www.refworld .org/country,,,COUNTRYNEWS,MMR,,564ee6fc40c,0.html.

24. Philip Kreager, "Aung Suu Kyi and the Peaceful Struggle for Human Rights in Burma," in *Freedom from Fear and Other Writings*, by Aung San Suu Kyi, ed. Michael Aris (New York: Penguin, 1991), 287.

25. Aung San Suu Kyi, "The Role of the Citizen in the Struggle for Democracy," in *Freedom from Fear and Other Writings*, by Aung San Suu Kyi, ed. Michael Aris (New York: Penguin, 1991), 219.

26. Wai Moe and Richard C. Paddock, "Myanmar to Create New Post for Aung San Suu Kyi, Cementing Her Power," *New York Times*, March 31, 2016.

27. Aradhana Aravindan and Yimou Lee, "Myanmar's Suu Kyi Says International Attention Fuelling Divisions in North," Reuters, December 2, 2016; "Aung San Suu Kyi Defends Myanmar's Reaction to Rohingya Muslim Crisis," NPR News, September 19, 2017.

28. Human Rights Council, "Report of the Special Rapporteur on the Situation of Human Rights in Myanmar," March 1, 2017, A/HRC/34/67, available at https://reliefweb.int/sites/reliefweb .int/files/resources/A_HRC_34_67_AUVFinal.pdf.

29. Charter of the Association of Southeast Asian Nations (adopted November 20, 2007, entered into force December 15, 2008) (hereafter ASEAN Charter), Article 1(7).

30. Ibid., Article 2(2)(h). The Preamble to the ASEAN Charter also refers to "the principles of democracy, the rule of law and good governance, respect for and protection of human rights and fundamental freedoms."

31. Association of Southeast Asian Nations (ASEAN), "Terms of Reference of the ASEAN Intergovernmental Commission on Human Rights" (hereafter TOR AICHR), July 2009, Article 1, available at http://www.refworld.org/docid/4a6d87f22.html.

32. ASEAN Charter, Article 2(f).

33. TOR AICHR, Article 2.1(b).

34. Ibid., Article 3.

35. Ibid., Article 2.4.

36. For example, see Chao-Tzang Yawnghe, "Burma: The Depoliticization of the Political," in *Political Legitimacy in Southeast Asia*, ed. Muthiah Alagappa (Stanford, Calif.: Stanford University Press, 1995).

37. Alan Saw U, "Reflections on Confidence-Building and Cooperation Among Ethnic Groups in Myanmar: A Karen Case Study," in *Myanmar: State, Society and Ethnicity*, ed. N. Ganesan and Kyaw Yin Hlaing (Singapore: Institute of Southeast Asian Studies, 2007).

38. The size of Myanmar's ethnic population is contested. One civil society organization claims minorities comprise around 40 percent of Myanmar's total population of around 53 million; see www.networkmyanmar.org. However, Alan Smith complicates attempts to delineate clear divides between different ethnic groups in Myanmar. Alan Smith, "Burma/Myanmar: The Struggle for Democracy and Ethnic Rights," in *Multiculturalism in Asia*, ed. Will Kymlicka and Baogang He (Oxford: Oxford University Press, 2015).

39. According to Smith ("Burma/Myanmar"), the British treated the ethnic Burmese majority (which became part of India) differently from the non-Burman minorities, playing a "divide and rule" game, favoring certain minorities in the army, as well as migrant Indians in the economy, at the expense of the ethnic Burmese majority.

40. Robert H. Taylor, "Burma's National Unity Problem and the 1974 Constitution," *Contemporary Southeast Asia* 1, no. 3 (1979): 236.

41. For example, see Richard Sollom et al., "Life Under the Junta: Evidence of Crimes Against Humanity in Burma's Chin State," Physicians for Human Rights, February 8, 2011, available at https://s3.amazonaws.com/PHR_Reports/life-under-the-junta-burma-chin-state.pdf.

42. United Nations Human Rights Commission, "UN Human Rights Commission Resolution 1992/58: Situation of Human Rights in Myanmar," March 3, 1992; UN General Assembly, "Memorandum of Allegations to the Government of Myanmar," November 16, 1993, UN Doc. A/48/578.

43. UN General Assembly, "Memorandum of Allegations to the Government of Myanmar."

44. Rajsoomer Lallah, "United Nations Special Rapporteur on the Situation of Human Rights in Myanmar," September 10, 1998, UN Doc. A/53/364.

45. UN General Assembly, *Universal Declaration of Human Rights*, December 10, 1948, 217 A (III), Article 21.

46. Amartya Sen, *Poverty and Famines: An Essay on Entitlement and Deprivation* (Oxford: Clarendon Press, 1981).

47. UN General Assembly, "Response by the Government of Myanmar to the Memorandum of the Special Rapporteur," November 16, 1993, UN Doc. A/48/578.

48. The NLD was subsequently stripped of its status as a legal political party. See "Suu Kyi's NLD Party to Boycott Burma Election," BBC News, March 29, 2010, available at http://news.bbc.co.uk/1/hi/world/asia-pacific/8592365.stm.

49. Aung Naing Oo, "Give Peace in Burma a Chance," *Irrawaddy*, December 13, 2011; BTI Project, "Myanmar Country Report," *Bertelsmann Stiftung* (2016): 4, available at https://www.bti -project.org/fileadmin/files/BTI/Downloads/Reports/2016/pdf/BTI_2016_Myanmar.pdf; Jonah Fisher, "Myanmar: Thein Sein Leaves Legacy of Reform," BBC News, March 30, 2016, available at www.bbc.com/news/world-asia-35916555.

50. See Human Rights Council, "Report of the Special Rapporteur on the Situation of Human Rights in Myanmar"; Amnesty International, "Myanmar: 'All the Civilians Suffer': Conflict, Displacement and Abuse in Northern Myanmar," June 14, 2017, available at www.amnesty.org/en/ documents/asa16/6429/2017/en/; Fortify Rights, "'I Thought They Would Kill Me': Ending Wartime Torture in Northern Myanmar," June 9, 2014, available at www.fortifyrights.org/downloads/ Fortify%20Rights_Myanmar_9_June-2014.pdf; Human Rights Watch, "'Untold Miseries': Wartime Abuses and Forced Displacement in Burma's Kachin State," March 20, 2012, https://www.hrw .org/report/2012/03/20/untold-miseries/wartime-abuses-and-forced-displacement-burmas -kachin-state; Bill Davis et al., "Under Siege in Kachin State, Burma," November 30, 2011, Physicians for Human Rights, http://burmacampaign.org.uk/media/Burma-Under-Siege-in-Kachin -State-PHR.pdf; Human Rights Watch, "Burma: Army Committing Abuses in Kachin State," October 18, 2011, available at Fortify Rights, "Myanmar: End Military Attacks on Kachin and Shan Civilians," November 6, 2014, http://www.fortifyrights.org/publication-20141106.html.

51. The Telecommunications Law (The Pyidaungsu Hluttaw Law No. 31, 2013), October 8, 2013, Section 66(d), available at http://www.burmalibrary.org/docs23/2013-10-08-Telecommunications _Law-en.pdf. Section 66(d) penalizes "extorting, coercing, restraining wrongfully, defaming, disturbing, causing undue influence or threatening to any person using any Telecommunications Network."

52. Salai Thant Zin, "Myanmar Activist Faces 5 Years in Jail for Facebook Post Mocking Army Uniform," *Global Voices*, October 14, 2015.

53. Lin Zueling, "Exclusive: Focus on Resolving Difficulties in Rakhine Rather than Exaggerating Them, Says Suu Kyi," Channel News Asia, December 2, 2016.

54. Human Rights Council, "Report of the Special Rapporteur on the Situation of Human Rights in Myanmar," para. 71.

55. Kyaw Myaing, "Rakhine Affair, Don't Try to Profit from Others' Woes," Republic of the Union of Myanmar Ministry of Information.

56. "Commentary: Shwe Maung Fails to Confess the Truth About Rakhine," *Global New Light of Myanmar*, November 4, 2016.

57. Ibid.

58. Oliver Holmes, "Myanmar Journalist Says She Was Fired over Story on Military Rape Allegations," *Guardian*, November 4, 2016.

59. United Nations Human Rights Commission, "Human Rights Council Decides to Dispatch a Fact-Finding Mission to Establish Facts on Violations, Especially in Rakhine State," March 24, 2017, Human Rights Council (Statement), available at http://www.ohchr.org/EN /NewsEvents/Pages/DisplayNews.aspx?NewsID=21443&LangID=E.

60. Stephanie Nebehay, "U.N. Will Investigate Crimes Against Rohingya in Myanmar," Reuters, March 24, 2017, available at https://www.reuters.com/article/us-myanmar-rohingya-un/u -n-will-investigate-crimes-against-rohingya-in-myanmar-idUSKBN16V15B; Nick Cumming-Bruce, "U.N. Rights Council to Investigate Reports of Atrocities in Myanmar," *New York Times*, March 24, 2017, available at https://www.nytimes.com/2017/03/24/world/asia/myanmar-rakhine -rohingya-un-rights-council.html.

61. "Aung San Suu Kyi Rejects UN Inquiry into Crimes Against Rohingya," *Guardian*, May 3, 2017, available at https://www.theguardian.com/world/2017/may/03/aung-san-suu-kyi-rejects-un-inquiry-into-crimes-against-rohingya.

62. Human Rights Watch, "Q&A: United Nations Fact-Finding Mission on Myanmar," August 2, 2017, available at https://www.hrw.org/news/2017/08/02/qa-united-nations-fact-finding-mission-myanmar.

63. United Nations Office at Geneva, "Human Rights Council Holds Interactive Dialogue with the Fact-Finding Mission to Myanmar," September 19, 2017.

64. Moe Myint, "Kofi Annan: Commission Will Not Do 'Human Rights Investigation' in Arakan State," *Irrawaddy*, September 8, 2016; President's Office, "Easing Rakhine Tension: Kofi Annan Calls for Cooperation Among Neighbouring Countries to Address Rakhine Issue," *Global New Light of Myanmar*, September 8, 2016.

65. "Interim Report of the Investigation Commission on Maungtaw," *Global New Light of Myanmar*, January 4, 2017.

66. See "Myanmar Commission Finds No Cases of Genocide, Religious Persecution of Rohingya in Rakhine," Radio Free Asia, January 4, 2017, available at https://reliefweb.int/report/myanmar/myanmar-commission-finds-no-cases-genocide-religious-persecution-rohingya-rakhine.

67. Investigation Commission on Maungtaw, "Interim Report of the Investigation on Maungtaw," January 3, 2017, available at http://www.moi.gov.mm/moi:eng/?q=news/4/01/2017/id-9542.

68. Press statement issued by Tatmadaw True News Information Team about accusations described in the report of the Office of the High Commissioner for Human Rights submitted to Human Rights Commission, May 23, 2017, available at https://www.facebook.com/Cincds/photos/a.530200420434161.1073741832.526503167470553/1339456762841852/?type=3&theater.

69. "Muslim Civilians 'Killed by Burmese Army,'" BBC News, November 7, 2016, available at http://www.bbc.co.uk/news/av/world-asia-37892512/muslim-civilians-killed-by-burmese-army.

70. Footage available at "Myanmar Detains Police Officers over Rohingya Beating Video," BBC News, January 2, 2017; "Muslim Civilians 'Killed by Burmese Army.'"

71. See "Rohingya Police Beating Footage: Myanmar Government to Investigate—Video," *Guardian*, January 2, 2017; see also "Myanmar: Crimes Against Humanity Terrorize and Drive Rohingya Out," *Amnesty International*, October 18, 2017.

72. Lee Jones, "ASEAN's Albatross: ASEAN's Burma Policy, from Constructive Engagement to Critical Disengagement," *Asian Security* 4, no. 3 (2008): 275.

73. Stephen McCarthy, "Burma and ASEAN: Estranged Bedfellows," *Asian Survey* 48, no. 6 (2008). For skeptical views on the effectiveness of the policy, see Deborah Toler, "Constructive Engagement: Reactionary Pragmatism at Its Best," *Issue: A Journal of Opinion* 12, no. 3/4 (1982); Sam C. Nolutshungu, "Sceptical Notes on 'Constructive Engagement,'" *Issue: A Journal of Opinion* 12, no. 3 (1982).

74. Hermann Kraft, "ASEAN and Intra-ASEAN Relations: Weathering the Storm?" *Pacific Review* 13, no. 3 (2000).

75. "ASEAN Prefers Soft Talk to Threats in Dealing with Yangon," *Strait Times*, August 26, 1992.

76. "Far Eastern Economic Review," August 15, 1996, quoted in Kraft, "ASEAN and Intra-ASEAN Relations," 464.

77. The *Sunday Times* reported a statement by the U.S. State Department's spokesperson declaring that the United States had "no objection to Laos and Cambodia. We have an objection

to Burma." April 6, 1997, quoted in C. K. Wah, "ASEAN: The Long Road to 'One Southeast Asia,'" *Asian Journal of Political Science* 5, no. 1 (1997): 1.

78. The permanent secretary of Singapore's Foreign Ministry stated in April 1997: "We have always adopted the attitude that we do not impose any political conditions on entry. Instead, the criteria today are, first, geographical, and second, economic, and Myanmar meets both the geographical and economic criteria." Foreign Broadcast Monitor No. 84/97, April 15, 1997.

79. See "Malaysia's Mahathir Calls for Myanmar to Release Aung San Suu Kyi," Agence France-Presse, June 17, 2005; Ruukun Katanyuu, "Beyond Non-Interference in ASEAN: The Association's Role in Myanmar's National Reconciliation and Democratization," *Asian Survey* 46, no. 6 (2006).

80. Keynote address by Mahathir Mohamed, prime minister of Malaysia, July 24, 1997, available at http://www.asean.org/3992.htm.

81. Opening statement by H. E. U. Ohn Gyaw, minister for foreign affairs of Myanmar, July 24, 1997, available at http://www.asean.org/communities/asean-political-security-community /item/opening-statement-by-he-u-ohn-gyaw-minister-for-foreign-affairs-of-myanmar.

82. Jones, "ASEAN's Albatross," 274.

83. Ibid.

84. "Different Concepts of Democracy," *Irrawaddy Magazine* 5, no. 2 (May 1, 1997).

85. "Mahathir to Make Business Visit to Myanmar, No Talks with Suu Kyi," *Burma Today*, August 16, 2002, available at http://www.burmatoday.net/newsarchives/news_020816_mahathir .htm.

86. Smith, *Burma*; Bertil Lintner, *Burma in Revolt: Opium and Insurgency Since 1948* (Boulder, Colo.: Westview Press, 1994); Hazel J. Lang, *Fear and Sanctuary: Burmese Refugees in Thailand* (Ithaca, N.Y.: Cornell University Press, 2002); Pim Koetsawang, *In Search of Sunlight: Burmese Migrant Workers in Thailand* (Bangkok: Orchid Press, 2001); Yuen Foong Kong, "ASEAN and the Southeast Asian Security Complex," in *Regional Orders: Building Security in a New World*, ed. David A. Lake and Patrick N. Morgan (University Park: Pennsylvania State University Press, 1997).

87. Katanyuu, "Beyond Non-Interference in ASEAN."

88. Jürgen Haacke, "The Concept of Flexible Engagement and the Practice of Enhanced Interaction: Intramural Challenges to the 'ASEAN Way,'" *Pacific Review* 12, no. 4 (1999); Donald Emmerson, "ASEAN's 'Black Swans,'" *Journal of Democracy* 19, no. 3 (2008): 77; Amitav Acharya, *Constructing a Security Community in Southeast Asia* (London: Routledge, 2001).

89. Indonesian foreign minister Ali Alatas argued, "If the proposition is to now talk publicly about internal problems we will be back to when ASEAN was not formed, when Southeast Asia was full of tension, mutual suspicion, and only because ASEAN was created, we have had more than 30 years of stability, of common progress." *Nation*, July 24, 1998, 1, quoted in Jürgen Haacke, *ASEAN's Diplomatic and Security Culture: Origins, Development and Prospects* (London: Routledge, 2009), 178.

90. See Jürgen Haacke, "'Enhanced Interaction' with Myanmar and the Project of a Security Community: Is ASEAN Refining or Breaking with Its Diplomatic and Security Culture?" *Contemporary Southeast Asia* 27, no. 2 (2005).

91. Premeditation and complicity of the regime were corroborated in a report by Special Rapporteur on Human Rights to Myanmar, Professor Paulo Sérgio Pinheiro, "Question of the Violation of Human Rights and Fundamental Freedoms in Any Part of the World: Situation of Human Rights in Myanmar," January 5, 2004, E/CN.4/2004/33 UN Economic and Social Coun-

cil, available at http://www.securitycouncilreport.org/atf/cf/%7B65BFCF9B-6D27-4E9C-8CD3
-CF6E4FF96FF9%7D/Myan%20E%20CN4%202004%2033.pdf.

92. "Remarks to the Media by Singapore Foreign Minister Prof. S. Jayakumar and Thai
Foreign Minister Surakiart After Their Bilateral Meeting on 15 June 2003, Phnom Penh," June
16, 2003, Ministry of Foreign Affairs, Singapore, available at https://www.mfa.gov.sg/content/mfa
/media_centre/press_room/if/2003/200306/infocus_20030616.html; "ASEAN's Myanmar Policy
May Face Review: Philippine FM," Agence France-Presse, June 18, 2003. Mahathir, who repeat-
edly urged the release of Aung San Suu Kyi, even suggested Myanmar might be expelled from
ASEAN if it remained intransigent. Mark Baker, "Mahathir Warns Burma over Suu Kyi," The Age,
July 22, 2003; "Malaysian Premier Urges Immediate Release of Burma's Aung San Suu Kyi," Ber-
nama, June 10, 2003; "Malaysia's Mahathir Again Urges Myanmar to Release Suu Kyi," Associated
Press, June 24, 2003. See also "Burma Told to Release Suu Kyi," BBC News, July 24, 2003, available
at http://news.bbc.co.uk/1/hi/world/asia-pacific/3091941.stm.

93. "Spotlight on Burma at ASEAN Meeting," Nation (Bangkok), June 18, 2003.

94. "Philippines Demurs as ASEAN Backs Burma," Nation, June 17, 2003; "Minister Says
ASEAN Forward on Political Reforms," Agence FrancePresse, June 20, 2003.

95. Jones, "ASEAN's Albatross."

96. Eileen Ng, "Myanmar Told That Suu Kyi's Detention a Slap to ASEAN, Says Official,"
Kyodo News, December 11, 2005.

97. United Nations Document No. A/C.3/61/SR.52, Special Rapporteurs Summary Record,
1–6.

98. Quoted in Wayne Arnold, "Malaysia, in Reversal, Condemns Myanmar," International
Herald Tribune, July 22, 2006.

99. ASEAN, "Statement by the ASEAN Foreign Ministers Vientiane," July 25, 2005, available at
http://asean.org/?static_post=statement-by-the-asean-foreign-ministers-vientiane-25-july-2005-2.

100. Jon Ungphakorn, "The Next Move to Help Myanmar Change," New Straits Times, October 7, 2005.

101. Andrew Selth, "Burma's 'Saffron Revolution' and the Limits of International Influence,"
Australian Journal of International Affairs 62, no. 3 (2008): 283.

102. Saffron is the color of the robes of Myanmar's Buddhist monks. It is estimated that
thirty-one protestors died and some three thousand were arrested in the Saffron Revolution.
Ardeth Maung Thawnghmung and Maung Aung Myoe, "Myanmar in 2007: A Turning Point in
the 'Road Map,'" Asian Survey?" 48, no. 1 (2008).

103. Selth, "Burma's 'Saffron Revolution.'"

104. The United Nations, the U.S. Department of State, Human Rights Watch, and other
NGOs have reported extensively on the military regime's record of human rights abuses, including denial of aid, forced labor, use of child soldiers, violence against ethnic minorities, forced
displacement, systematic and widespread rape, torture and extrajudicial killings, and religious
persecution. See U.S. Department of State, Bureau of Democracy, Human Rights and Labor,
"2008 Human Rights Report: Burma," February 25, 2008, available at http://www.state.gov/g/drl
/rls/hrrpt/2008/eap/119035.htm; Human Rights Watch, "Burma's Forgotten Prisoners," September 16, 2009, available at https://www.hrw.org/report/2009/09/16/burmas-forgotten-prisoners;
UN Human Rights Council, "Report of the Special Rapporteur on the Situation of Human Rights
in Myanmar, Tomás Ojea Quintana," June 3, 2008, A/HRC/8/12, available at https://reliefweb.int
/report/myanmar/report-special-rapporteur-situation-human-rights-myanmar-tom%C3%A1s
-ojea-quintana-ahrc812.

105. Paul Eckert, "ASEAN Voices, 'Revulsion' at Myanmar Violence," Reuters, September 27, 2007, available at https://www.reuters.com/article/us-myanmar-asean/asean-voices-revulsion-at-myanmar-violence-idUSN2736930120070927.

106. "Interview with Singapore Foreign Minister George Yeo," *New Straits Times*, October 2–3, 2007.

107. Ibid.

108. Ibid. ASEAN's exasperation with Myanmar may have been increased by Myanmar's actions in relation to North Korea earlier in 2007, when North Korea signed an agreement with Myanmar in relation to the Tatmadaw's access to military equipment that had been blocked by U.S. and EU sanctions. "Myanmar Denies Trying to Obtain N. Korean Nukes," *Straits Times*, January 31, 2012, available at http://sg.news.yahoo.com/myanmar-denies-trying-obtain-n-korean-nukes-052659723.html.

109. Julian Borger and Ian MacKinnon, "Bypass Junta's Permission for Aid, US and France Urge," *Guardian*, May 9, 2008, available at https://www.theguardian.com/world/2008/may/09/cyclonenargis.burma; Gareth Evans, "Facing Up to Our Responsibilities," *Guardian*, May 12, 2008, available at https://www.theguardian.com/commentisfree/2008/may/12/facinguptoourresponsbilities.

110. Sheldon W. Simon, "Southeast Asian International Relations: Is There Institutional Traction?" in *International Relations in Southeast Asia: Between Bilateralism and Multilateralism*, ed. N. Ganesan and Ramses Amer (Singapore: Institute of Southeast Asian Studies, 2010), 48.

111. Aung Hla Tun, "Foreign Powers Lean on Myanmar to Open Up Aid," Reuters, May 15, 2008, available at https://www.reuters.com/article/idUSMAN146707._CH_.2400.

112. Jürgen Haacke, "Myanmar's Foreign Policy: Domestic Influences and International Implications," *Adelphi Papers* 381 (2006): 58–59.

113. ASEAN Parliamentarians for Human Rights (APHR), "The Rohingya Crisis and the Risk of Atrocities in Myanmar: An ASEAN Challenge and Call to Action (Report)," April 16, 2015, http://burmacampaign.org.uk/media/APHR-Report-Rohingya-Crisis-and-Risk-of-Atrocities-in-Myanmar-final.pdf.

114. TOR AICHR, Article 4.10.

115. Joe Cochrane, "In Reversal, Myanmar Agrees to Attend Meeting on Migrant Crisis," *New York Times*, May 21, 2015.

116. "Intervention by YB Minister of Foreign Affairs at the ASEAN Foreign Ministers' Retreat Yangon, Myanmar" (Speech, ASEAN-Malaysia National Secretariat, December 19, 2016). See also "Aung San Suu Kyi Discusses Rakhine Crisis with ASEAN Foreign Ministers," Radio Free Asia, December 19, 2016.

117. United Nations Human Rights Office of the High Commissioner, "Interviews with Rohingyas Fleeing from Myanmar Since 9 October 2016: Flash Report," February 3, 2017, https://reliefweb.int/sites/reliefweb.int/files/resources/FlashReport3Feb2017.pdf.

118. Ibid., 42.

119. ASEAN, "Chairman's Statement: Partnering for Change, Engaging the World," April 29, 2017, http://asean.org/storage/2017/04/Chairs-Statement-of-30th-ASEAN-Summit_FINAL.pdf.

120. Kyaw Tint Swe and Aung Htoo, "Myanmar in ASEAN: Cooperation for Development," in Proceedings of the Symposium on "Interaction for Progress: Myanmar in ASEAN," Myanmar (1998), 177.

121. Ibid.

122. Jon C. Pevehouse, *Democracy from Above: Regional Organisations and Democratisation*

(Cambridge: Cambridge University Press, 2005); Peter Schraeder, "The State of the Art in International Democracy Promotion: Results of a Joint European-North American Research Network," *Democratization* 10, no. 2 (2003).

123. On shaming, see Thomas Risse and Kathryn Sikkink, "The Socialization of International Human Rights Norms into Domestic Practices: Introduction," in *The Power of Human Rights: International Norms and Domestic Change*, ed. Thomas Risse, Stephen C. Ropp, and Kathryn Sikkink (Cambridge: Cambridge University Press, 1999); Oran Young, "The Effectiveness of International Institutions: Hard Cases and Critical Variables," in *Governance Without Government: Order and Change in World Politics*, ed. James N. Rosenau and Ernst-Otiel Czempiel (Cambridge: Cambridge University Press,1992); Abram Chayes and Antonia Chayes, *The New Sovereignty: Compliance with International Regulatory Agreements* (Cambridge, Mass.: Harvard University Press, 1996); Douglass Cassel, "Does International Human Rights Law Make a Difference?" *Chicago Journal of International Law* 2, no. 1 (2001); Alastair Johnston, "Treating International Institutions as Social Environments," *International Studies Quarterly* 45, no. 4 (2001).

124. Anne-Marie Slaughter, "Government Networks and Traditional International Organisations: Interconnected Worlds," in *A New World Order* (Princeton, N.J.: Princeton University Press, 2004).

125. See also Anne-Marie Slaughter, *A New World Order* (Princeton, N.J.: Princeton University Press, 2004); Robert Keohane and Joseph Nye, *Power and Interdependence* (London: Book Service Ltd., 1977), 25–26.

126. Dr. Termsak Chalermpalanupap, assistant director for programme coordination and external relations, ASEAN Secretariat, "ASEAN-10: Meeting the Challenges" (Paper presented at the Asia-Pacific Roundtable, Kuala Lumpur, June 1, 1999), http://www.asean.org/news/item/asean-10-meeting-the-challenges-by-dr-termsak-chalermpalanupap-assistant-director-for-programme-coordination-and-external-relations-asean-secretariat-2.

Conclusion

1. Thomas Thomas and Alexander Chandra, "Thematic Study on CSR and Human Rights in ASEAN" (2014), available at http://aichr.org/?dl_name=AICHRs_Thematic_Study_on_CSR_and_Human_Rights_in_ASEAN.pdf.

2. Amitav Acharya, "Comparative Regionalism: A Field Whose Time Has Come?" *International Spectator* 47, no. 1 (2012).

INDEX

abduction (kidnaping), 125, 129
Abdullah, Muhammad Shafee, 72, 85
abortion, 84, 198n85
accountability, 24, 89, 180n7 (Part I)
Aceh/Sumatra National Liberation Front
    (Indonesia), 63, 196n46
Acharya, Amitav, 24
ACWC (ASEAN Commission on the
    Promotion and Protection of the Rights of
    Women and Children), 116–118, 121, 139,
    173n3, 211nn108–110, 212n115
adultery, 83, 84, 109, 208n63
Africa, 4, 5–6, 174n17
African Charter on Human and People's
    Rights (Banjul Charter), 40, 74, 174n17,
    199n102; rights limitations and, 74; on
    right to peace, 203–204n181
African Court on Human and People's
    Rights, 6, 174n17
AHRD (ASEAN Human Rights Declaration),
    2, 13, 57, 151, 167, 169; Article 1, 65–69;
    Article 2 (nondiscrimination), 69–73;
    Article 4, 58, 118; Article 6 (duties), 73–78;
    Article 7 (indivisibility of rights), 78–82;
    Article 8 ("public morality"), 82–88;
    Article 9 (particularization), 89; Article 38
    (right to peace), 170; drafting of, 47,
    48–56, 98, 190n71, 190n84; failure to meet
    international standards, 168; potential to
    effect change, 91–93; Preamble, 64, 74,
    196n52; solidarity rights, 90–91
AHRD-UDHR similarities and differences,
    58–60, 193nn4–8, 194n19; Article 1,
    65–66; duties in relation to rights, 74, 75,
    77–78; "general principles," 64; "public
    morality" limitations, 83, 201n138
AICHR (ASEAN Intergovernmental

Commission on Human Rights), 2, 17,
    117, 167, 173n3, 181n8; activities of,
    12–13; Cha-am Hua Hin Declaration, 50;
    drafting of AHRD and, 48–55, 58;
    establishment and early years of, 6, 44–47;
    noninterference principle and, 151; report
    on corporate social responsibility, 169;
    Rohingya crisis and, 164; Terms of
    Reference (TOR), 18, 45–46, 50, 170,
    192n107, 211n110; trafficking in persons
    and, 139, 146
AIDS (Acquired Immune Deficiency
    Syndrome), 60, 141
Alatas, Ali, 226n89
Algeria, 32
Alliance on Global Justice, 43
American Convention on Human Rights, 65,
    74
American Declaration on the Rights and
    Duties of Man (1948), 5, 65, 74, 199n100
Americas, 4, 5, 174n16
Amin, Azril Mohd, 71
Amnesty International, 153, 192n110
Annan, Kofi, 156
APEC (Asia Pacific Economic Cooperation),
    9
APF (Asia Pacific Forum of National Human
    Rights Institutions), 144
Aquino, Benigno, III, 62
Aquino, Corazon, 12, 130
Arab Charter of Human Rights, 6, 83, 174n18
Arab Court of Human Rights, 171
Arab Human Rights Committee, 6, 171
Arab League, 174n18
Arakanese ethnic minority (Myanmar), 152
arms trafficking, 128
arrest, arbitrary, 68

ASEAN (Association of Southeast Asian Nations), 2, 124, 170, 173n1; ACTIP (ASEAN Convention Against Trafficking in Persons), 124, 139, 146; ACW (ASEAN Committee on Women), 115–116, 210n89; AEC (ASEAN Economic Community), 140, 219n116; AFAS (ASEAN Framework Agreement on Services), 21; AFTA (ASEAN Free Trade Area), 9, 21; AIA (ASEAN Investment Area), 21; AMMTC (ASEAN Ministerial Meeting on Transnational Crime), 141; APHR (ASEAN Parliamentarians for Human Rights), 163–164; ARF (ASEAN Regional Forum), 9; ASC (ASEAN Security Committee), 40–41; ASCPA (ASEAN Security Community Plan of Action), 41; ASEM (ASEAN-Europe Meeting), 9; authoritarian leaders in early years, 10; Civil Society Conference (2012), 70; Commission on Human Rights, 41; Convention on Human Rights, 50; Declaration Against Trafficking in Persons, 124, 139, 142; Declaration of ASEAN Concord (1976), 8–9, 20, 21; Declaration on the Advancement of Women in the ASEAN Region (1988), 115; Declaration on Transnational Crime, 141; Declaration on Zone of Peace, Freedom and Neutrality (1971), 8; denounced as tool of U.S. imperialism, 7; "development divide" within, 21; economic interdependence of, 21–22; formation (1967), 7–8; HRWG (Human Rights Working Group), 52, 72, 74, 77, 170, 191n99; human rights in Myanmar and, 165–166; IAI (Initiative for ASEAN Integration), 21; Inter-Parliamentary Organization, 139; nascent human rights system of, 13, 18, 37, 38; Political-Security Community Blueprint (2009), 142; regional approaches to combat trafficking, 139–147; regional human rights system of, 7; relationship with Myanmar, 157–163, 228n108; Rohingya crisis and, 151, 163–164; Senior Officials Meeting (SOM), 55; tension between democratic and nondemocratic member states, 57; treaty monitoring system and, 2–3; Women's Leaders Conference, 113, 210n89. See also ACWC; AHRD; AICHR; Bangkok Declaration

ASEAN + 3 (with Japan, South Korea, China), 9
ASEAN + 6 (with Japan, South Korea, China, India, Australia, New Zealand), 9
ASEAN Charter, 12, 33, 36, 51, 140, 167, 192n107; ACWC and, 211n110; AHRD and, 81; ASEAN Political-Security Council, 220n138; Bali Concord II, 43; democracy mentioned in, 39–44, 151, 166, 187n3, 223n30; drafting processes for, 18, 56; EPG (Eminent Persons Group) and, 41–42, 44–45, 188n21; HLTF drafting of, 38, 41–42; political character of member states and, 165–166; on sustainable development, 90–91
"ASEAN Economic Community," 21, 140
ASEAN-PMC (ASEAN Post-Ministerial Conference, 1998), 142
ASEAN Vision 2020, 21, 219n116
"ASEAN Way," 9, 10, 159, 226n89
Asian Convention on Human Rights, 176n39
Asian financial crisis (1997), 3, 10, 23, 124, 142
"Asian values" debate, 3, 23, 81, 167; CEDAW and, 101–102; end of, 116; relativism and, 82; skepticism about democracy and, 28, 31–35
assembly, right of, 19, 23, 180n7 (Part I); in AHRD, 59; limitations on, 83; as requirement of democracy, 26
association, freedom of, 11, 24, 26, 59
Association of Southeast Asia (ASA), 8
Aung Bwa, 38, 44
Aung San, General, 150
Aung San Suu Kyi, 154–155, 160; as Nobel laureate and human rights icon, 1, 150; Rohingya crisis and, 150–151, 164
Aung Win, 157
Australia, 9, 125
authoritarianism, 10, 12, 152, 166; concept of duty and, 76; economic development and, 24, 33
Aye Win, Lieutenant General, 156
Azril Mohd Amin, 71n89

Bakti, Ikrar Nusa, 40
Bali Democracy Forum, 74
Bangalore Principles of Judicial Conduct (2002), 106

Bangkok Declaration (1967), 8, 19, 91, 177n57; AHRD Article 9 and, 89, 203n174; "Asian values" debate and, 31, 32; on context of human rights, 81; liberal peace thesis and, 21; peace as raison d'être of, 90, 203n179; Preamble to, 32; UDHR and, 56, 193n114

Bangkok Declaration on Irregular Migration (1999), 143

Bangladesh, 148, 149, 165

Barisan Nasional coalition (Malaysia), 27

Beijing Statement of Principles of the Independence of the Judiciary, 106

Beitz, Charles, 67

BIFF (Bangsamoro Islamic Freedom Fighters), 62, 195n34

Binay, Jejomar C., 134

bodily integrity, right to, 111–112

borders, integrity of, 129–130

Bosnia, 118

Bouhours, Thierry, 128–129

Brunei, 18, 53, 167, 208n65; anti-trafficking legislation in, 131; ASEAN Charter and, 44, 45; as ASEAN member, 2, 9, 173n1; CEDAW and, 103, 104, 109–110, 119, 120; drafting of AHRD and, 54, 55; majority-Muslim population of, 70; polygamous marriage in, 107; "public morality" limitations in, 85; response to global anti-trafficking regime, 127–128; Sharia law in, 109–110, 208n63; SOGI rights opposed in, 70, 72

Buddhism/Buddhists, 34, 149, 152, 154, 157; equality and karma, 66; Saffron Revolution and, 161, 227n101; view of women, 112

Bunch, Charlotte, 118

Burma. See Myanmar (Burma)

Cambodia, 1–2, 21, 225n77; anti-trafficking legislation in, 131; as ASEAN member, 2, 9, 173n1; ASEAN relationship with Myanmar and, 161; CEDAW and, 101, 102, 105, 111, 205n18, 206n36; chaos following democratic transition, 12; dam in Lower Mekong and, 90; domestic violence legislation, 116; electoral authoritorianism in, 2; famine in, 22; genocidal rule of Khmer Rouge, 10; Marxist-Leninist ideology in, 29; nonalignment policy in Cold War, 8; "public morality" limitations

in, 83, 84–85, 201n141; response to global anti-trafficking regime, 128; SOGI rights opposed in, 70; trafficking in persons from, 125, 129; Vietnam's invasion of, 20, 22

Cambodian People's Party (CPP), 12, 27

capitalism, 35, 36

caste system, 66–67, 68, 69

Catholic Church, 85, 87–88, 112

CEDAW (Convention on the Elimination of All Forms of Discrimination Against Women), 99–101, 117, 173n10; ASEAN member states and, 101–113, 121; issue of violence against women, 100, 111, 113, 204n8; Optional Protocol, 101, 205n19; ratified as tactical concession, 119, 169; reservations to elements of, 103–104

censorship, 1, 67

Chalermpalanupap, Termsak, 45

children, rights of, 117, 118, 121, 211n110; child betrothal and marriage, 112; child labor, 60, 135; enlisted by Myanmar military, 154, 227n104; trafficking in persons and, 125, 142, 145–146

China, People's Republic of, 8, 21, 74, 171; abstention on human rights resolution, 26, 183n49; ASEAN and regional ambitions of, 158; rise of, 7, 8; Tiananmen Square massacre (1989), 32; trafficking in persons and, 125

Chin ethnic minority (Myanmar), 152

Chuang, Janie, 135

civil liberties, 32, 73, 123

civil rights, 5, 10; "Asian values" debate and, 32; in communist states, 37; of women, 67

civil society, 12, 13, 14, 49, 170, 191n91; in absence of democracy, 47, 92; AHRD and, 81; civil society actors, 18, 46, 57–58, 78, 143; in Indonesia, 40; SOGI rights and, 72; UN women's conferences and, 102. See also CSOs (civil society organizations)

CLMV group (Cambodia, Laos, Myanmar, Vietnam), 18, 44, 172

Coalition Against Trafficking in Women in Asia-Pacific, 146

Cohen, Joshua, 24

Cold War, 5, 7, 9, 10, 99

colonialism, 6, 60, 89; end of, 7; Rohingya crisis in Myanmar and, 149; skepticism about democracy and legacy of, 28–30, 184n61

communism, 1, 28; anticolonial struggles
and, 29; end of Cold War and, 9, 17;
incompatibility with democracy, 36;
insurgencies in Southeast Asia, 20; in
Malaysia, 10; rights and duties under,
36–37, 77; "woman question" and, 103. See
also Laos; Vietnam
community (family, society), 33, 34, 199n108;
community building process, 91; conflated
with the state, 34; debates and, 92; duties
owed to, 78; market forces and, 35; "nation
before community," 76
community, international, 102, 132; "outside
pressure" from, 13, 14, 105; universality of
human rights and, 78
Conference on Security and Cooperation in
Europe, 3
conflict resolution, 40
Confucianism, 33, 35, 66, 67, 197n65;
conservative views on family and gender
roles, 102; inferior status of women in, 112
Confucian Traditions in East Asian Modernity
(Tu Wei-Ming), 33
Confucius, 67
conscience, freedom of, 59, 69
constitutional government, 39, 42, 151, 166
"constructive engagement," 157–158
Cordillera indigenous peoples (Philippines),
62–63
corruption, 24, 27, 35, 146
Council of Europe, 5
crime, transnational, 123, 128, 141–142, 143,
220n133
Cristobal, Ging, 72
cronyism, 24
CSOs (civil society organizations), 46, 80, 91,
120; AHRD Article 1 and, 65, 66; "Asian
values" debate and, 81–82; CEDAW and,
104, 107, 108, 110; drafting of AHRD and,
49–55, 89, 191n91; on relation of rights
and duties, 74, 77, 200n122; SOGI rights
and, 70; solidarity rights and, 90;
trafficking in persons and, 146. See also
civil society
Cuba, abstention on human rights resolution,
26, 183n49
customary law, 80
Cyclone Nargis (2008), 153, 162–163, 164

Dansalan Declaration (1935), 61

Déclaration des Droits de l'Homme et du
Citoyen (France, 1789), 65
decolonization, 28
deforestation, 90
democracy, 5, 26, 76, 158; absence of, 18, 56,
92–93, 167; ASEAN Charter and, 39–44;
definition of, 19, 167, 180n4; economic
development and, 24, 185n87; "established" (in place before 1920), 181n8;
failure to develop in Myanmar, 152–153; as
necessary condition for human rights, 11,
19–20, 167; "new" (established 1920–50),
181n8; "partial democracy," 105; regional
shifts toward and away from, 172;
skepticism about, 28–37; "true" or
"guided," 34
democracy–human rights link, 11, 26;
democracy itself as human right, 24;
incentive for governments to protect
rights, 22; liberal peace thesis, 19–20. See
also liberal democracy
democratization, 20, 22–23, 121, 149, 167
Derks, Annuska, 128
deterrence, against perpetrators of abuse, 5,
175n26
development, right to, 90–91
DEVW (Declaration on the Elimination of
Violence Against Women in the ASEAN
Region, 2004), 116, 117, 121, 212n115
diffusion, regional, 102, 119
dignity: human, 17, 22, 59, 67–68; national,
142, 143
Dili massacre (East Timor, 1991), 10, 177n60
discrimination, 83, 97; gender, 107;
gender-based violence and, 100; against
indigenous populations, 62; racial, 113;
"sexual identity" and, 55; sexual minorities
and, 85; UDHR prohibition of, 59, 69–73,
89; against women, 104, 106, 110–111, 120
disease, elimination of, 8–9
Djamin, Rafendi, 47
Djani, Triansyah, 40
Domestic Application of International
Human Rights Norms (India, 1988), 106
domestic violence laws, 112, 209n79
Donnelly, Jack, 36, 68
Dosch, Jörn, 188n21
Draft Declaration of Human Responsibility
(1997), 75
drug trafficking, 128, 141, 219n125

Duterte, Rodrigo, 1, 62, 63
duties, rights and, 34, 46, 199nn100–102, 199n108; in AHRD (Article 6), 73–78; communist view of, 37; in Confucian philosophy, 197n65; controversy over universality of rights, 48, 190n76
Dworkin, Ronald, 77

Earthrights International, 52, 192n110
East Asian Summit (EAS), 9
ECHR (European Convention on Human Rights), 49, 74; as "early warning system," 5; Preamble to, 19
Economic Community of West African States, 3
economic security, 22, 23
education, right to, 79, 150
elections, 17, 57, 180n7 (Part I); absence of, 110; ASEAN Charter and, 41; "Asian values" debate and, 34; in Myanmar, 154, 172, 222n10; UN General Assembly resolution on, 25
electoral authoritarianism, 2, 23
Engels, Friedrich, 37, 103
Enlightenment, Western, 115
environment, sustainable, 90
environmental crises, 10
equality, 33, 79, 97, 103, 149, 169; gender equality legislation, 111; between men and women, 100, 103, 204n4; of opportunity, 24; principles in the Quran and Sunnah, 103
ethnic cleansing, 1, 118, 148
Europe: regional human rights institutions in, 4, 174n15; trafficking in persons to, 125
European Convention on Human Rights, 39
European Court of Human Rights, 5, 13, 39, 170, 174n15
European Union, 32, 39, 178n69; AICHR and, 46; ASEAN relationship with Myanmar and, 158, 160, 161
exploitation, 32, 123; defined in UN Trafficking Protocol, 131, 216n57; of labor, 127, 129, 216n57; sexual, 125, 127, 129, 213n16, 216n57
extradition treaties, 132

famines, 22
female genital cutting, 83, 112, 115

feminism, 103, 108, 115, 208n61
Fernandez, Beatrice, 107
Fernandez case [Beatrice Fernandez v. Sistem Penerbangan Malaysia & Anor] (Malaysia, 2004), 107, 207n50, 207n52, 207n54
foot-binding, 115
Fortify Rights, 153
France, 74
free expression, 19, 23, 24, 180n7 (Part I); limitations on, 83; as requirement of democracy, 26
free press, 22, 153, 165
Fretelin, of East Timor, 63
"front state principle," 9
Funcinpec faction (Cambodia), 12

Gallagher, Anne, 126–127, 135, 136, 144
Gandhi, Mahatma, 75
gender identity, 53, 69, 70, 72
gender mainstreaming, 119
General Comment 25 (UN Human Rights Committee), 26, 183n47
genocide, 11, 29, 68, 101, 151
Ghai, Yash, 34
Global Alliance Against Trafficking in Women, 146
globalization, 49
"global society," 14
good governance: ASEAN Charter and, 39, 41, 151, 166, 223n30; communist states and, 35; socialization toward, 157
Goodman, Ryan, 137
Great Powers, 7, 8
Guerrero, Amado, 29

Hai Noi Declaration on the Enhancement of Welfare and Development of ASEAN Women and Children (2010), 118
Hamid, Syed, 160–161
Hanoi Plan of Action (1999–2004), 21
Hatta, Mohammad, 184n61
health, right to, 60
Hinduism, caste system and, 66–67
HLTF (High Level Task Force), 33, 38, 41–42, 44, 45
Ho Chi Minh, 35
Holocaust, 5
homosexuality, 84, 85, 86, 141, 202n162
Howard, Rhoda, 36
Htein Lin, Colonel, 155

human rights: in absence of democracy, 56;
communism at odds with, 36–37; core
inviolable rights, 68–69, 198n85; democracy
as necessary condition for, 11, 19–20, 167;
global and regional dynamics of, 12–14;
global and regional regimes of, 4–7;
indivisibility and interrelatedness of, 78–82;
institutionalization of, 3, 17; international
court of, 5, 175n26; international treaties,
12, 13; liberal democracy codependent
with, 17; regional systems, 1, 12; as secular
religion, 89; seen as Western imposition, 68,
172; spiral theory of, 13–14, 105, 132; treaty
monitoring system, 2–3; universality of, 32,
48, 89, 190n76, 203n174; weak institutions
in nondemocratic regions, 7. *See also*
NHRIs
human rights activists, 18, 46, 81, 91
human rights instruments, international, 25,
50, 55, 57–58
human rights norms, 14, 98, 111; change
among community of states and, 132;
communism and, 36; incentive for
compliance with, 136; internalization of, 4,
124, 136
human rights treaties, international, 2, 12, 54,
101; "contagion" effect in ratification of,
102–103; hierarchy of rights and, 80;
signing of treaties as tactical concession,
13, 103, 104–105
Human Rights Watch, 80, 153, 227n104
hunger, elimination of, 8–9
Hun Sen, 1, 2, 9, 12, 27
Huntington, Samuel, 185n87

Ibrahim, Anwar, 86, 203n163
ICCPR (International Covenant on Civil and
Political Rights), 3, 173n10, 174n12,
192n108; Article 25 of, 25, 26; Brunei
outside of, 109, 208n65; drafting of AHRD
and, 54, 192n108; inviolability of rights in,
68–69; Preamble to, 199n101; rights
limitations and, 201n137; right to
self-determination and, 60; UDHR's
evolution into, 50; wording of, 196n62
ICESCR (International Covenant on
Economic, Social and Cultural Rights), 3, 22,
173n10, 174n12; drafting of AHRD and, 54;
right to self-determination and, 60; UDHR's
evolution into, 50; wording of, 196n62

illiteracy, elimination of, 8–9
imperialism, 28, 32
imprisonment, arbitrary, 68
India, 9, 106, 107, 165, 171
indigenous people's rights, 53, 60, 62–64
individual, the, 5, 86, 199n101, 199n108;
communist view of rights/duties of, 36–37;
community/social order and, 33, 68, 78;
"society before self," 76; Western
philosophical emphasis on, 33
individualism, 33, 34, 76, 77
Indochina War, Second (1954–73), 8
Indonesia, 18, 40, 91, 171, 172; AHRD and,
53–54, 65, 66; anti-trafficking legislation
in, 133–134, 137; ASEAN Charter and,
40–41, 42–43; as ASEAN member, 2, 7,
173n1; Asian financial crisis (1997) and,
23, 24; "Asian values" debate and, 3, 31–32;
CEDAW and, 101, 105, 110–111, 112, 119,
120, 205n18; drafting of AHRD and, 55; as
"established democracy," 181n8; forest fires
(1997), 90; *gotong rojong* (mutual aid) in,
34; independence from the Netherlands,
63; international norms of democracy and,
26; intolerance and extremism in, 2;
invasion of East Timor (1975), 10; Justice
and Prosperity Party (PKS), 142;
konfrantasi period, 8, 20; multiparty
democracy in, 2; National Commission on
Violence Against Women (Komnas
Perempuan), 110; NHRIs (national human
rights institutions) in, 144, 146; polygamous marriage in, 107; "public morality"
limitations in, 83, 201n141; response to
global anti-trafficking regime, 128;
response to "World Plan of Action" on
women's rights, 114; Rohingya crisis and,
163, 164; role of military in politics, 30;
self-determination sought by ethnic
groups within, 63; Sharia law in, 110;
trafficking in persons from, 125, 142; as
world's third largest democracy, 40
infanticide, 112, 198n85
institution building, 2, 8, 13
Inter-American Commission on Human
Rights, 79
Inter-American Convention on Human
Rights, 5
Inter-American Court of Human Rights, 5
Inter-American Democratic Charter, 39–40

International Commission of Jurists, 6, 176n39

International Court of Justice, 34, 55, 192n110; CEDAW and, 100, 103; states' reservations to jurisdiction of, 103; Trafficking Protocol and, 128

International Criminal Court, 101, 148

International Gay and Lesbian Human Rights Commission (IGLHRC), 70

international law, 43, 50, 170; domestic issues and, 107–108; international human rights law, 24, 38, 57, 74, 75; trafficking in persons (TIP) and, 127

Islam and Muslims, 35, 59; conservative views on family and gender roles, 102, 113; Islam as state religion of Malaysia, 85; Moro people in the Philippines, 30, 61–62, 194n31; polygamous marriage, 107–108. *See also* Rohingya people; Sharia law

Jakarta Legal Aid, 55

Japan, 7, 21, 140

Jayakumar, S., 160

Jinks, Derek, 137

Jones, Lee, 160

Jones, Simon, 68

judiciary, impartial and independent, 53, 106

Kachin ethnic minority (Myanmar), 61, 152, 154

Kadir, Abdul, 202n162

Karen ethnic minority (Myanmar), 152

Karenni ethnic minority (Myanmar), 152

Keck, Margaret E., 111

Khin Maung Win, U., 29, 30, 34

Khmer Rouge, 10, 22

kidnaping (abduction), 125, 129

Koh, Tommy, 33

Korea, North, 228n108

Korea, South, 9, 21

Kuala Lumpur Declaration (1993), 65, 81, 199n108, 201n133

Lacierda, Edwin, 134

Laos (Lao PDR), 21, 26, 52, 130, 225n77; anti-trafficking legislation in, 130, 131, 135, 216n50; ASEAN Charter and, 44; as ASEAN member, 2, 9, 116, 141, 173n1; ASEAN relationship with Myanmar and, 161; CEDAW and, 101, 103, 104, 105, 111,

112, 206n30; Communist Party, 27–28; dam in Lower Mekong and, 90; drafting of AHRD and, 55; economic liberalization in, 35; elections in, 27–28; imprisonment of dissidents and activists in, 1; indigenous populations of, 63; Marxist-Leninist ideology in, 29; polygamous marriage in, 207n55; "public morality" limitations in, 83, 201n141; relation of rights and duties in, 77; as single-party communist state, 10, 28, 35, 167; trafficking in persons from, 125, 127, 129; understanding of democracy in, 35–36, 186n103

League of Arab States (LAS), 6

Lee, Yanghee, 151

Lee Kuan Yew, 3, 23, 56, 76

LGBTIQ rights, 53, 70, 72, 86, 202n151

liberal democracy, 7, 26, 79; emphasis on liberty and autonomy, 3; human rights codependent with, 17; resistance to ideas of, 38, 39. *See also* democracy

liberty, 3, 77, 149; "Asian values" debate and, 28, 33; liberty and security of the person, 123; in Marx's theory, 36

Malaysia, 11, 18, 44; AHRD and, 53–54, 200n122; anti-trafficking legislation in, 131; as ASEAN member, 2, 7, 173n3; Asian financial crisis (1997) and, 23; "Asian values" debate and, 3, 102; CEDAW and, 101, 103, 104, 105–109, 119–120, 207n43; civil society activism in, 121; dispute with neighboring states, 8; domestic violence legislation, 116; drafting of AHRD and, 55; drug trafficking as threat to national security, 141; elections and reform in, 23–24; electoral authoritarianism in, 23; Federal Court of Malaysia, 107, 207n44; High Court of Malaysia, 106, 207n44; Internal Security Act (ISA), 30, 183n54; Kelantan Islamic Family Law Enactment (2002), 108; majority-Muslim population of, 70, 71; NHRIs (national human rights institutions) in, 144, 146; polygamous marriage in, 107–108, 208n58; "public morality" limitations in, 83, 85–86, 201n141, 202n159, 202n162, 203n163; response to "World Plan of Action" on women's rights, 114; Rohingya crisis and, 149, 163, 164; as "semi-authoritarian" state,

Malaysia (*cont.*)
27; Sharia law in, 112; SOGI rights
opposed in, 70–71, 72; states of emergency
in, 10, 30; SUHAKAM (National Human
Rights Commission), 104, 106, 145
Malaysian Bar Association, 53, 54, 192n104
Malik, Adam, 7
Manila consultation, 72, 89
Maphilindo, 8
Marcos, Ferdinand, 1, 10, 11, 20
Maritain, Jacques, 66, 67
Marx, Karl, 36, 37
Marxist-Leninist ideology, 28, 29, 35. *See also*
communism
Mekong Lawyers Network, 192n110
Mencius, 67
Middle East, 4, 6, 171, 174n18
migrant workers, 53, 58, 118, 133
migration, illegal, 129, 130
MILF (Moro Islamic Liberation Front), 62,
194–195n34, 195n37
*Minister for Immigration and Ethnic Affairs v.
Teoh* (Australia, 1995), 106
Mjotowijono, Umarjadi, 114
MNLF (Muslim National Liberation Front),
61, 62, 194n34
Mohamad, Mahathir, 3, 27, 76, 86, 177n60;
Myanmar membership in ASEAN and,
159; Western pressure on ASEAN and, 158
Molland, Sverre, 128, 129
Mon ethnic minority (Myanmar), 152
money laundering, 128, 220n133
Moravcsik, Andrew, 180–181n8 (Chap. 1)
Moro people (Philippines), 30, 61–62,
194n31
movement, freedom of, 59, 153
Musawah (Islamic women's group), 208n58,
209n67
Muslim Lawyers Association of Malaysia, 71
Myanmar (Burma), 9, 32, 171; anticolonialist
ideology in, 29; anti-trafficking legislation
in, 131, 135; ASEAN Charter and, 44; as
ASEAN member, 141, 159; "Asian values"
debate and, 34; Border Guard Police
(BGP), 148; British colonial rule in, 30,
223n39; CEDAW and, 101, 102, 111; dam
in Lower Mekong and, 90; Depayin
incident (2003), 159–160; drafting of
AHRD and, 54; drug trafficking from, 142;
ethnic minorities, 61, 152, 154, 223n38,

227n104; human rights in, 165–166;
military junta, 9, 32, 42, 165; name change
to Myanmar (1988), 204n1 (Part II);
National Law on Protection and Prevention of Violence Against Women (2017),
111; NHRIs (national human rights
institutions) in, 144; NLD (National
League for Democracy), 1, 152, 154, 172,
223n48; nonalignment policy in Cold War,
7, 8; "public morality" limitations in, 85;
role of military in politics, 30, 150, 166;
"Saffron Revolution" (2007), 11, 152,
161–162, 227n101; SLORC (State Law and
Order Restoration Council), 10–11; SOGI
rights opposed in, 70; SPDC (State Peace
and Development Council), 11, 165;
trafficking in persons from, 125; transition
from military dictatorship to democracy,
2, 28, 149, 152–155; Union Solidarity and
Development Party, 154, 160. *See also*
Rohingya people
Myint Swe, 156

Nagel, Thomas, 67, 68, 73, 198n84
National Council for Peace and Order
(Thailand), 1
nationalism, 30
natural law, 68
Nelson, Joan M., 185n87
neocolonialism, 30
nepotism, 24
Ne Win, General, 149
New Zealand, 9
NGOs (nongovernmental organizations), 12,
13, 14, 43; anti-trafficking measures and,
127; ASEAN Civil Society Conference and,
70; drafting of AHRD and, 50, 51, 191n93;
human rights abuses in Myanmar and,
153, 227n104; SOGI rights and, 72;
trafficking in persons and, 139, 145, 146;
women's NGOs in Malaysia, 106
NHRIs (national human rights institutions),
138, 139, 144–146
Nickel, James, 80
9/11 (September 11, 2001) terrorist attacks,
10
Noorfadilla binti Ahmad Saikin, 106
Noorfadilla case [*Chayed bin Basirun & Ors v.
Noorfadilla binti Ahmad Saikin*] (Malaysia,
2009), 105–107, 120

OAS (Organization of American States), 3, 39, 174n16; Charter (1948), 19
OAU (Organization of African Unity), 40, 174n17
occupied territories, Palestinian, 6
Official Secrets Act (Malaysia), 30
Ohn Gyaw, 158
Om Yintieng, 50
Ong KengYong, 160
Ople, Blas, 160
Organic Acts (Philippines), 62–63
organized crime, 125
organ trade, 129

Pan-American Declaration of Rights and Duties (1948), 65
Panikkar, R., 67–68
Paribatra, M. R. Sukhumbhand, 9
particularism, 75, 81, 97, 157
Patra, Pengiran Dato Paduka Osman, 45
patriarchy, 83, 84
Paust, Jordan J., 74
peace: democracy and, 20, 21; right to, 90, 170, 203–204n181
Permanent Arab Commission on Human Rights, 6
Philippines, 18, 30, 160, 172, 187n19; AHRD and, 53–54, 65, 66; anti-trafficking legislation in, 130–131, 134, 137; ASEAN Charter and, 188n39; as ASEAN member, 2, 173n1; Asian financial crisis (1997) and, 23; in Association of Southeast Asia (ASA), 8; beginning of democracy in, 180n8 (Chap. 1); CEDAW and, 101, 103, 105, 112, 205n18; colonialism in, 29, 30; drafting of AHRD and, 55; as "established democracy," 23, 181n8; indigenous people's rights in, 62–63; international norms of democracy and, 26; Magna Carta for Women Act (2008), 111; martial law regime (1972–81), 10; minority Islamic population, 113; Moro peoples, 61; NHRIs (national human rights institutions) in, 144, 146; "People Power" revolution (1986), 11–12; "public morality" limitations in, 83, 85, 87–88, 202n151; Reproductive Health and Population Development Bill, 87–88; response to global anti-trafficking regime, 128; role of military in politics, 30; SOGI rights

opposed in, 70; state-sanctioned judicial violence in, 1; trafficking in persons from, 125
Philippine Society and Revolution (Guerrero), 29
Pillay, Nava, 49, 91
pluralism, 10, 25, 32, 86
Pogge, Thomas, 75
political participation, right of, 24, 25, 26; Constitution of Myanmar and, 149; drafting of AHRD and, 55, 56; economic/social conditions and, 79
political rights, 2, 5, 78, 79, 192n108; AHRD and, 55, 58, 196n52; "Asian values" debate and, 3, 31–33; duty and constraint on, 77; in the Philippines, 12; violations of, 10
pollution, 90
Pol Pot, 10
polygamy, 107–108, 207n55, 208nn58–59
pornography, 3, 84, 202n149
poverty, 23, 26, 88; Asian financial crisis (1997) and, 142; elimination of, 8–9; as obstacle to human rights, 31; trafficking in persons and, 129, 140, 146
Power of Human Rights, The (Risse, Bopp, Sikkink), 13, 132
Prayuth Chan-ocha, General, 11, 27
privacy, right to, 33, 83
private property, right to ownership of, 149
Proclamation of Teheran (1968), 79
"Promoting and Consolidating Democracy" (Resolution 2000/47), 26
prostitution, 129, 141, 213n16, 216n57
"public morality" limitations, 53, 54; absence of democracy and, 92; in AHRD Article 8 clause, 82–88; political diversity of ASEAN member states and, 48; SOGI rights and, 72, 73

racism, 113
Ramos, Fidel, 141
rape, 1, 125; marital rape, 112, 209n79; perpetrated by Myanmar military, 148, 154, 155, 156, 157, 164
Raz, Joseph, 74–75
Razak, Datuk Seri Najib, 86, 183n54
relativism, 32, 81, 82, 91, 98
religion, freedom of, 18, 59, 69, 202n158; Constitution of Myanmar and, 149; limitations on, 83

religious fundamentalism, 99
Renteln, Alison Dundes, 68
Risse, Thomas, 13, 132
Roadmap for the Integration of ASEAN
    (RIA), 21
Rohingya people (Myanmar), 1, 11, 97, 151;
    ASEAN's role in addressing situation of,
    151, 163–164; Aung San Suu Kyi and,
    150–151, 164; "clearance operation"
    against, 1, 148–149, 155, 164; crimes
    against humanity by Myanmar military,
    98; denied constitutional protection,
    149–150; described as "Bengalis," 149;
    flight to Bangladesh, 148, 149; government
    response to crisis in Rakhine state,
    155–157; historical persecution by
    Burmese governments, 149; mass killings
    of, 148
"Role of National Institutions in Advancing
    the Human Rights of Women, The"
    (Gallagher, 2002), 144
Rome Statute (International Criminal Court,
    1998), 101
Ropp, Stephen, 13, 132
Rorty, Richard, 67
Rousseau, Jean-Jacques, 34
rule of law, 2, 17, 27, 39, 42, 45
Russell, Bertrand, 36
Rwanda, 118

Santiago Declaration, 40, 187n8
Santi Promphat, 134
SAPA (Solidarity for Asian People's
    Advocacy), 52
Sardjoro, Roesiah, 113
Saul, Ben, 75
SEANF (Southeast Asian NHRI Forum), 144,
    146
SEATO (South East Asian Treaty Organisa-
    tion), 8
security, "comprehensive" or "overall," 140
Sedition Act (Malaysia), 30
self-determination, right to, 53, 54, 60–64,
    137, 138
Selth, Andrew, 161
"semi-democracies," 181n8
Sen, Amartya, 22, 34–35, 75
Severino, Rudolf, 23
sexual and reproductive rights, 53

sexual orientation, 53, 69–70; "public
    morality" limitations and, 84–85; SOGI
    (sexual orientation and gender identity),
    70–71, 72–73
sexual violence, 148
shame/shaming, 14, 18, 152
Shan ethnic minority (Myanmar), 61, 194n30
Sharia law, 18, 53, 67, 112; penal code of
    Brunei, 109–110, 208n63; polygamous
    marriage and, 108; "public morality"
    limitations and, 85; SOGI rights and, 70
Sihanouk, Prince, 12
Sikkink, Kathryn, 13, 111, 132
Simmons, Beth, 99
Singapore, 22, 53, 112; AHRD and, 53–54;
    anti-trafficking legislation in, 131,
    137–138; ASEAN Charter and, 44; as
    ASEAN member, 2, 7, 173n3; Asian
    financial crisis (1997) and, 23; "Asian
    values" debate and, 3, 33, 102; CEDAW
    and, 101, 103; domestic violence
    legislation, 116; drafting of AHRD and, 55,
    56; ejection from Malaysia (1965), 8;
    electoral authoritarianism in, 23; Myanmar
    membership in ASEAN and, 158, 226n78;
    one-party rule in, 10; polygamous
    marriage in, 107; "public morality"
    limitations in, 85; response to global
    anti-trafficking regime, 128; response to
    "World Plan of Action" on women's rights,
    114; as "semi-authoritarian" state, 27;
    Shared Values white paper, 75–76; SOGI
    rights opposed in, 70, 72
Sisters in Islam (SIS), 108–109, 121, 208n58
Sivaraksa, Sulak, 67
Slaughter, Anne-Marie, 107
slavery, 6, 32, 59, 89; as exploitation, 216n57;
    universal condemnation of, 68
socialization, 4, 14, 119, 157; mechanisms of,
    168; modes of influence at global level and,
    124
social justice, 8, 23, 24
South Asia, 4, 124, 171
South China Sea, conflict in, 10, 164, 171
Southeast Asia, 1, 3, 172; democratic deficit
    in, 17; economic development in, 22;
    human rights in, 10–12; as a region, 7–10;
    skepticism about democracy in, 28–37;
    state of democracy in, 37–38; trafficking in

persons in, 124, 128–129; violent struggles for self-determination in, 61

South Moluccas independence movement (Indonesia), 63, 196n47

sovereignty, 31, 42, 139, 140

Soviet Union, 8, 25, 74, 77

Sriphapa Petcharameesri, 47

Suharto, 3, 8, 10, 76; Dili massacre and, 177n60; toppled by Asian economic crisis (1997), 23, 24

Sukarno, 8, 34

Surayud Chulanot, General, 188n29

Surin Pitsuwan, 22, 162

Susilo, Djoko, 43

suttee (sati), 69, 115

Sydney Centre for International Law, 192n110

tactical concessions, by authoritarian states, 13, 14, 103, 104–105; motivated by sanctions and rewards, 132; women's rights and, 119, 169

Taylor, Charles, 68

territorial disputes, unsettled, 7, 20

terrorism, international, 141, 164

Thailand, 18, 112, 130, 159, 172; AHRD and, 53–54, 65, 66; anti-trafficking legislation in, 131, 134–135, 137; ASEAN Charter and, 42, 188n29, 188n39; as ASEAN member, 2, 7, 173n1; ASEAN response to military coup (2014), 11, 178nn68–69; Asian financial crisis (1997) and, 23; in Association of Southeast Asia (ASA), 8; beginning of democracy in, 180n8 (Chap. 1); Buddhism in, 34; CEDAW and, 101, 102, 103; drafting of AHRD and, 55; drug trafficking in, 142; Gender Equality Act (2015), 111; lèse-majesté laws, 11; lethal crackdown on demonstrators (1992), 10; military coup d'état (May 2014), 1, 11; minority Islamic population, 113; NHRIs (national human rights institutions) in, 144, 146; Rohingya refugees in, 149, 163; role of military in politics, 30; SOGI rights in, 70; trafficking in persons and, 125; unelected institutions of, 27

Thaksin Shinawatra, 27

Thaung Tun, 160

Thein Sein, 154

thought, freedom of, 59, 69, 201n137

"tiger economies," 3, 23

Timor Leste (East Timor), 10, 32, 63, 173n1

TIP reports, U.S. State Department: Gallagher's critique of, 126–127, 135, 217n90; tiers of compliance with TVPA, 126. See also trafficking in persons

tolerance, 34, 36, 72, 86

torture, 67, 153, 154, 198n84; prohibition of, 58, 68; UN convention against, 109; universal condemnation of, 68

totalitarianism, 5

"Towards Regional Cooperation on Undocumented/Illegal Migration" (international symposium, 1998), 143

trade unions, 154, 194n19

trafficking in persons (TIP), 46, 59, 97, 123–124, 168; definition of, 213n16; domestic response of ASEAN states to, 130–133; global regime to prevent, 124–127; multilateral approaches by states to combat, 98; regional approaches to problem of, 139–147; response of ASEAN states to global regime against, 127–130; Rohingya crisis and, 149, 163; TVPA as external motivator for ASEAN states, 133–138. See also TIP reports, U.S. State Department; TVPA (Trafficking Victims Protection Act)

Trafficking Protocol, UN (2000): anti-trafficking legislation in ASEAN states and, 130–131; ASEAN states' response to, 127–130; as centerpiece of global effort to end trafficking, 125

transnational judicial networks, 107

"transnational society," 18

Treaty of Amity and Cooperation (1976), 9, 20, 140–141

Turley, William, 103

Tu Wei-Ming, 33

TVPA (Trafficking Victims Protection Act) (United States, 2000), 124, 125–127, 130, 133, 136, 146

UDHR (Universal Declaration of Human Rights), 2, 3, 5, 32, 57; Article 1, 24; Article 21, 25, 153, 187n18; Article 24, 190n76; Article 29, 182n41. See also AHRD-UDHR similarities and differences

United Nations, 6, 12, 38, 124; Charter, 50,
60, 64, 204n4; Commission on Human
Rights, 17, 25, 26, 100, 118, 119, 175n24;
Commission to Study the Organization of
Peace, 4; Convention Against Torture, 109,
208n65; Convention on the Rights of the
Child, 118, 121; "Decade for Women"
(1975–85), 99, 102; Declaration on the
Rights of Indigenous Peoples, 60; Entity
for Gender Equality and the Empowerment of Women (UN Women), 112; ethnic
independence movements in Indonesia
and, 63; Human Rights Committee, 25, 26,
84, 201n144; Human Rights Council, 148,
156; International Women's Year
Conference, 113; Organised Crime
Convention (2000), 126, 133, 213n10,
214n23; Rohingya crisis in Myanmar and,
155–156; Security Council, 160, 162;
Special Rapporteurs Reports, 11, 153, 154,
226n91; UNESCO (UN Educational,
Scientific and Cultural Organization), 19,
75; World Conferences on Women, 101,
102, 106, 119, 120. See also CEDAW;
Trafficking Protocol, UN; UDHR
United Nations General Assembly, 11, 25,
160, 162; CEDAW adopted (1979), 99;
Declaration on the Elimination of Violence
Against Women (1993), 100, 101, 111, 116,
117, 139; Resolution 46/137 (1991), 25,
182–183n46
United Nations High Commissioner for
Human Rights, 1, 74, 91; on civil society
and drafting of AHRD, 49, 52, 74; on
NHRIs, 144; plight of Rohingya in
Myanmar and, 148, 164; "public morality"
limitations and, 83; seminar on democracy,
17
United States of America, 3, 32, 39, 168;
ASEAN relationship with Myanmar and,
158, 161; colonial rule over the Philippines, 29, 30, 61; "A Right to Democracy"
resolution sponsored by, 26; trafficking in
persons to, 125; war in Vietnam, 29. See
also TVPA (Trafficking Victims Protection
Act)
universalism, 55, 81, 167

Vejjajiva, Abhisit, 11
Vienna Declaration and Programme of
Action (1993), 6, 50, 64; Article 5, 78, 80;
UDHR and, 65; women's rights in, 100
Vienna World Conference on Human Rights
(1993), 12, 182–183n46; Bangkok
Declaration and, 31, 81, 89; debate about
universality, 66; on democracy, 187n18;
Kuala Lumpur Declaration and, 65;
universality of human rights and, 48
Vientiane Action Program, 139
Vietnam, 21, 26, 52; anti-trafficking
legislation in, 131; ASEAN Charter and,
44; as ASEAN member, 2, 9, 116, 173n1;
CEDAW and, 101, 103, 105, 111, 205n18;
Communist Party, 23, 27–28, 29; dam in
Lower Mekong and, 90; drafting of AHRD
and, 55; economic liberalization in, 35;
elections in, 27–28; imprisonment of
dissidents and activists in, 1; indigenous
populations of, 63; Marxist-Leninist
ideology in, 29; North and South Vietnam,
8; "public morality" limitations in, 85;
relation of rights and duties in, 77;
response to global anti-trafficking regime,
128; as single-party communist state, 10,
28, 35–36, 167; trafficking in persons from,
125, 130; understanding of democracy in,
35–36; war with Khmer Rouge in
Cambodia, 10, 20, 22
Vishaka v. State of Rajasthan AIR (India,
1997), 106

Wahyuningrum, Yuyun, 53, 72
Waldron, Jeremy, 77
war, 14, 19–20
War on Terror, 10, 135
Weeramantry, Christopher, 34
West, the, 38, 172; accused of double
standards, 32, 89; differences from
Southeast Asia, 20; individualism in, 33;
liberal democracy associated with, 28
West Papua independence movement
(Indonesia), 63
Williams, Bernard, 68
women, rights of, 97–98, 122, 168–169;
conflated with children's rights, 118, 121;
emerging regional order and, 113–119;
human rights in relation to, 118–119;
international norms and regional
legitimacy regarding, 119–122; Marxist
principles of sexual equality and, 116; as

matters of domestic politics, 97; polygamous marriage and, 107–108, 208nn58–
59; "public morality" limitations and,
83–84, 87–88; Sharia law and, 108, 109;
trafficking in persons and, 139, 142,
145–146; violence against women, 100,
111, 113, 116–117, 121, 204n8; voting
rights in Western states, 89. *See also*
CEDAW
Women's Caucus (Southeast Asia Women's
Caucus), 52, 53, 83, 84, 85

Yasuaki, Onuma, 68, 184n61
Yee, Sienho, 28
Yeo, George, 162
Yingluck Shinawatra, 27
Yokota, Yozo, 153
Yudhyono, Susilo Bambang, 11
Yugoslavia, 32

Zaleha, Justice (High Court of Malaysia), 106
ZOPFAN (Zone of Peace, Freedom and
Neutrality) Declaration, 20

ACKNOWLEDGMENTS

What motivated this book was the commonplace observation that global human rights institutions, with their plethora of unenforceable declarations, hortatory statements, and overblown bureaucracies, are very distant from the ordinary realities of people's lives and the injustices and persecutions that plague them. Regional levels of governance, on the other hand, seem both more modest and more successful—if success can be measured by the willingness of states to subscribe to binding mechanisms for monitoring human rights and compliance with the decisions of regional institutions. My theory was that regional human rights systems must carry a degree of legitimacy that the global human rights system does not. This book is in part an attempt to see how this theory measures up against the experience of one of the world's emerging regional human rights systems in Southeast Asia.

At the outset, it seemed important that I try to understand the relationship between the Association of Southeast Asian Nations (ASEAN) and the region's "pariah state," Myanmar. Myanmar is a case study in the book and will remain a lifelong research interest. In the period during which this book as written, the country took what seemed to be its first tentative steps toward democracy after decades of direct military rule. But by 2017, the military had reasserted its power, carrying out a campaign of what the United Nations called "ethnic cleansing" against the country's minority Muslim population, the Rohingya. Aung San Suu Kyi had undergone a spectacular fall from grace.

My fieldwork in Myanmar was extremely productive. Although not everyone I spoke to was comfortable about being recorded or signing official ethics documents, everyone was willing—indeed, eager—to talk. I thank all those in Yangon who gave me their time and assistance by agreeing to be formally interviewed or by informally sharing their experiences with me. Thanks are due to David Kinley and to two of Australia's former ambassadors to Myanmar, Christopher Lamb and Trevor Wilson, for helping me get ethics clearance to do interviews in Myanmar at a time when no one was quite sure how the political tumult would end.

I wrote this book while I was at the University of Sydney. There, I was supported and encouraged by the many colorful and collegial scholars who populate the law school: Ben Saul, who was my mentor throughout the process of writing the book; Terry Carney, who inspired and influenced a generation of scholars; Mary Crock, who showed me that one could be both brilliant *and* kind; Wojciech Sadurski, whose exuberant confidence in me I eventually thought I had better try to justify; and Emily Crawford, who gave advice, guidance, and encouragement at times when these things were most needed. Scholars from other institutions were generous in their interest and support: Alison Duxbury from the University of Melbourne; Tan Hsien-Li from the National University of Singapore; Hilary Charlesworth and Mathew Davies from the Australian National University; Susan Armstrong from Western Sydney University; and Andrew Byrnes from the University of New South Wales. It was Andrew who first introduced me to the fecund field of human rights research in Southeast Asia. The book benefited from the extensive feedback and helpful critiques I received from Simon Chesterman from the National University of Singapore, Sarah Joseph from Monash University, and Dinah Shelton from George Washington University.

My involvement in the Mekong Lawyers Network, and a particularly illuminating meeting of that network that I attended in Chiang Mai prior to the drafting of the ASEAN Human Rights Declaration, gave me access to civil society members from Laos, Vietnam, Myanmar, and Cambodia. This opened up possibilities for researching attitudes in the CLMV countries, which are too often ignored by scholars of Southeast Asia. I owe thanks to Daniel King and Earthrights International for inviting me to this meeting. I am also grateful to Rafendi Djamin, former Indonesian human rights commissioner, and Dato' Sri Muhammad Shafee Abdullah, former Malaysian human rights commissioner, for their efforts to give me access to a critical meeting in Kuala Lumpur between civil society and the ASEAN Human Rights Commission.

Great thanks go to Anne Dacey, who undertook the horrible task of converting footnotes from the Cambridge style to the U.S. humanities style and did it with her customary competence and grace. Her predecessors in the unglamorous but vital task of checking footnotes and citations include Kathleen Heath, research assistant par excellence, Alice Gardoll, and Sally Asnicar. Peter Agree at the University of Pennsylvania Press connected me with Kathleen Kearns, whose wisdom and talent helped reshape the book.

Aspects of this book have previously been published as "Global or Regional? Realising Women's Rights in Southeast Asia," *Human Rights Quarterly* 39 (2017); "Human Trafficking in Southeast Asia: Uncovering the Dynamics of State Commitment and Compliance," *Michigan Journal of International Law* 37 (2017): 611–59; and "The ASEAN Human Rights Declaration," *Human Rights Law Review* 13 (2013): 557–79. I am grateful to the editors and publishers of these journals for allowing me to reproduce parts of these articles.

Finally, thanks go to my family: my husband, John; my sons, Jack and Marcus; and my daughter, Madelaine. Throughout the course of writing this book, Jack shared with me the kind of wise insights that only a teenager can have about endeavors like mine being a mere meaningless flicker in a solar system of irrelevance. Marcus was steady in his kind attempts to dispel the resulting despair. Madelaine, who traveled with me in Myanmar, understood what drove me to begin the book and what made me stay the course. This book is for Madelaine, for whom nothing is impossible.